Earth negotiations

D1570406

Earth negotiations: Analyzing thirty years of environmental diplomacy

Pamela S. Chasek

**United Nations
University Press**

TOKYO · NEW YORK · PARIS

© The United Nations University, 2001

The views expressed in this publication are those of the authors and
do not necessarily reflect the views of the United Nations University.

United Nations University Press
The United Nations University, 53-70, Jingumae 5-chome,
Shibuya-ku, Tokyo, 150-8925, Japan
Tel: +81-3-3499-2811   Fax: +81-3-3406-7345
E-mail: sales@hq.unu.edu
http://www.unu.edu

United Nations University Office in North America
2 United Nations Plaza, Room DC2-1462-70, New York, NY 10017, USA
Tel: +1-212-963-6387   Fax: +1-212-371-9454
E-mail: unuona@igc.apc.org

United Nations University Press is the publishing division of the United Nations
University.

Cover design by Joyce C. Weston

Printed in the United States of America

UNUP-1047
ISBN 92-808-1047-2

Library of Congress Cataloging-in-Publication Data

Chasek, Pamela S., 1961–
Earth negotiations : analyzing thirty years of environmental diplomacy /
Pamela S. Chasek.
    p. ;   cm.
Includes bibliographical references and index.
ISBN
1. Global environmental change-International cooperation. 2. Environmental
policy-International cooperation. I. Title.
[DNLM: 1. United Nations. 2. Environment. 3. Economics. 4. International
Cooperation. 5. Negotiating-methods. HC 79.E5 C487e 2000]
GE149 .C42 2000
363.7'0526—dc21   00-012568

Contents

Tables and figures

Tables

Figures

Acknowledgements

Trying to acknowledge everyone who has made this book possible is a humbling task. At the same time, I take great pleasure in thanking those who have encouraged my efforts. In particular, I would like to thank my doctoral dissertation advisers, I. William Zartman and Charles Pearson at the Paul H. Nitze School of Advanced International Studies, Johns Hopkins University, for supporting me since the very beginning. To Lance Antrim go my thanks for introducing me to the world of multilateral environmental negotiations first-hand. I must also thank Daniel Druckman for giving me the idea and the challenge to work with statistics.

I have also been fortunate in receiving a great deal of moral and technical support from the United Nations diplomatic community. I particularly want to thank Oscar Avalle, Burhan Gafoor, Tehmina Janjua, Alison Drayton, Hugo Maria Schally, Frederick Mallya, David Elliot, Mostafa Tolba, Ismail Razali, Tommy T. B. Koh, Bernardo Zentilli, Robert Ryan, Hama Arba Diallo, Richard Benedick, Peter Thacher, Janette Ryan, Penelope Wensley, Kevin Stairs, Marilyn Yakowitz, and countless others.

I must thank everyone who took the time to fill out questionnaires for different cases of negotiations. They include: Peter Haas, Alexander Timoshenko, Andrey Vasilyev, A. L. Alusa, Richard Benedick, UNEP Ozone Secretariat, UNEP Basel Convention Secretariat, Wolfgang E. Burhenne, Michael Monaghan, Simone Bilderbeek, and David Elliot.

Special thanks also go to Bertram Spector and the Processes of International Negotiation project at the International Institute for Applied

Systems Analysis (IIASA) in Laxenburg, Austria, for providing a wonderful environment in which to work in the early stages of my research during the summer of 1992.

The cases, analyses, and proposals presented in this book have been developed as part of an interesting experiment in combining research and writing a book with the conception and production of a new tool to add transparency and understanding to the multilateral environmental negotiation process – the *Earth Negotiations Bulletin*. Conceived during the preparations for the 1992 UN Conference on Environment and Development, the *Earth Negotiations Bulletin* has been recognized as the most reliable, unbiased source of information and analysis about ongoing environment and development negotiations within the United Nations system. As one of the founders, writers, and editors of the *Bulletin*, I had the unparalleled opportunity to attend and participate as an observer and adviser in more than 10 different negotiating processes from 1992 to 1995. As a result, my research benefited from the access and experiences gained while producing the *Bulletin* and the *Bulletin* has benefited from the analytical tools that a political scientist can provide. I am confident that this experiment in participatory research will continue to help both students of multilateral environmental negotiation and practitioners better understand and improve the processes through which international environmental law is developed.

Finally, I thank my family and my friends for supporting me and accepting my itinerant travels during the dissertation period. I especially thank Langston James Goree VI "Kimo," my husband and partner in the *Earth Negotiations Bulletin*, for all he has done to support me in my work.

This research was supported by a Peace Scholar award from the United States Institute of Peace, an independent, non-partisan federal institution created and funded by Congress to expand available knowledge about ways to achieve a more peaceful world. The opinions, findings, and conclusions or recommendations expressed in this dissertation are those of the author and do not necessarily reflect views of the Institute of Peace.

Abbreviations

AGBM	Ad Hoc Group on the Berlin Mandate
AIA	advance informed agreement
BSWG	Open-ended Ad Hoc Working Group on Biosafety
CANZ	Canada, Australia and New Zealand
CBD	Convention on Biological Diversity
CCAMLR	Convention on the Conservation of Antarctic Marine Living Resources
CEQ	Council on Environmental Quality
CFC	chlorofluorocarbon
CITES	Convention on International Trade in Endangered Species
COP	Conference of the Parties
COW	crude-oil washing
EC	European Community
ECE	Economic Commission for Europe
ECOSOC	Economic and Social Council
EEC	European Economic Community
EU	European Union
ExCOP	extraordinary meeting of the Conference of the Parties
FAO	Food and Agriculture Organization
FCCC	Framework Convention on Climate Change
G-77	Group of 77
GEF	Global Environment Facility
HCFC	hydrochlorofluorocarbon

IMCO	Intergovernmental Maritime Consultative Organization
IMO	International Maritime Organization
INC	Intergovernmental Negotiating Committee
INCD	Intergovernmental Negotiating Committee to elaborate an international convention to combat desertification in those countries experiencing serious drought and/or desertification, particularly in Africa
IPCC	Intergovernmental Panel on Climate Change
ITTA	International Tropical Timber Agreement
ITTO	International Tropical Timber Organization
IUCN	World Conservation Union
IWGMP	Intergovernmental Working Group on Marine Pollution
LMO	living modified organism
LRTAP	Convention on Long-Range Transboundary Air Pollution
MAP	Mediterranean Action Plan
MARPOL	International Convention for the Prevention of Pollution from Ships
NGO	non-governmental organization
OAU	Organization of African Unity
OECD	Organisation for Economic Co-operation and Development
OPEC	Organization of Petroleum Exporting Countries
SAEP	Senior Advisors to ECE Governments on Environmental Protection
SBT	segregated ballast tanks
TSPP	Tanker Safety and Pollution Prevention
UN	United Nations
UNCED	United Nations Conference on Environment and Development
UNCHE	United Nations Conference on the Human Environment
UNCTAD	United Nations Conference on Trade and Development
UNDP	United Nations Development Programme
UNEP	United Nations Environment Programme
WEOG	Western European and Others Group
WHO	World Health Organization
WMO	World Meteorological Organization
WTO	World Trade Organization

1

Introduction

"Getting action in the United Nations," a diplomat once complained, "is like the mating of elephants. It takes place at a very high level, with an enormous amount of huffing and puffing, raises a tremendous amount of dust and nothing happens for at least 23 months" (Gardner 1972, 70).

Taking into account the slow process of negotiating international agreements within the framework of the UN system, including the acknowledged "huffing and puffing," global environmental problems, while raising a certain amount of dust, pose important diplomatic and legal challenges to the international community in general and the United Nations in particular. Many who see the urgent need for action on environmental problems are skeptical of entrusting responsibilities to the slow and often cumbersome multilateral negotiating process within the United Nations. Not all international environmental treaties have been negotiated under the auspices of the United Nations or one of its specialized agencies or programs, but, ever since the 1972 UN Conference on the Human Environment in Stockholm, the United Nations has been increasingly recognized as the habitat for addressing environmental issues that are too large to be handled by any state, or even by a limited group of states. Although there are frustrations inherent in the UN system and the international treaty-making process, governments are not ready to surrender environmental decision-making and their own sovereignty to a supranational body with legislative and enforcement powers. As a result, the international community is forced to employ some method of intergovernmental cooperation – usually multilateral negotiation (even though it may take an average of 23 months).

Over the past three decades, multilateral environmental negotiation has become increasingly prominent within the UN system. The United Nations Environment Programme (UNEP) lists over 155 environmental agreements that have been negotiated at the regional and global levels since 1921, more than 90 of these negotiated since the 1972 United Nations Conference on the Human Environment. Despite the fact that the oldest historical international treaties deal with the use of natural resources (waterways), international environmental negotiation is a comparatively recent phenomenon. As a result, although there is a large body of research on international environmental law and global environmental governance, there has been only limited research on the negotiation process itself.

The task of achieving international agreement on any issue is extremely difficult. Environmental issues, which combine scientific uncertainty, citizen and industry activism, politics, and economics, may be among the most complicated and difficult to resolve. In environmental negotiations, the characteristics of the actors, the issues, and the outcome all point to the need for strategies and processes that may be different from those used in other multilateral negotiations, such as those on arms control, trade, or peace. The negotiations themselves are both complex and time-consuming. They are usually preceded by extensive scientific fact-finding. The debate then centers on various response strategies. Any solution is constrained by the costs of deploying new technologies and concerns about the fair allocation of the costs involved. Discussions about the best ways of enforcing treaties often fall victim to political rivalries and national sovereignty concerns (Susskind and Ozawa 1992, 143).

Given these inherent difficulties, how do governments negotiate international environmental treaties? The process used to produce international agreements is often considered to be among the most cumbersome and archaic means of multilateral negotiation. Yet, time after time, consensus is achieved and a new treaty or agreement is adopted, signed, and ratified. How does this process work? Although there are numerous approaches to the study of multilateral negotiation oriented to international relations, I have decided that phased process analysis lends itself to the study of multilateral environmental negotiation. A complete study of multilateral environmental negotiation requires an examination of the precipitants to the negotiations, the prenegotiation process, the actual process and procedures that diplomats use to negotiate the text of a treaty, and the post-agreement negotiation phase. In other words, the life-cycle of an environmental treaty begins long before delegates are bargaining over specific issues and may even continue once agreement is reached as governments determine that scientific and/or political and economic realities dictate the need for amendments or protocols to the original convention.

Phased process analysis is based on the understanding that the process has to meet certain procedural imperatives in order to arrive at substantive goals (Zartman 1987, 8). The notion of stages or phases of negotiation is purely an analytic one that, while corresponding to reality, is far sharper in concept than it is in practice. For analytical purposes of identification and discussion, phases can be isolated and examined in detail, but in reality they tend to overlap and have indistinct borders. The sequencing of these phases and the length of time that each takes vary greatly. Nevertheless, by viewing the negotiation process as a succession of phases, in each of which there is a particular focus of attention and concern by the negotiators, it is possible to identify relationships between variations in process and outcome. Thus, phased process analysis can be used as both a framework that reduces some of the complexities inherent in multilateral environmental negotiation to a more manageable level as well as a framework for understanding what negotiators have to do in different phases to advance the negotiations towards a successful outcome.

The purpose of this book is to develop a model that will facilitate understanding of the process by which international environmental agreements are negotiated. Using phased process analysis, 11 cases of environmental negotiation between 1972 and 1992 were studied in depth to determine the relationship among different phases in the process and the outcome. The cases represent the range of different environmental issues, including marine pollution, forests, biological diversity, atmosphere, air pollution, endangered species, and marine living resources. The cases characterize negotiations on both the global and regional levels and both within and outside the United Nations system. My analysis of each of these cases was based on answering the following four questions: (1) Are there discernible phases within the negotiation process? (2) If there are phases, what key events or "turning points" enable the negotiations to move from one phase to the next? (3) Is there any relationship among the phases and turning points in the process and the outcome? and (4) Can these phases and turning points be developed into a model to help guide or explain future or ongoing multilateral environmental negotiations?

To answer these questions, I begin in Chapter 2 with an examination of the nature of the problem of international environmental management to determine why negotiation is the tool of choice and how the United Nations became the de facto forum for many of these negotiation processes. From the perspectives of both the political scientist and the economist, international environmental management poses a dilemma since there is no international or multinational "government" that can enforce international environmental policy. As a result, effective environmental management seems to demand that countries cooperate openly and put their signatures on international agreements, treaties, and conventions. Many realist and neo-realist scholars argue that no effective collective environmental protection is possible through the negotiation of treaties. Nevertheless, negotiation has been the primary means for reaching these agreements and, thus, managing transboundary environmental problems.

Within this context, Chapter 3 examines multilateral negotiation more closely and defines the complexities brought about by multiple issues, parties, and roles, as well as the use of consensus decision-making, which have led to the development of practices and procedures that are quite different from those used in bilateral negotiation. Given these complexities, it is often difficult to understand how agreements are actually reached. I explain some of the different approaches that policy analysts and practitioners can use to compare new, impending negotiations with past negotiations to help them determine whether or not the presence or absence of certain factors within the negotiation process will help or hinder the prospects for a strong outcome. Of these different approaches, I chose phased process analysis as the theoretical basis upon which to build the model. I explain phased process analysis and examine the literature so that its theoretical aspects can be applied to the 11 cases of multilateral environmental negotiation to develop the model.

Chapter 4 summarizes the 11 cases of multilateral environmental negotiation that were used to develop the model: the 1972 Convention on the Prevention of Marine Pollution by Dumping of Wastes and Other Matters (London Convention); the 1973 International Convention for the Prevention of Pollution from Ships (MARPOL) and the 1978 Protocol; the 1973 Washington Convention on International Trade in Endangered Species (CITES); the 1976 Barcelona Convention for the Protection of the Mediterranean Sea against Pollution; the 1979 Geneva Convention on Long-Range Transboundary Air Pollution; the 1980 Convention on the Conservation of Antarctic Marine Living Resources (CCAMLR); the 1983 International Tropical Timber Agreement (ITTA); the 1987 Montreal Protocol to the Vienna Convention for the Protection of the Ozone Layer on Substances that Deplete the Ozone Layer; the 1989 Basel Convention on the Control of Transboundary Movements of Hazardous Wastes and Their Disposal; the 1992 Convention on Biological Diversity; and the 1992 Framework Convention on Climate Change. The main purpose of the research on these cases was to determine what phases the negotiations passed through from the time the decision was taken to negotiate a treaty until the time that the treaty was adopted. As a result, rather than focusing in detail on the issues being negotiated, these case studies focus on the process – the phases and turning points of the negotiations and how they were influenced by specific internal or external events or activities.

In Chapter 5, I use phased process analysis to develop the model. During the examination of the cases, it became clear that there were six loosely defined phases that each of the cases had in common:

- **Precipitants:** this phase identifies the events that bring the environmental problem to the attention of the international community.
- **Issue definition:** this is where government delegates and/or scientists and other technical experts work together to define the nature of the problem at hand, determine its scope and magnitude, and develop a common body of knowledge before beginning actual negotiations.
- **Statement of initial positions:** in this phase governments state their initial positions on the environmental problem at hand, its causes, effects, and possible solutions, and start to form initial coalitions.
- **Drafting/formula-building:** this is the phase where delegates begin to forge consensus on the nature and provisions of the basic agreement.
- **Final bargaining/details:** this is where governments have to work out the final, often contentious details of the agreement.
- **Ratification/implementation:** this phase takes place after the agreement has been adopted. During this phase, the agreement usually is ratified, enters into force, and is, it is hoped, implemented by the parties.

After defining these phases in the negotiation process, the model is expanded to include "turning points" – the decisions, compromises, or events that enable the negotiations to pass from one phase to the next. Although identifying the phases of the multilateral environmental negotiation process is important, it is the understanding of how and why the negotiations move from phase to phase that brings the model to life. To identify these turning points, the phases in the overall negotiating process were examined once again to answer the following questions: (1) When did the negotiations move from one phase to the next? (2) What was the event or activity that led to the turning point? (3) Was this event triggered by an event external to or from within the negotiations themselves?

The next step in developing this model was determining whether there is any relationship among characteristics or attributes of the process (within the phases or at the turning points) and between these characteristics and the outcome. In Chapter 6, I look for correlations or relationships between the phases and the turning points to determine if the presence of certain characteristics in the process has any discernible relationship to subsequent phases and turning points or the outcome in terms of the following two hypotheses or guiding statements:

(1) The characteristics of the phases and turning points late in the process are influenced by which type of actor plays the lead role in the
early phases.

(2) The outcome, as measured by the strength of the resulting agreement
and ratification time, is shaped more by the nature of the final phases
and turning points than by the earlier ones.

The correlation analysis highlights several aspects of the negotiation
process that the case-study method did not reveal. First, it appears that
the characteristics of the phases and turning points late in the process are
influenced by which type of actor plays the lead role in the early phases:
individual states or intergovernmental organizations. In cases where an
intergovernmental body, such as one of the UN agencies, takes the decision to begin negotiations, the intergovernmental body tends to play a
strong role throughout the process. On the other hand, in the cases where
the decision to begin addressing the problem in the international arena is
the result of an initiative of a state, group of states, or non-governmental
organization, the nature of the subsequent phases and turning points is
quite different.

With regard to the second hypothesis, there is not as strong a relationship between process and outcome as one might imagine. In the five cases
where the final bargaining/details phase focused on outstanding peripheral details in the final agreement (core issues and/or a formula had
already been agreed to in the previous phase), the final turning point
was usually brought about by postponing consideration of a difficult issue,
the ratification/implementation phase was characterized by inaction until
the agreement entered into force, and the resulting agreement was often
weaker than when negotiations took a different path.

Based on the correlation analysis, two different negotiating paths or
processes have emerged. The first path can be called "UN-centered negotiations," where the United Nations or one of its specialized agencies
tends to be the focal point throughout the negotiating process. A second
path can be called "State-centered negotiations." Even though "UN-
centered negotiations" feature states as the primary actors, the United
Nations plays a major role as the initiator and host of the negotiating
process. State-centered negotiations are those where a state or group of
states initiate the negotiating process and guide it through until there is
agreement on a final treaty.

In Chapter 7, I evaluate the phased process model to determine if it can
be used to explain future or ongoing negotiations as a means of clarifying
the process, reducing the complexities, and explaining the evolution of
international environmental treaties. As new developments in the international arena and within the UN system have evolved in recent years,
this model must be adaptable and flexible to accommodate changing cir-

cumstances. Some of these recent developments include the 1992 United Nations Conference on Environment and Development (UNCED); the end of the Cold War; the increasing use of negotiation as a means of managing the global environment; the increased transparency in the negotiations themselves, as evidenced by the growing participation of non-governmental organizations (NGOs); and the growing awareness of the relationship between environment, social development, economic development, and security. As a test, the model is applied to two cases of post-UNCED negotiations: the Cartagena Protocol on Biosafety to the Convention on Biological Diversity, and the Kyoto Protocol to the UN Framework Convention on Climate Change. The results indicate that, in spite of the growing complexities in negotiating environmental agreements since 1992, the phased process model is a useful tool for understanding the process and explaining the evolution of international environmental treaties.

Finally, in Chapter 8, the model is reviewed in terms of lessons for both analysis and practice. The model has also provided a number of insights that can help negotiators navigate through the complex process of multilateral environmental negotiation:

(1) If negotiations are influenced by the occurrence of a natural or human-induced disaster early in the process, ratification time tends to be longer.

(2) Do not underestimate the importance of defining the issues in the beginning of the process.

(3) When the first draft of the agreement is prepared by the chair or the secretariat, rather than a state or group of states, the ratification time for the final agreement is shorter.

(4) When the negotiating time is shorter, the provisions in the resulting agreement are generally stronger.

(5) If there are still outstanding core issues towards the end of the process, it is better to resolve them (even if the final compromise text is weak) rather than postpone further consideration of the issue.

(6) A recent trend in multilateral environmental negotiations is the establishment of mechanisms so that governments can meet during the interim period before the agreement enters into force.

(7) Time pressure inevitably affects the final phases of the negotiating process but, if managed properly, deadlines can be beneficial to the process.

(8) There are two approaches to negotiating an agreement: deductive and inductive. There is no indication that one approach results in a better outcome than the other; however, negotiations on different topics may be better suited to the use of different approaches.

(9) Although non-governmental actors appear to have had a minimal impact on the negotiations, governments should continue to encourage their participation in the negotiating process since NGOs and scientists often play a crucial role in bringing environmental issues to the attention of the world community.

(10) Finally, one of the most important ways for governments to improve the negotiation of environmental agreements is to keep abreast of the phases and the process.

In spite of the difficulties and frustrations inherent in the UN system and the international treaty-making process, multilateral negotiation is currently the only game in town. As long as governments are not ready to surrender environmental decision-making and their own sovereignty to a supranational body with legislative and enforcement powers, multilateral negotiation will continue to be the best means of managing global and transboundary environmental problems.

2

International environmental management

Environmental problems do not respect national boundaries. Transboundary air pollution, the degradation of shared rivers, and the pollution of oceans and seas are just a few examples of the international dimensions of environmental problems. Population growth, in combination with resulting urbanization and industrialization, has served only to increase the amount and frequency of major international environmental problems. The cumulative impact that human beings have had on the earth, together with an increased understanding of ecological processes, means that the environment cannot be viewed as a relatively stable background factor. Rather, the interaction between economic development and the complex, often fragile ecosystems on which that development depends has become an international political and economic issue (Hurrell and Kingsbury 1992, 2).

Not only have the number and scope of transboundary environmental problems increased, but a new category of global environmental issues has emerged. First, humanity is now faced by a range of environmental problems that are global in the strong sense that they affect everyone and can be effectively managed only on the basis of cooperation between all, or at least a very high percentage, of the countries in the world. These global issues include controlling climate change and the emission of greenhouse gases, the protection of the ozone layer, safeguarding biodiversity, protecting special regions, such as Antarctica or the Amazon, the management of the seabed, and the protection of the high seas (Hurrell and Kingsbury 1992, 2).

Second, the increasing scale of many regional or local environmental problems, such as extensive urban degradation, deforestation, desertification, salinization, denudation, or water or fuelwood scarcity, means that they now have broader international repercussions. These problems can undermine the economic base and social fabric of weak and poor states, generate or exacerbate intra- or inter-state tensions and conflicts, and stimulate increased flows of refugees. As a result, environmental degradation in diverse parts of the developing or even the industrialized world can affect the political and security interests of countries thousands of miles away (Hurrell and Kingsbury 1992, 3).

Perspectives on international environmental management

The management of international environmental problems has been an area of concern for both political scientists and economists. From the political scientist's point of view, international environmental management is marked by the dichotomy between ecological interdependence on the one hand and the fragmentation of the international political system on the other (Hurrell and Kingsbury 1992, 4). A single, complex, and highly integrated ecosystem has to be managed within the constraints of a political system comprised of over 180 states, each claiming sovereign authority within its territory. According to Richard Falk (1971, 37–38):

A world of sovereign states is unable to cope with endangered-planet problems. Each government is mainly concerned with the pursuit of national goals. These goals are defined in relation to economic growth, political stability, and international prestige. The political logic of nationalism generates a system of international relations that is dominated by conflict and competition. Such a system exhibits only a modest capacity for international cooperation and coordination.

For some, the logical answer to this dilemma is to curtail the sovereign powers of states and move towards a greater degree of supranational authority. Others believe, however, that the prospects for extensive supranationalism and world government are inevitably remote and open to several objections. First, the nation state remains extremely resilient as a structure for the exercise of political power. Second, claims about the need to abolish or limit sovereignty have to be considered within the context of all the other issues and problems of international life. Third, it is not clear that the creation of some supranational authority would in fact lead to more effective environmental management. The negotiations over the nature of a new political authority in themselves would be very difficult and time-consuming and would generate much conflict. Finally, there is the basic paradox that, if there were sufficient consensus to move beyond the state system, there would also be sufficient consensus to ensure a degree of inter-state cooperation that would make such a move largely unnecessary.[1]

An alternative solution supports not the creation of a global Leviathan, but rather the decentralization of power and authority. Proponents of this approach believe that it would weaken the competitive drives of the global economy that intensify the depletion of natural resources and the degradation of the environment. This approach would also empower local communities that have a greater understanding of the specific eco-systems on which their economic livelihoods depend. Although there are arguments in favor of greater decentralization and empowerment of local communities, there are also important limitations: empowerment of local communities and rational ecological management are not always consistent; decentralization neglects the broader functions of the state system in the many other fields of human activity; the costs of disrupting the global economic system would be enormous and would prove a potent source of conflict; and there would continue to be a need for some degree of global coordination, either for effective ecological management or for social equity, but such coordination would be infinitely more difficult in such a system because of the increased numbers of communities involved (Hurrell and Kingsbury 1992, 8–9).

In spite of the fact that new forms of cooperation will likely be required and further constraints on state sovereignty may emerge, for the time being states will continue to play the major part in international environmental management. One aspect of this management is the negotiation of international environmental agreements.

From the economist's point of view, international environmental problems are the result of resource misallocation caused by "externalities" – unintended consequences or side-effects of one's actions that are borne by others. Externalities have always existed but, as the planet grows more crowded and per capita consumption rises, accompanied by the emergence of new polluting technologies such as chlorofluorocarbons (CFCs), synthetic fertilizers, pesticides, herbicides, and plastics, externalities become more critical (Dorfman and Dorfman 1993, 75).

In this sense, the externalities that lead to environmental degradation have been called the "tragedy of the commons." Garrett Hardin (1968) observed that overgrazing unrestricted commonlands, prior to their enclosure, was a metaphor for the overexploitation of the earth's land, air, and water resources that are common property. The root cause of overgrazing was the absence of a mechanism for obliging herders to take into account the harmful effects of their own herds' grazing on all of the other herders who shared the common. The solution lay in assigning property rights so that owners could limit the use of the commons. Yet, Hardin also recognized that air, water, and many other environmental resources, unlike the traditional commons, could not readily be fenced and parceled out to private owners who would be motivated to preserve them. This observation raised a central question in the fields of both environmental economics and environmental governance: how can we oblige users to internalize the damages they inflict on environmental resources that, by their very nature, cannot be owned by anyone?

Demsetz (1967, 354–355) argued that users of a community-owned resource would fail to come to an agreement on managing the resource, even though it is in the interest of all users to cooperate and reduce their rate of use of the resource. If this improved situation is attained, every user will earn even higher returns by free-riding on the virtuous behavior of the remaining cooperators. As a consequence, united action on the part of users can be expected to be unstable; cooperative agreements, even if they are reached, will not persist. The only way out of the common property dilemma, according to Demsetz, is intervention by "the state, the courts, or the leaders of the community."

Barrett (1990, 68–69) sees this view as disquieting because in the case of global common property resources there is no "world government" empowered to intervene for the good of all. Because national sovereignty must be respected, the problem of conserving global common property resources is no different from that described by Demsetz. The only way out of the global common property dilemma is agreement. Yet, just as in the situation that Demsetz describes, there are strong incentives for governments not to cooperate, or to defect from an agreement should one be reached.

Pearson (1975, 2–3) explains the problem of common property resources using the economic concept of optimality. A particular allocation of resources is said to be optimal if it is impossible to reallocate them so that one individual's or group's welfare is improved without necessarily harming the welfare of others (Pareto optimality). Examples of suboptimal situations are found when national tariffs distort the free flow of trade and limit the full exploitation of comparative advantage, or when monopoly power restricts output and raises prices. One of the conditions necessary to achieve optimum resource allocation is that market prices should be equal to the full marginal social costs of production, including the costs to society of using environmental resource services. However, a central feature of common property resources that have an economic, or scarcity, value is that the users of the resource do not have to pay a price. In spite of their economic value, these environmental resources are considered "free goods." Accordingly, a divergence between the social costs of the activity and the private costs to individuals and firms occurs, and prices fail to reflect all social costs.

Given the inherent problems of common property resources and the lack of a single authority with the right to control and decide on a solution to this problem, effective management of global environmental resources seems to demand that countries cooperate openly and put their signatures on international agreements, treaties, and conventions. Barrett (1990, 74) offers several explanations for why cooperation of this kind might emerge. Suppose a group of countries "collude" by signing an international environmental agreement and that the remaining countries continue to act non-cooperatively. Suppose further that the signatories to the agreement choose their collective abatement level while taking as given the abatement decision functions of the non-signatories. Meanwhile, the non-signatories choose their abatement levels on the assumption that the abatement levels of all other countries are fixed. That is, the signatories act as "abatement leaders" and the non-signatories as "abatement followers."

The solution to this problem exhibits many of the features of actual agreements. The net benefits realized by both signatories and non-signatories to an agreement are higher than in situations where negotiation is ruled out. Moreover, the signatories would like the non-cooperators to sign the agreement. However, non-signatories do better by free-riding in the short term. In the long run, however, the incentives to be a free-rider will diminish, argues Mäler (1990), because the temporary gains from free-ridership will not be sufficient to compensate for the long-term losses if cooperation breaks down.

Although they approach the problem from different perspectives, many economists and political scientists reach the same conclusion – international environmental management is best served by cooperation among states. The primary means of cooperation has been through the negotiation of agreements, often in the form of treaties, conventions, or protocols. Negotiation takes place when states consider the status quo unacceptable. Quite often states anticipate high costs, even crisis, if existing trends continue. Although it is in every state's interest to reach agreement on how to manage the problem, it is also in their interest to give up as little and gain as much as possible. Nevertheless, the expected value of the outcome to each state, and hence the total value of the outcome, must be positive, or there would be no incentive to engage in negotiations or to accept the outcome. In multilateral negotiations, all states must win (or be better off than with no agreement) or they will not come to agreement.[2]

Nevertheless, not all scholars view the negotiation of treaties as the solution to the management of international environmental problems. Many realist and neo-realist scholars argue that no effective collective environmental protection is possible through the negotiation of treaties. The absence of any central authority – the existence of anarchy between states – is seen as the defining principle of international relations and the source of inevitable insecurity and conflict. The existence of anarchy fuels the foreign policies of states, which are dominated by the need to survive and to accumulate power in order to guarantee their survival. As Robert Jervis (1978, 167) notes:

Because there are no institutions or authorities that can make and enforce international laws, the policies of cooperation that will bring mutual rewards if others cooperate may bring disaster if they do not. Because states are aware of this, anarchy encourages behavior that leaves all concerned worse off than they could be.

According to Peter Haas and Jan Sundgren (1993, 402), much of current realist-derived writing in international relations is skeptical about the possibility of controlling environmental problems by modifying state sovereignty. They continue:

A conventional Realist understanding of international relations suggests that environmental problems are particularly difficult to resolve collectively. Bargaining is necessary to formulate international agreements, but strong systemic factors exist that inhibit obtaining significant collective benefits.

The "logic of collective action" suggests that individual countries will not cooperate on issues that seriously challenge their sovereignty and if they fear that their own actions will not be reciprocated. They will not participate if they suspect that others' defections will not be observed, or even if they are not sure that other parties' actions can be effectively monitored (Haas and Sundgren 1993, 403; Olson 1971).

Realists propose that the extent to which effective treaties are concluded and enforced is the result of the exercise of power. Hans Morgenthau and Kenneth Thompson (1985, 296) argue that international law owes its existence and operation to two factors: identical or complementary interests of individual states and the distribution of power among them. Where there is neither community of interest nor balance of power, there is no international law. The balance of power operates as a decentralizing force only in the form of a general deterrent against violations of international law and in the exceptional cases when a violation of international law calls for a law-enforcement action.

Realists and neo-realists have also placed a great deal of emphasis on the role of dominant actors or hegemons in compelling others to cooperate or mobilize others' action (Haas and Sundgren 1993, 411; Young 1994, 87). They believe that the presence of such a hegemon, exerting the type of leadership that the United States has since World War II, constitutes a critical or even necessary condition for treaty negotiation and regime formation at the international level. Without the presence of a hegemon, international negotiations are likely to fail. Furthermore, environmental negotiations run the risk of failure because not only do they often lack a hegemon, but they deal with issues that threaten national sovereignty and often have a large number of actors.

However, contrary to what many realists believe, environmental treaties have been concluded that actually stipulate reasonably stringent standards that will improve environmental cooperation (Haas and Sundgren 1993, 413). And many of these agreements have been completed without the presence of a hegemon or dominant actor. In fact, according to Young (1994, 89), true hegemony is the exception rather than the rule in international society. First, power in the sense of control over material resources or tangible assets is often difficult to translate into power in the sense of the ability to determine collective outcomes. Situations in which other states coalesce in opposition to a state that appears to have hegemonic pretensions are routine in international society. Furthermore, there are many situations where states possess blocking power or the capacity to veto institutional arrangements they dislike, such as in the regulation of the emission of greenhouse gases. In such cases, Young argues, it is hard to see how any international regime could be effective if it failed to satisfy the concerns of both industrialized and developing countries. For all practical purposes, then, the great powers today routinely find themselves in situations in which they must negotiate the terms of international agreements covering specific issue areas whether they like it or not (Young 1994, 90).

The environment, multilateral negotiation, and the United Nations

Negotiation has been the primary means of managing conflict between nations on environmental and natural resource issues. Since the 1972 United Nations Conference on the Human Environment, the UN system has become the focal point for numerous multilateral environmental negotiations. This is quite a development, particularly since the United Nations Charter makes no specific mention of environmental protection, preventing pollution, or conserving resources. As Patricia Birnie (1993, 330) points out, following the League of Nations' failure to prevent World War II, the primary objective of the founders of the United Nations was to remedy the deficiencies that were thought to have contributed to the League's failure together with the violation of human rights that had occurred in the course of these events. As a result, the UN Charter provides for the United Nations "to achieve international cooperation in solving international problems of an economic, social, cultural or humanitarian character and in promoting and encouraging respect for human rights and for fundamental freedoms for all." To accomplish this, the founders gave the United Nations five principal organs: a General Assembly, a Security Council, a Trusteeship Council, an Economic and Social Council (ECOSOC), an International Court of Justice, and a Secretariat. ECOSOC has since become the main UN organ responsible for environmental concerns yet, when it was established, it was charged with the following functions: promoting higher standards of living, full employment, and conditions of economic and social progress and development; developing solutions to international economic, social, health, and related problems; encouraging international cultural and educational cooperation; and promoting universal respect for and observance of human rights and fundamental freedoms.

For a number of years, ECOSOC's responsibility for economic and social matters led it to consider environmental issues only indirectly, as its functional commissions were more involved in developmental and human rights issues than in environmental ones. This was largely due to the fact that in 1945 there was no consciousness of any need to protect the environment, except on an ad hoc basis outside the United Nations. In fact, after the establishment of the United Nations, most cooperative action on environmental issues continued to take place as before – outside the United Nations, mainly through the convening of meetings by non-governmental organizations. Although the United Nations convened some conferences on environmental issues during its first 25 years, their scope was limited. For example, the 1949 UN Scientific Conference on the Conservation and Utilization of Resources was limited by ECOSOC to exchanging experiences in resource use and conservation techniques. Even the 1968 UNESCO Conference of Experts on a Scientific Basis for Rational Use and Conservation of the Resources of the Biosphere, which was a landmark at the international level in recognizing the relationship between humans and nature, addressed the problems only in so far as they were relevant to the life-support systems of plants and animals (Birnie 1993, 336).

Whereas in 1945 environmental awareness was low, the situation changed dramatically by 1972 when the concerns of private citizens and emerging environmental organizations led certain states to place environmental issues on their political agenda. Two events of particular importance occurred in the 1960s that sparked the industrialized world's awareness of the need for environmental concern. First, the publication of Rachel Carson's *Silent Spring* brought to light the devastating impact of DDT on bird populations and the deleterious effect of industrial chemicals on the earth's natural resources. Not long thereafter, in 1967, an oil tanker, the *Torrey Canyon,* spilled most of its cargo in the English Channel, destroying hundreds of sea birds and polluting the British coast.

It was at this time that the industrialized countries identified the need for multilateral action. Even though the international community had already adopted a number of multilateral environmental treaties, there was no framework within the United Nations for comprehensive consideration of the problems of the human environment. Thus, in 1968, Sweden called for a United Nations environmental conference to encourage "intensified action at national and international levels to limit, and where possible, eliminate the impairment of the human environment" (UN Resolution 1346 (XLV), 30 July 1968). The General Assembly approved this proposal in 1969 and decided that the conference would take place in 1972. Sweden volunteered to host the conference in Stockholm.

Six subjects were placed on the agenda of the United Nations Conference on the Human Environment (UNCHE): planning and management of human settlements for environmental quality; environmental aspects of natural resource management; identification and control of pollutants and nuisances of broad international significance; educational, informational, social, and cultural aspects of environmental issues; development and environment; and international implications of action proposals.

After more than two years of preparation, representatives from 113 states gathered in Stockholm from 5 to 16 June 1972. By the conclusion of the conference, delegates had established a UN environment program consisting of four major elements: an Action Plan; an Environment Fund to be established by voluntary contributions from states; a new UN mechanism (the United Nations Environment Programme) for administering and directing the program; and a declaration of 26 principles on the human environment. Not only did the 1972 UN Conference on the Human Environment legitimize environmental policy as an issue of international concern, but for the first time environmental issues received a place on many national agendas.

The Stockholm Conference also enlarged and facilitated means toward international action previously limited by inadequate perception of environmental issues (Caldwell 1984, 49). This international action took numerous forms, including the development of international environmental law. The establishment of the United Nations Environment Programme (UNEP) in itself led to the development and codification of a new body of international law to meet new requirements generated by environmental concerns and the Declaration on the Human Environment adopted in Stockholm. Other UN specialized agencies, such as the International Maritime Organization (IMO), the International Labour Organization (ILO), the Food and Agriculture Organization (FAO), the UN Educational, Scientific and Cultural Organization (UNESCO), and the World Meteorological Organization (WMO), also continued to or began to contribute to the development of international environmental law.

The process leading towards international lawmaking within the United Nations system was also established during this period. The first step is usually a proposal to ECOSOC, the General Assembly or one of the specialized agencies to establish a committee or to convene an international conference to consider a major issue of international concern. Then preparatory committees, working groups, regional meetings, and symposia are organized. Usually, but not always, preconference preparation assures substantial agreement on official conference action. In the end it is not the action of an international conference that confers legal status; rather it is the effective consensus of nations that makes it law (Caldwell 1984, 102). This process is known as conference diplomacy.

Conference diplomacy

The majority of multilateral negotiations on the environment within the United Nations system take the form of conference diplomacy – the management of relations between governments and intergovernmental organizations that occurs in international conferences. Conference diplomacy involves the conduct of multilateral diplomacy before, during, and after an international conference, when the drafting and implementation of the conference decisions are the subject of consultations, negotiation, and review.

Conference diplomacy can be traced back to the 1815 Congress of Vienna, the first major international gathering to bring together hundreds of participants to redraw the frontiers of Europe after the Napoleonic wars. The most significant innovation of the Congress of Vienna consisted precisely in enlarging participation to admit the representatives of small territories or cities who were not given a hearing in the earlier conclaves of monarchs that dominated the eighteenth century. The apparent progress towards some measure of representative democracy was, however, seriously flawed by the secret agreement reached among the four great powers of the Quadruple Alliance of the time (Austria, Prussia, Russia, and the United Kingdom – subsequently the Group of Five when France was readmitted) to settle among themselves the issues that they considered to be of major importance. This practice of bilateral or restricted multilateral understandings being negotiated behind closed doors, rather than in plenary sessions of a conference, has survived to this day (Scott 1985, 42).

Another feature of the Congress of Vienna included the arrangements, sketchy as they were, for the conduct of negotiations in which so many representatives were entitled to participate. In every conference the problem of organization, the actual plan of procedure, acquires a significance that is often underestimated. As a result, the initial problem of organization, unless carefully prepared before the conference assembles, is apt to become a disintegrating problem (Nicolson 1961).

Conference periodicity received a strong impulse after World War I with the formation of the League of Nations and the International Labour Organization. A superficial comparison between the period after World War II and the one before World War I, with the interwar period as a transition, reflects the following developments:

- The number of international conferences increased at an impressive rate.
- Before World War I, international conferences were usually called by one, or sometimes several, of the major powers, or occasionally by one of the smaller powers after close consultations with the great powers. During the interwar period, the League of Nations system already had what might be called a self-propelling system for organizing conferences. Since World War II, most conferences have been convened within the framework of the United Nations or its specialized agencies. Conferences convened by individual countries have become the exception rather than the rule.
- Economic, financial, social, and cultural questions have increasingly become agenda items, whereas questions of peace and war once dominated the international conference scene (Kaufmann 1996, 9–10).

Today, conference diplomacy has evolved to become an integral part of international organization, both within and outside the United Nations system. For example, in the East–West setting the Four Power conferences of the post-1945 period have been superseded, since the early 1970s, by the Conference on Security and Co-operation in Europe. In the North–South setting, conference diplomacy outside the United Nations system was practiced in the cases of the Conference on International Economic Cooperation in Paris (1975–1977) and the Cancún Summit (1981). In the South–South setting, conference diplomacy, as manifested by the meetings of the non-aligned countries and by the consultative mechanisms of the Group of 77, has played a decisive role in articulating and aggregating the interests of developing countries and non-state actors such as dependent territories and liberation movements. Among the industrialized countries, conference diplomacy has become a seemingly indispensable facet of everyday political life encompassing almost every sector of public policy-making (Rittberger 1983, 169).

Within the United Nations system, conference diplomacy refers to processes of internationally coordinated policy-making through negotiation that takes place at the regular or special sessions of the main intergovernmental bodies and at ad hoc world conferences, which deal with almost every conceivable issue of international concern. UN conference diplomacy is all encompassing not only with respect to the themes under consideration and the number of states participating, but also with regard to the specific policy-making functions upon which a conference tends to concentrate. These functions include problem identification, goal definition, programming, budgeting, implementation oversight, and evaluation. Clearly, every conference fulfills multiple policy-making functions. One may assume, however, that regular sessions of the main intergovernmental bodies of the United Nations are likely to be found at the upper end of a continuum, whereas ad hoc world conferences tend to cluster at the opposite end, with a smaller number of policy-making functions being served (Rittberger 1983, 171).

According to Rittberger (1983, 171), ad hoc world conferences have become so frequent, particularly since the early 1970s, that they warrant special attention within the overall analysis of conference diplomacy. Their dominant function can be said to be the injection of new impulses for innovative programming in a certain issue area that has become part of the international political agenda. "Programming" as a core element of policy-making can be used in a somewhat looser way and in a narrower meaning. In the first instance, world conferences enunciate and/or affirm basic principles governing the interaction of states (and, to some extent, non-state actors) in a certain issue area, and promulgate broad mandates or guidelines for collective action at the national, regional, and global level. In the second instance, world conferences focus on the drafting of a convention, treaty, or other international legal instrument with the intent of codifying, altering, or adding to the existing body of international law. Illustrative of the first category (action-oriented conferences) are the United Nations Conference on Environment and Development (UNCED, June 1992, Rio de Janeiro), the International Conference on Population and Development (ICPD, September 1994, Cairo), and the Fourth World Conference on Women (FWCW, September 1995, Beijing). The second category (rule-making conferences) is epitomized by the Third United Nations Conference on the Law of the Sea. Both types of ad hoc world conference differ significantly with respect to the outcome and the process of negotiation while being part of the same pattern of conference diplomacy (Rittberger 1983, 171–172).

International conferences can also have a variety of objectives. Kaufmann (1996, 11–16) distinguishes the following eight general objectives:
(1) To serve as a forum for general discussion of broad or specific issues.
(2) To make non-binding recommendations to governments or international organizations.

   These two objectives can be found together in the annual conferences of the major organs of the United Nations and the specialized agencies, which serve as a forum for general discussion and for possible adoption of non-binding recommendations to governments. In some cases, such as the World Bank and the International Monetary Fund, general discussion takes place but the practice of making recommendations to governments on the basis of draft resolutions submitted by delegations is exceptional.
(3) To make decisions binding upon governments.
(4) To make decisions giving guidance or instructions to the secretariat of an intergovernmental organization, or on the way in which a program financed by governments should be administered.

   These two objectives can also be found in the periodic plenary conferences of the major organs of the United Nations and the specialized agencies that supervise the work of an international secretariat and certain jointly financed programs. One of the principal binding decisions taken is the one approving the budget of the organization and the way it is assessed.
(5) To negotiate and draft a treaty or other formal international instrument.

   Over the years a number of special conferences have been convened to negotiate treaties or international instruments, including the San Francisco Conference of 1945 that adopted the text of the United Nations Charter, the Law of the Sea conferences, the conferences that led to the convention prohibiting the production of chemical weapons, and the conferences that have led to the adoption of numerous environmental agreements. Some periodic conferences also serve to negotiate international agreements, including the UN General Assembly, which adopted the International Human Rights Covenants in 1966, followed by a series of other rights-related conventions.
(6) To provide for the international exchange of information.

   All international conferences involve exchanges of information to varying degrees. Intergovernmental conferences specifically organized to exchange information on a certain subject or series of related subjects are similar in character to private scientific congresses. On a smaller scale, many committees, subcommittees, and working parties of the United Nations and the specialized agencies work for the exchange of information.

(7) To provide for the pledging of voluntary contributions to international programs.

Annual conferences are held for the United Nations Development Programme (UNDP), the program of the UN High Commissioner for Refugees, and the World Food Programme, among others, where governments announce their voluntary contributions for the next year. These pledging conferences are useful in that they indicate how much financial support a program should receive in the coming year.

(8) To review progress under an agreement or a treaty concluded earlier.

Agreements and treaties are regularly reviewed during meetings of the Parties or during specially convened conferences for this purpose. For example, the Treaty on Non-Proliferation of Nuclear Arms is reviewed every five years.

Some of these conferences involve only a few countries meeting on a regional or subregional basis. Others may involve most of the 185 members of the United Nations. Since most conferences are currently held under the auspices of an international organization, the question of participation is settled either by the constitution or other basic instruments of the organization, or by an ad hoc decision of the organization (Kaufmann 1996, 44). In addition to government delegates, representatives of various intergovernmental organizations as well as non-governmental organizations also attend many conferences.

Some conferences are not intended to arrive at decisions and do not go beyond general debate or the exchange of information. Most intergovernmental conferences, however, end with some sort of conclusions or decisions, or the adoption of a treaty. The procedure by which decisions are taken and the form in which they are cast differ from conference to conference, depending on the objective of the conference, its rules of procedure, and traditional practices that may have been formed over the years.[3]

Summary

From the perspectives of both the political scientist and the economist, international environmental management poses a dilemma since there is no international or multinational "government" that can enforce international environmental policy. As a result, effective environmental management seems to demand that countries cooperate openly and put their signatures on international agreements, treaties, and conventions. Negotiation has been the primary means for reaching these agreements and, thus, managing the international environment.

As global concern for the environment has grown, the number of multilateral negotiations addressing the ways states can safeguard the natural environment has also increased. The intergovernmental conference is the most conspicuous and probably the most frequent vehicle of multilateral cooperation and confrontation. Since the 1972 United Nations Conference on the Human Environment, negotiations within the framework of the UN system have become commonplace. Many of these multilateral negotiations have taken the form of conference diplomacy – the management of relations between governments and intergovernmental organizations that occurs in international conferences.

Conference diplomacy and multilateral negotiation are characterized by complexity – multiple parties addressing multiple issues, playing multiple roles based upon multiple values. Both negotiators and analysts are always searching for new ways to manage these complexities and increase both the understanding and the effectiveness of the process of multilateral environmental negotiation. The next chapter will examine these complexities and explore ways of analyzing multilateral negotiations that can provide added understanding and improved management of the process.

Notes

1. This discussion is based on Hurrell and Kingsbury (1992). Others who have written about or criticized centralization of power as the solution to collective action problems include William Ophuls, *Ecology and the Politics of Scarcity* (San Francisco: W. H. Freeman, 1977); Elinor Ostrom, *Governing the Commons: The Evolution of Institutions for Collective Action* (New York: Cambridge University Press, 1990); and Hedley Bull, *The Anarchical Society: A Study of Order in World Politics* (London: Macmillan, 1977).
2. This paragraph is adapted from Zartman (1983, 9–10).
3. For more information about how conference diplomacy works, see Kaufmann (1996).

3

Multilateral negotiation

International negotiation is the process by which divergent values are combined into an agreed decision (Zartman and Berman 1982, 1). Multilateral negotiation can be defined as the process of simultaneous negotiation by three or more parties over one or more issues that aims at agreement acceptable to all participants (Touval 1991, 351). Multilateral negotiation is characterized by the complexities brought about by multiple issues, parties, and roles as well as the use of consensus decision-making, which have led to the development of practices and procedures that are quite different from those used in bilateral negotiation. Yet, although the study of negotiation has received considerable attention during the past three decades, most of the theoretical literature addresses bilateral negotiation. Some of this literature is relevant to multilateral negotiation, yet theories of bilateral processes can provide only a starting point for considering the added complexities of multilateral negotiation (Midgaard and Underdal 1977, 330). For example, theories of bilateral negotiation are not always applicable. It is seldom feasible to collapse multilateral negotiations into two-sided bargaining processes by grouping the players into two coalitions or blocs. This means that analytic constructs closely tied to a two-party view of the world, such as the Edgeworth box, cannot really help analysts come to terms with multilateral negotiation (Young 1989, 360).

This chapter will examine the complexities of multilateral negotiation and the ways in which it differs from bilateral negotiation. Given these complexities, different analytic constructs have been developed to study and understand just how these negotiations work. Some of these approaches to the analysis of multilateral negotiation will be outlined and one approach in particular – phased process analysis – will be discussed in detail. This will then set the stage for the development of a model that will help explain multilateral environmental negotiation.

Characteristics of multilateral negotiation

According to Gilbert Winham (1977, 350–353), the overarching characteristic of multilateral negotiation is the task of making some order of a complexity of issues, parties, and roles. Winham argues that complexity in international negotiation can result from various factors, including the size of the negotiation or the variety in the decision-making environment that is faced by the negotiators. International negotiations become complex when there are a lot of "things" to be kept in mind, either issues being debated or positions taken by different parties, or implications that the negotiations may have for the external environment. Complexity is also created under conditions of uncertainty, when information needed for decision-making is difficult or costly to obtain or is simply unavailable. Size or variety create problems of processing and are best understood in the sense of information overload.

To better understand these complexities, it is useful to identify the minimal and basic characteristics that define multilateral negotiation and distinguish it from bilateral agreement. These characteristics include the nature of multilateral negotiations: they are multi-party, multi-issue, and multi-role. There is also a multiplicity of different types of participants, including governments, the scientific community, secretariats, non-governmental organizations (NGOs), and the public/media. The negotiations often continue over long periods of time. Within the negotiations themselves, multilateral negotiations are distinguished by the difficulties in the identification of appropriate criteria for evaluating an outcome, the processes used, such as consensus decision-making, and their focus on rule-making rather than on the redistribution of goods. Group dynamics also play an important role in the process, especially with regard to coalition formation, the role of interpersonal relationships, the development of leadership, and the institutional context within which many multilateral negotiations take place.

Multiple parties

First, multilateral negotiations are multi-party negotiations. Although any party may agree with any other party, and eventually all parties presumably reach agreement, the multi-party assumption implies the existence of autonomous entities each with interests and interest groups of their own that underpin their separate positions. This characteristic constitutes a challenge to the reconciliation of multifaceted interests (Zartman 1994, 4).

An increase in the number of parties often causes more heterogeneity in terms of interests and perceptions as well as more uncertainty within each party as to the preferences of others. Thus, the search for fair or integrative solutions becomes more difficult as the number of parties increases. Midgaard and Underdal (1977, 339) state two propositions concerning the implications of size for the outcome of multilateral negotiations. First, the larger the number of parties, the more likely it is that an agreement, if concluded at all, will be "partial" in at least one of three ways: (a) covering only some of the agenda topics; (b) leaving some disagreement latent in an ambiguous text; or (c) being signed and accepted by only some of the parties. Second, the risk of suboptimal outcomes seems to increase with size, at least as far as collective goods are concerned. A collective good, as defined by Mancur Olson (1971, 14–15), is any good such that, if any person in a group consumes it, it cannot feasibly be withheld from the others in that group. In other words, those who do not purchase or pay for any of the public or collective good cannot be excluded or kept from sharing in the consumption of the good, as they can where noncollective goods are concerned. Olson argues that the provision of collective goods is inversely related to the size of the group owing to increasing organizational costs, declining individual benefits, and declining possibilities of strategic interaction as group size increases.

Touval (1991, 353) also examines the complexities caused by the number of participants in multilateral negotiations. Each participant has interests that require accommodation. The larger the number of participants, the greater the likelihood of conflicting interests and positions, and the more complex the interconnections among the parties. In addition, as the number of participants increases, the sheer volume of communication becomes difficult to manage. As a result, each participant is likely to experience difficulty in orchestrating the different signals that are to be sent – sometimes simultaneously – to different audiences, and interpreting the statements and signals made by the other participants. Inconsistent or contradictory messages, as well as errors in interpretation, may cause friction, generate distrust, and hinder the successful conclusion of negotiations. Another impediment, according to Nye (1986, 90), is the tendency of participants to engage in oratory and grandstanding. Even when the public and the press are excluded from the meeting, the presence of a sizeable number of delegates – along with their attendant staff – often tempts participants into posturing. Such behavior, in turn, may lead to the development of extreme positions from which the parties are not inclined to yield.

Multiple issues

The complexity of multilateral negotiations is also shaped by their multi-issue nature. Although multilateral negotiations can address only one issue, multiplicity of issues is the norm. In addition to complicating the negotiations, multiple issues provide the means as well as the subject of agreement, since they allow for trade-offs that can lead to a successful outcome. They also allow for diversity in the negotiations, since different parties have different levels of interest in the various issues (Zartman 1994, 4). According to Homans' Maxim, the greater the number of items at stake that can be divided into goods valued more by one party than they cost to the other and goods valued more by the other party than they cost to the first, the greater the chances of a successful outcome (Homans 1961, 62).

The multi-issue nature of negotiations can also have other implications. The technicality of many of these issues, particularly in the environmental field, often requires the diplomats to deploy technical expertise in addition to diplomatic experience (Scott 1985, 45). Another consequence of multiple issues is the interlinkages between issues and between negotiations. These interlinkages can lead to the intrusion of politics into technical matters and introduce an additional process of "lagged" bargaining where support from another party or parties for a national position or interest at a future or parallel negotiation or conference can be obtained in exchange for support for (or non-opposition to) the latter's interest at the current negotiation or conference.

Multiple roles

A third defining characteristic is the multi-role nature of the negotiations. Just as texture is present on the issue dimension, combining intensity and interest, so it is present on the parties dimension, adding role differential to numbers and interest groups. But role presents its own dimension beyond the simple matter of intensity. In the process of being more or less active in multilateral negotiations, Sjöstedt, Spector, and Zartman (1994, 11) claim that parties select from a limited list of roles. They can Drive, Conduct, Defend, Brake, or Cruise. Drivers try to organize the participation to produce an agreement that is consonant with their own interests. Conductors also seek to produce an agreement but from a neutral position, with no interest axe of their own to grind. Defenders are single-issue participants, concerned more with the issue than with the overall success of the negotiations. Brakers are the opposing or modify-ing resistance, brought into action by the progress being made either on the broad regime or on specific issue items. Cruisers are filler, with no strong interests of their own and, thus, available to act as followers. This role diversity can allow the issue and party complexities to be combined in an agreeable outcome.

Multiplicity of participants

Although all multilateral negotiations have a multiplicity of participants, environmental negotiations are particularly influenced by this factor. Bertram Spector (1992, 2–6) identifies five types of participants in envi-ronmental negotiation: governments, the scientific community, secre-tariats, non-governmental organizations (NGOs), and the public/media.

Government participation in these types of negotiations is complicated in itself. Many different ministries may be involved in setting a national position, including foreign affairs, environment, science and technology, industry, finance, trade, defense, foreign aid, planning, energy, agricul-ture, and transport. As these ministries have different constituencies and interests, there are likely to be considerable internal conflicts before a national delegation can advance a firm position. In addition to the execu-tive branch, national legislatures play an increasingly important role by holding hearings for airing scientific theories and exploring conflicting economic and social interests as well as by actually participating on offi-cial government delegations.

The scientific community also plays an important role. It is essential to build an international scientific consensus that can agree on basic parameters and narrow the ranges of uncertainty to ensure the success of negotiations. In recent years, an international network of cooperating scientists and scientific institutions has developed as a major new actor on the negotiating scene. Scientists have counterbalanced the industrial lobby, worked closely with government officials and assumed a new re-sponsibility for the implications of their findings for policy options.

Another influential party to negotiations is secretariats and other inter-national organizations. Often playing the role of a third-party mediator, the secretariat may supply objective information needed to clarify issues, summarize proceedings, and undertake systematic comparison of key elements in national position papers. According to Scott (1985), the role of the secretariat can range from an "activist" approach to one of a purely technical and servicing nature. In some cases, delegations prefer the technical/servicing role, because an activist secretariat may be inimi-cal to their interests. In some cases, the secretariat can have its own agenda and try to influence the process in such a way that its desired outcome is guaranteed. Sometimes this agenda can be ideological in nature and other times it can be practical. For example, if the number of negotiating sessions is increased, the members of the secretariat will have jobs for a longer period of time.

The fourth type of participant is the non-governmental organization. NGOs can include public advocacy groups, environmental organizations, development and social welfare organizations, and the business community. The rate of participation of NGOs in environmental negotiations has increased in recent years. Not only do they have greater access to the negotiations themselves, but they are increasingly serving as a catalyst to initiate such negotiations and to assist in the implementation of the resulting agreements.

The public also have a role to play. Policy makers may become complacent if the public do not lobby them to act on vital environmental issues. With assistance from creative use of the media, press conferences, speeches, television, radio, and educational campaigns, the public can become a major force in keeping their governments accountable in the international environmental arena.

Time

Multilateral negotiations are distinguished by two different characteristics related to time: the length of the negotiating process and its ongoing nature. The analysis of issues, communication and information processing, decision-making, and development of plans for implementation and monitoring the behavior of the parties to the agreement all take time (Touval 1991, 356). In the case of multilateral environmental negotiations, many participants and observers have commented on the length of time it takes to negotiate a treaty and bring it into force. Sometimes the length of this process actually undermines the goal of environmental protection. By the time the treaty goes into force, the nature or effects of the environmental problem may have changed or worsened.

One of the reasons that environmental negotiations take a long period of time relates to the unique role of scientific evidence. Scientific evidence places conflicting demands on the negotiation process: negotiators need sufficient data to understand the problem and formulate effective solutions, but at the same time they may have to act quickly to prevent the problem from worsening or becoming irreversible (Benedick 1991, 201). Because scientific evidence is often uncertain, and because research is expensive and time-consuming, states face a dilemma: to act in the face of uncertainty or not to act at all. Scientific uncertainty invariably complicates the decision-making process. If one country thinks it will be disadvantaged by a particular policy proposal, it can easily locate sympathetic experts to raise doubts about the adequacy of the scientific evidence put forward by others (Susskind and Ozawa 1992, 152). Scientific evidence also competes with considerations of economic feasibility; this too reflects the underlying conflict of interests between antagonistic lobbies (Lang 1991, 355).

Regardless of the role of scientific evidence, the nature of inter-governmental relations requires a significant amount of time. Delegates cannot always agree to provisions without approval from their capitals. The intersessional periods, sometimes lasting as long as four to six months, are needed to give the chairperson, their bureau, and the secretariat sufficient time to draft text and consult with key governments. Governments also need time to formulate or reconsider positions.

Complex multilateral negotiations also have an ongoing nature, which is punctuated by outcomes that are rarely final. Although this is occasionally a trait of bilateral negotiations and multilateral negotiations on trade and disarmament, it has become a common feature of multilateral environmental negotiations. Bertram Spector (1993) refers to the ongoing nature of negotiations after the initial agreement has been reached as "post-agreement negotiation." He defines post-agreement negotiation as the dynamic and cooperative systems, procedures, and structures that are institutionalized to sustain dialogue on issues that cannot, by their very nature, be resolved by a single agreement. The purpose of post-agreement negotiations is to continue the dialogue to push forward the development of the agreement and its implementation in an evolutionary fashion. According to Spector, this notion is similar to Howard Raiffa's (1985) concept of post-settlement settlements.

However, while Raiffa discusses the benefits of sometimes returning to the table after an agreement has been reached to seek a yet improved settlement, the goal of post agreement negotiations encompasses this function plus the additional tasks of implementation, feedback, and adjustment of agreed formulas over the longer term. These sustained negotiations are the dynamic mechanism by which international cooperation can be enhanced by improving and adding to past agreements, completing or modernizing them, operationalizing their effects, and attempting to perfect solutions so that all participants feel satisfied with the outcome.

One manifestation of the ongoing nature of multilateral negotiation is the convention–protocol approach. According to Susskind and Ozawa (1992, 144), the process begins with several years of multilateral negotiations aimed at getting a group of nations to acknowledge the need for action. These discussions usually culminate in the signing of a treaty or convention, offering a general policy framework or a set of goals. Once a convention is signed, the countries involved begin negotiations on one or more protocols – discrete actions directed at achieving concrete objectives or technical standards consistent with the convention. While the convention phase of treaty negotiations focuses on developing a general statement of the problem and a possible solution, protocols typically deal with the details of implementation.

Criteria for evaluating an outcome

The fact that there are many parties and issues naturally enhances complexity. Yet the processes and strategies used within multilateral negotiations give this complexity an additional dimension. Hopmann (1996, 246) points out that the identification of appropriate criteria for evaluating an outcome is much more complicated in the multilateral case.

It is often hard enough for two parties to identify the range of available bargaining space on any given issue and locate a point that may serve as a fair and optimal solution, even though that may be depicted in two-dimensional space. This is especially serious when there are multiple issues and/or multiple outcomes, which can lead to multiple preferences about which outcomes are favored.

There is usually no one outcome that dominates all others and, as a result, there may be no clear solution that satisfies the preferences of all parties at the same time. The result, Hopmann (1996, 246) continues, is often that multilateral negotiations proceed in a trial and error fashion, employing an inductive search strategy as negotiators "float trial balloons" concerning various possible agreements until finding one that appears to be acceptable to most parties.

Consensus decision-making

Another element of complexity is found in the difficulty in arriving at a decision rule. In bilateral negotiations, it is clear that the agreement of both parties is always required to reach agreement. In many multilateral negotiations this decision rule is not quite so obvious, especially since it may breed stalemate with regard to all but the most innocuous decisions. Parties to multilateral negotiations usually find themselves confronted with a procedural trade-off between efficiency, fairness, or legitimacy, meaning a recognition by all participants that their interests and views have been taken into account in the resulting decision (Hopmann 1996, 247). Therefore, majority rule or the "one state, one vote" voting procedure do not always work in multilateral negotiations. In fact, the most common decision rule has been the attainment of consensus – a decision rule in which, essentially, abstention is an affirmative rather than a negative vote (Zartman 1994, 5).

Consensus involves the continuation of negotiations in an endeavor to reach a compromise that will be reasonably acceptable to all, so that even states with some objections will not press them by insisting on a vote, but will content themselves with making statements on their position before or after the adoption of the agreement. In this way, although the resultant agreement will generally, in order to attract consensus, be expressed in more general or "constructively" ambiguous terms, the expectation is that it is more likely to be put into practice by all states affected than if it was adopted by a divisive vote (Birnie and Boyle 1992, 19).

The implications of this condition are significant. Unlike bilateral negotiations where each party has a veto, which creates a basic element of equality, the veto rarely exists in multilateral negotiation. Parties that disagree with the proposed treaty (or a section thereof) can abstain without blocking the outcome. Pressure to accept consensus language is often so high that parties may agree to the text at the eleventh hour so as not to be blamed for the failure of the negotiations. At the same time, the attempt to reach consensus usually means that lowest common denominator agreements without teeth are residual possibilities. Such agreements may form the basis of an incremental process that creates international socio-political pressures rather than legal obligations to conform, although this is not always the case.

Outcomes

Unlike many bilateral negotiations, the outcomes of multilateral negotiation are usually matters of rule-making rather than the redistribution of tangible goods. In this context, rule-making is defined to include both the negotiation of legally binding instruments, such as treaties, conventions, or protocols, as well as the negotiation of non-legally binding agreements, such as declarations, action plans, and recommendations. Rarely are the basic characteristics of division and exchange present in multilateral negotiations; instead, the main goal is to harmonize national legislation or establish rules that can be applied by and to states (Winham and Kizer 1993). This does not mean that tangible goods are not affected, but it does mean that the effect is uncertain, long range, and universal, instead of simply being contingent on the other party's actions. It also means that the importance of finding a mutually acceptable formula is even greater than in bilateral negotiations, since the adoption of a rule depends more on convincing justification or a notion of justice than on exchanged concessions in detail. Trade-offs between rules, however, are often a major part of the structure of multilateral agreements.

Group dynamics

The complexity of multilateral negotiations is also shaped by the group dynamics, including coalition formation, interpersonal relationships, and leadership.

The formation of coalitions is one of the many ways in which parties in multilateral negotiations handle their own large number by bringing it down to a manageable size. But coalition formation is not just a mechanism available to the many parties. Coalition is also applicable to the many issues, as it can reduce their complexity and make them manageable. Packaging, linkages, and trade-offs are all ways of making coalitions among issues, interests, and positions.

Norman Scott (1985, 45–46) adds that in some cases of multilateral negotiation the scale of participation is so large that special procedures have to be devised for consultations and decision-making. One such procedure is the emergence of the "group" system, where countries with common interests – geographical, socio-economic, or ideological, to name a few – form negotiating groups. Each group usually elects a spokesperson, often on a rotating base, and this serves to minimize the number of individual actors participating in the negotiations while increasing the leverage or bargaining position of many of the smaller, less influential countries.

The effective negotiating structure that emerges as a result of coalition formation may, in fact, be reduced to very few negotiators. Nevertheless, bargaining among a small number of groups is still more complex than any bilateral negotiation. Even when the structure is reduced to merely two coalitions, the complexities of intra-group negotiations and the problems of maintaining group cohesion result in a process that is far more difficult than bilateral negotiation (Touval 1991, 356–357). For example, the process of coalition formation is likely to be accompanied by an increasing differentiation among groups (Hopmann 1996, 261). Coalitions may establish internal cohesion through negative reference to other coalitions. The coalition formation process may break down some social bonds, thereby intensifying conflicts among members of opposing coalitions (Pruitt and Rubin 1986, 68–70). These conflicts may create obstacles to the negotiation process as a whole if they prevent members of different coalitions from setting aside their differences in order to achieve a satisfactory outcome.

Another aspect of group dynamics – interpersonal relationships – often plays the strongest role in negotiations within the UN system where negotiators often work with each other in many different forums over the course of a year. Not only do UN-related negotiations take place over a long period of time, but some are actually ongoing. As a result, reputation, trust, credibility, and friendships outside of the conference room can have an impact on the process and outcome of multilateral negotiations. This focus on relationships has been largely neglected in the literature. According to Rubin (1991, 226), in keeping with the cultural traditions of the United States and Western Europe – rather than cultures such as those of the Middle East, South and East Asia, and Africa, where on-going relationships among parties to a negotiation are the norm rather than the exception – the emphasis in negotiation writings has largely been placed on economic and political considerations.

Zartman and Berman (1982, 29) mention the positive impact that a good personal working relationship can have on the negotiations and a negotiator's credibility. They argue that contacts away from the bargaining table in a relaxed atmosphere may contribute to the creation of good working relationships. Along these lines, Benedick (1991, 48–50) describes the role that personal relationships played in the negotiations that resulted in the Montreal Protocol on Substances that Deplete the Ozone Layer. In 1986, two informal workshops were held that were able to break down the problems into smaller components, develop consensus by incremental stages, and establish a degree of rapport and mutual confidence among future participants in the diplomatic negotiations. During the September 1986 workshop in Leesburg, Virginia, participants were together day in and day out. Benedick described the workshop: "The shirt-sleeve working sessions were supplemented by evening barbecues, square dancing, a Southern-style plantation garden party, and bluegrass music – all of which helped to build personal relationships that were to carry over into the formal negotiations."

Of the many aspects of group dynamics, leadership is of especially great significance. Without effective leadership, the negotiations may get bogged down in the complexity of the issues and the multiplicity of interests that must be reconciled. Young (1989, 355) argues that leadership in multilateral environmental negotiation is a matter of entrepreneurship involving a combination of imagination in inventing institutional options and skill in brokering the interests of numerous actors to line up support for such actions.[1] A leader, in this context, is an actor who, desiring to see the successful conclusion of the negotiations and realizing that imposition is not feasible, undertakes to craft attractive proposals and to persuade others to come on board as supporters of such proposals. Examples of this type of leadership include the role played by the United Nations Environment Programme in the development of the Mediterranean

Action Plan in the early 1970s and the role the United States played in gaining support for the 1987 Montreal Protocol.[2]

Analyzing multilateral negotiations

Given the complexity of multilateral negotiation, it is often difficult to understand how agreements are actually reached. Policy analysts and planners need a way to compare new, impending negotiations with past negotiations to help them to determine whether or not the presence or absence of certain factors within the negotiation process will help or hinder the prospects of a strong outcome. To better understand multilateral negotiation, it is necessary to explain the process by which the participants adjust their interests and make concessions and compromises in order to reach agreement.

One can take a number of different approaches in the study of multilateral negotiations. This section summarizes some of these different means of analysis – decision, strategic, organizational, small group, coalition, leadership and phased process – focusing on their methods and utility. There is no single approach that is better than another, but some approaches can provide a better view of a particular negotiating process by virtue of their specific parameters or techniques.

Although all of these approaches have merit and can add different perspectives to the study of multilateral negotiation, *phased process analysis* will be used here to help construct a model for the study of multilateral environmental negotiation. Phased process analysis is based on the understanding that the process has to meet certain procedural imperatives in order to arrive at substantive goals (Zartman 1987, 8). Phased process analysis can provide a framework that reduces some of the complexities of multilateral negotiation to a more manageable level for understanding and analysis. It essentially divides the negotiation process into a number of successive, often overlapping phases in each of which negotiators have a particular focus of attention and concern. Although it could be said that progress in one phase opens the way to the succeeding phase with a different concentration, this is not necessarily the case. It is not unusual for two or even three phases to overlap in time. It is also possible for negotiators to return to an earlier phase, in effect or by deliberate intent. They may wish to take up previously neglected matters, to clarify others, or to start fresh in the light of new information or experience (Gulliver 1979, 121).

Phased process analysis was chosen over the other means of analysis because, by viewing the negotiation process as a succession of phases and turning points, it is possible to examine the actions of the negotiating parties to determine how international environmental agreements are arrived at, from the decision by the international community to address a particular issue to the ratification and implementation of the final agreement. A comparative study of different methods of phased process analysis appears in the next section.

So what are some of the other ways of analyzing complex multilateral negotiations? One method is *decision analysis*,[3] which is based on "seriatim consideration of each player's outcome values, followed by comparison among them" (Zartman 1994, 7). Although it is usually applied in a prescriptive mode to assist a single decision maker deal with one issue at a time, decision analysis can be used to explain multilateral negotiations. According to Spector (1994, 91), this technique is best suited to address "the process by which negotiators consider trade-offs across multi-issue formulas and modify their preferences, thus yielding a convergence of interests and compromise agreements." Decision analysis can help clarify why a party or a coalition chooses particular strategies and rejects others, the attractiveness of strategy options, the perceived likely outcomes of alternative strategies, and the probabilities of the occurrence of other-party strategies and other uncontrollable events. However, this approach is not suited for the analysis of other dimensions of the negotiation process, such as structure, the effects of situation, power, and strategy. It can nonetheless enhance a larger analysis of such negotiation processes in collaboration with other approaches.

Another method for analyzing multilateral negotiation is *strategic analysis* using game theory. This approach is based on the structure of values the parties assign to different outcomes, yet it pluralizes decision analysis because it considers outcomes to be the product of social interaction (Zartman 1994, 7). The multilateral form of strategic analysis, known as *n*-person game theory, is based on coalitions. Beginning with the coalitions' security points, game theory determines outcomes that can be achieved by coalitions or individuals acting rationally, according to formulas for agreement that embody various notions of justice (Rapoport, 1970). The strength of strategic analysis is that it can explicate the dynamics of negotiation processes and shed light on unfolding positions and possible changes of support patterns, as players offer compromises and respond to each other over time. In modeling negotiations, however, game theory has been used primarily, but not exclusively, to study two-person strategic situations.[4] Although multilateral negotiations can be reduced to bilateral negotiations, or a series of bilateral negotiations, they often resist such a simplification and the reduction of the negotiations to two-person games "would do violence to reality" (Brams, Doherty and Weidner 1994, 109).

A third method is *organizational analysis*, which is based on the institutional setting of multilateral negotiations. It explains outcomes through parties' behavior as determined from their position within an organization or from their need to find their way through the constraints of the organization (Zartman 1994, 8). Negotiations often replicate characteristics of the mother organizations that house them. Thus, the structure of the organization, its culture, its modes of decision-making, and its approaches to managing conflict influence each particular negotiation and, in turn, are affected by them (Kolb and Faure 1994, 129–130).[5] When analyzed by organization theory, international multilateral negotiations are viewed as processes that are set and managed by organizations. Since the majority of multilateral environmental negotiations have taken place within the United Nations system, it is safe to assume that the culture and modes of decision-making are representative of the United Nations. Thus, to a certain degree, the subsequent analysis of multilateral environmental negotiations does take organization analysis into account.

Small group analysis can be used to explain outcomes of interaction in a restricted pluralist setting. Like other approaches, small group analysis handles the complexity of multilateral negotiations by assuming a reduced number of players and focusing on within-group and among-group interactions, both seen as small group behavior (Zartman 1994, 8–9). Also, as in many of the other approaches, the focus is on process yet, by acknowledging that small groups are made up of individual actors interacting in face-to-face encounters, this approach looks more at social-psychological behaviors than at organizational characteristics. Small group analysis examines leadership, group composition, group history, and group cohesiveness in its attempt to explain multilateral negotiation.[6]

Coalition analysis examines multilateral negotiation in terms of building and working with coalitions. Dupont (1994, 148) defines coalitions as cooperative efforts for the attainment of short-range, issue-specific objectives. In multilateral negotiation, coalitions form and act according to the amount of congruence in the aspirations, goals, and purposes of the actors concerned. Thus, coalition analysis can be used to explain negotiations in terms of: the kind of coalition patterns that can be identified and decoded in a relevant taxonomy; the extent to which observed coalitions developed distinctive behavioral roles and strategies; and the extent to which the coalitions proved effective in making significant contributions to outcomes and in ensuring their own durability.[7]

Leadership analysis focuses even more sharply than coalition analysis on the negotiating agent, analyzing the tactics and strategies used to reduce the complexity both of parties and of issues to the point where a consensual decision emerges (Zartman 1994, 9). Underdal (1994, 178) defines leadership as "an asymmetrical relationship of influence in which one actor guides or directs the behavior of others toward a certain goal over a certain period of time." Leadership analysis can be used to identify the behavioral strategies available to negotiators and can provide important clues to how capabilities and behavior interact to affect outcomes. Underdal (1994, 180) points out that students of negotiation have had little interest in the study of leadership in multilateral negotiations. Likewise, students of leadership have paid little attention to the specifics of international negotiations. Nevertheless, existing theories of leadership are able to predict the capabilities required to provide different modes of leadership (and thus to identify potential leaders) and can identify the principal behavioral strategies available to these actors; they can thus provide important clues on how capabilities and behavior interact to affect outcomes (Underdal 1994, 193).[8]

Phased process analysis

Phased process analysis is characterized by its focus on the phases of negotiation. The notion of stages or phases of negotiation is purely an analytic one that, while corresponding to reality, is far sharper in concept than it is in practice. For analytical purposes of identification and discussion, phases can be isolated and examined in detail, but in reality they tend to overlap and have indistinct borders. The sequencing of these phases and the length of time that each takes vary greatly. The following is an overview of some of the studies that analyze the process of bilateral and multilateral negotiations using this approach.

I. William Zartman and Maureen R. Berman (1982) identify three phases in the negotiation process and associate different types of problems and behaviors with each phase.

(1) *Diagnostic phase.* Long before the first formal session opens, the negotiation process begins with the decision by each party to explore the possibility of negotiating. Although sometimes it is determined that the dispute or issue is non-negotiable, in many cases the interested parties agree that they need a solution and that the decision to negotiate must be unanimous. When this important "turning point of seriousness" has been reached – the perception by each party that the others are serious about finding a negotiated solution – this phase comes to a close and the actual negotiations begin.

(2) *Formula phase.* During this phase the parties negotiate a formula or common definition of the conflict in terms of a framework for agreement. Finding a formula means that the parties confront the basic elements of the controversy and either deal with them all or recognize their existence and put some aside for later consideration. Although there is no way of telling why or when a proposed formula

will be accepted by the other parties, acceptability is in some part a function of the formula's relevance, comprehensiveness, flexibility, coherence, balance, and uniqueness, as well as of the skill with which it is proposed and defended. Once a formula is proposed, the parties will study it for implications, applying it to details on a trial basis to see what it means. This process is brought out into the open when the formula seems suitable to both sides, is agreed upon, and is used to start addressing the details.

(3) *Detail phase.* Once the formula has been established, it can provide guidelines and referents for the solution of more precise problems and the search for detailed agreements can begin. There is often movement back and forth between this phase and the formula phase. Addressing the details is often the most complex part of the negotiation. Usually the number of details agreed upon increases as the end of negotiations approaches, and the existence of a specific deadline generally causes parties to hold out until they are ready to establish final positions just before time runs out.

Whereas Zartman and Berman's analysis is based on bilateral negotiation, Saadia Touval (1991) focuses on multilateral negotiation and also divides the process into three distinct phases.

(1) *Prenegotiation phase.* This phase is characterized by informal contact among the parties. Several important aspects of the negotiation are typically addressed during this preliminary phase: a list of participants is agreed upon; initial coalitions emerge; role differentiation takes place among the participants; and substantive and procedural issues are addressed. During this phase the parties learn more about the problems, develop an agenda, and search for a formula or general framework within which an agreement can be reached.

(2) *Formal negotiation phase.* This is where the exchange of information and the negotiation proper over the detailed terms of an agreement take place. The participants explore various alternative packages and may reach some tentative, conditional understandings.

(3) *Agreement phase.* In this phase, the participants translate tentative understandings into legally phrased agreements. During this phase, the participants often have second thoughts about the terms that they have agreed upon. Furthermore, concerns about the implementation of the agreement tend to increase. Such misgivings may prompt efforts to obtain new assurances about compliance and implementation. These last-minute problems, according to Touval, may prolong the agreement phase, the end of which is sometimes facilitated by deadlines. Owing to the large number of participants, such reservations and the introduction of any new proposals at this stage are both likely to delay the conclusion of a multilateral negotiation.

P. H. Gulliver (1979) describes two distinct though interconnected processes going on simultaneously: a repetitive, cyclical one and a developmental one. The cyclical process is composed of the repetitive exchange of information between parties, its assessment, and the resulting adjustments of expectations and preferences. The developmental process involves the progression from the initiation of the negotiations to their conclusion. It comprises a series of overlapping sequences or phases, each with a particular emphasis and kind of interaction that opens the way for the succeeding phase in a complex progression. These phases are not in practice, or in conception, altogether congruent with linear, chronological time. Nor is it unusual for two, or even three, phases to overlap in time. In fact, at any given time negotiators may return to an earlier phase, in effect or by deliberate intent. Although Gulliver's model was developed specifically for bilateral negotiation, his phases can easily be used for analyzing multilateral negotiation.

Gulliver defines his eight phases as follows:

(1) *Search for an arena.* Once the parties recognize that disagreement and conflict are not immediately resolvable and prepare to negotiate a mutually tolerable resolution, there is a need to agree to some place where the negotiations will take place.

(2) *Composition of an agenda and definition of issues.* During this phase each party takes stock of the situation and of the possibilities now open. Agenda formulation is not always problematic and can often be resolved before proceeding to the next phase. However, even when the parties agree upon the agenda, this does not necessarily mean that it is adhered to faithfully thereafter. Either party may later wish to introduce new issues or redefine existing ones.

(3) *Establishing maximal limits to issues in dispute.* This phase is often characterized as the beginning of real negotiations. Each party reiterates and develops initial stands, both in general and on particular issues, and continues to elaborate on them. In the course of these exchanges, each party attempts to extract greater precision and firmer commitment from the others.

(4) *Narrowing the differences.* This phase begins when there is a shift in orientation by the parties and the interaction between them. The emphasis changes from differences, separateness, and antagonism toward coordination, collusion, and even cooperation. Where a dispute includes several or many issues, this phase is generally prolonged as the parties grapple with the considerable complexities involved. The difficult issues are identified and the parties are faced with the necessity of somehow dealing with them in order to obtain final agreement.

(5) *Preliminaries to final bargaining.* When the parties' differences are more starkly revealed and the outstanding issues reduced to a small

number, the parties move into the final bargaining phase. Before that, they often (but not always) engage in further explorations that can bring additional clarification and set the stage for final bargaining. These preliminaries are concerned with one or more purposes: the search for a viable bargaining range, the refining of persisting differences, the testing of trading possibilities, and the construction of a bargaining formula.

(6) *Final bargaining.* This phase consists of the exchange of more or less specific, substantive proposals about the terms of agreement for the outcome of one or more issues under negotiation.

(7) *Ritual affirmation.* A negotiated outcome prescribing novelty of some kind is usually given some type of formal affirmation, such as a ceremony, to make it clear and to mark and seal it. Not all outcomes require formal affirmation, however. The culmination of the negotiations may be an impasse or breakdown such that the outcome is a return to the status quo.

(8) *Execution of the agreement.* This post-negotiation phase involves carrying out the provisions of the agreement. Often the execution of the agreement is handed over to specialists such as administrative or judicial officials, political leaders, lawyers, or a standing committee.

Robert L. Friedheim (1987) defined a series of phases with respect to the negotiations during the Third United Nations Conference on the Law of Sea. Although Friedheim built his model around a series of negotiations that lasted for more than 15 years, his phases can also be applied to other, less complex, multilateral environmental negotiations. Friedheim defined his five phases as follows:

(1) *Stating basic orientations; exploring others' positions; looking for coalition partners.* There is little concern in this phase for movement toward an outcome. The issues are new and often technically demanding. Many of the participants may need time to acquaint themselves with the issues and determine their positions.

(2) *First statement of formal proposals; firming up of coalitions.* During this phase the initial debate takes place and agreement on basic principles, trade-offs, and formulas may begin.

(3) *Informal drafting groups.* During this phase, informal drafts showing patterns of agreement on some issues emerge. Whether the text is a chairperson's draft or a compilation of ideas from an informal working group, this text often becomes the basis for further negotiation.

(4) *Single negotiating text.* This phase is primarily a process of refinement where the parties work toward making marginal improvements on a general outcome that they essentially have decided upon. It presupposes the acceptance by the parties, willingly or unwillingly, of a conceptual framework.

(5) *Endgame.* During this phase it is possible that some parties insist on major revisions or changes to the text of the agreement at the last minute. It is also during this phase that the final treaty is adopted.

Volker Rittberger (1983) analyzes the processes of global conference diplomacy as represented by ad hoc world conferences by delineating four principal phases.

(1) *Conference initiation.* This phase is characterized by a succession of exploratory talks and contacts among governments, sometimes also involving agencies and bodies within the United Nations system and other intergovernmental organizations. Their purpose is to determine whether or not there exists a general consensus, or at least a widely shared view, that an issue of international concern warrants a collective diplomatic effort. This phase comes to an end with the formal decision to convene a conference.

(2) *Conference preparation.* This phase centers on the identification of specific aspects of the issue to be dealt with by the conference and surveys the options for collective action. This is where the analytical and strategic groundwork for conference decision-making has to be laid. During this phase, there may be several sub-phases. First, experts are often brought together to help develop a general framework for negotiation. Then a committee of governmental experts is established and charged with elaborating an outline of an international legal instrument and pinpointing areas of controversy. Sometimes participants in this preparatory process are even able to complete a draft text to forward to the conference itself.

(3) *Conference decision-making.* This phase coincides with the conference itself. Occasionally, the conference outcome has been pre-negotiated and pre-decided to such an extent that the conference has only to give its formal endorsement to the draft text elaborated during the preparatory phase. More frequently, however, the conference itself is characterized by intense negotiations, not only about format and scope, but also about many detailed provisions.

(4) *Conference implementation.* During this post-negotiation phase, the policy program that was agreed to as a result of the negotiations has to be translated into policy measures by the participating states and – in most cases – by one or more international organizations.

Abiodun Williams (1992) identifies three phases in the negotiation process that are characteristic of many multilateral negotiations.

(1) *Deciding to negotiate.* Parties may enter negotiations in order to bring an end to a military conflict, to further their security interests, to address trade and development issues, to deal with environmental dangers, to resolve competing claims over natural resources, or to deal with the activities of certain actors in the international system.

(2) *Reaching an agreement.* Negotiators have to take into account not only the positions of their respective governments and domestic interest groups but also those of the regional bloc or coalition to which their country belongs. The ability to work within a coalition and with other coalitions is an important element in this phase of the process.

(3) *Endgame.* During many multilateral negotiations, the final elements of a treaty or agreement are usually hammered out under significant time pressure during this last phase of the process. The setting of deadlines and the awareness that time is limited often create a certain momentum that causes the different parties to shift their positions and compromise. It is during this phase of negotiations that final decisions are usually reached, either by consensus or by vote.

Gareth Porter, Janet Welsh Brown, and Pamela Chasek (2000) focus their attention on the multilateral negotiation process that results in the development of global environmental agreements. They identify three phases.

(1) *Issue definition.* This phase brings the issue to the attention of the international community and identifies the scope and magnitude of the environmental threat, its primary causes, and the type of international action required to address the issue. The actors who introduce and define the issue often publicize new scientific evidence or theories, as in the case of ozone depletion, acid rain, and climate change. An issue may be placed on the global environmental agenda by one or more state actors, by an international organization, or by a non-governmental organization.

(2) *Fact-finding.* This phase may be well developed or only minimal. In some cases, a mediating international organization has brought interested parties together in an attempt to establish a baseline of facts on which there is agreement and to clarify the scope and nature of differences in understanding the problem and possible policy options for international action. This phase often overlaps with and becomes indistinguishable from the bargaining phase.

(3) *Bargaining.* During this phase, a lead state may start to advance a proposal for international action and try to build consensus behind it. International cleavages and coalitions begin to form. The outcome of this phase depends on the bargaining leverage and cohesion of the veto coalition – the group of states that can block a strong international regime on the issue if they choose to since their cooperation is necessary for its effectiveness.

Fen Osler Hampson (1995) identifies three phases in his study of multilateral negotiations.

(1) *Prenegotiation.* This is the period when parties define the problem, search for options, and develop a commitment to negotiate. Essen-

tially, prenegotiation is the prelude to formal negotiations, marked by a decision by one or more parties to consider negotiation as a behavioral option. In a multilateral setting, prenegotiation is useful in managing complexity when many potential parties and issues are involved and the risks of formal negotiation are high. For example, prenegotiations can set the basic principles and rules that will guide the negotiations themselves, identify and select participants, and set the agenda (which issues should be included or kept off the negotiating table).

(2) *Negotiation.* During the formal negotiation phase, participants exchange information, discuss alternative negotiation packages, and move from a general formula to the details of an agreement.

(3) *Agreement and implementation.* At the agreement phase, parties will reach a preliminary settlement and seek to translate that settlement into a concrete package of mutual commitments and undertakings. In multilateral negotiations, the process can be prolonged and difficult as efforts are made to accommodate the varying interests and concerns of the various parties to the final settlement. Verification and compliance considerations also have to be taken into account. Sometimes new or unanticipated problems emerge, and this may require further negotiations or discussions.

A comparison of different examples of phased process analysis

Each of the eight examples of the phased process analysis described above concentrates on different types of negotiation (bilateral, multilateral, or conference diplomacy) and identifies varying numbers of phases. Whether or not one example is better than the next is not important here. What is notable, however, is that there are a number of similarities between the examples. Perhaps the most important of these similarities is that, in effect, all of these variations can be consolidated into four main phases (see figure 3.1). Using a slightly modified version of Zartman and Berman's (1982) terminology, these four main phases can be defined as: diagnosis, formula, details, and implementation.[9]

Diagnosis or prenegotiation phase

In the diagnosis or prenegotiation phase, the parties analyze the situation, develop an information base, and make the decision to explore the possibility of negotiating. I. William Zartman (1989, 4) argues that pre-

PHASES OF MULTILATERAL NEGOTIATION							
	TOUVAL	GULLIVER	FRIEDHEIM	RITTBERGER	WILLIAMS	PORTER et al.	HAMPSON
D I A G N O S I S	Pre negotiation	Search for an arena Defining agenda and issues	Exploring positions; forming coalitions	Initiation of conference project	Deciding to negotiate	Issue definition	Prenegotiation
F O R M U L A	Formal negotiation phase	Establishing maximal limits Narrowing differences Preliminaries to final bargaining	Making formal proposals; firming up coalitions Informal drafting groups	Conference preparation	Reaching an agreement	Fact-finding process Bargaining process	Negotiation
D E T A I L S	Agreement phase	Final bargaining Ritual affirmation	Single negotiating text Endgame	Conference decision-making	Endgame	Bargaining process	Negotiation
I M P L E M E N T A T I O N		Execution of the agreement		Conference implementation			Agreement and implementation

Fig. 3.1 Phases of multilateral negotiation: A comparison of different approaches

negotiation or diagnosis begins when one or more parties consider negotiation as a policy option and communicate this intention to other parties.
The phase ends when the parties agree to formal negotiations (an exchange of proposals designed to arrive at a mutually acceptable outcome
in a situation of interdependent interests) or when one party abandons
the consideration of negotiation as an option. Harold Saunders (1985)
describes the prenegotiation phase as containing two sub-phases. During
the first sub-phase the parties aim to achieve a shared definition of the
problem. In the second sub-phase, parties commit to a negotiated settle-

ment if they conclude that a fair settlement is likely. Brian Tomlin (1989, 22) defines the prenegotiation phase as the period in relations between parties when negotiation is considered, and perhaps adopted, as an option. The onset of the prenegotiation process is marked by a turning point in the relations between parties, when negotiation is added to the range of options being considered.

This phase of the negotiation process serves a number of functions. According to Janice Gross Stein (1989, 251–252), prenegotiation reduces uncertainty and manages complexity at lower cost. It provides valuable information and reduces risk by defining the structure of negotiation through the specification of boundaries, the participants, and even the agenda for the negotiations that may follow.

Touval (1991), Friedheim (1987), Rittberger (1983), Williams (1992), Porter, Brown, and Chasek (2000), and Hampson (1995) each outline a prenegotiation or diagnosis phase in their analyses of bilateral and multilateral negotiation. Touval's prenegotiation phase and Rittberger's "conference initiation" phase are similar to Zartman's diagnosis phase – each focuses on developing an information base and ends with the decision to begin negotiations. Williams focuses primarily on "deciding to negotiate," whereas Friedheim assumes that the decision to negotiate has already been taken and looks primarily at issue definition and exploring positions. Porter et al.'s "issue definition" phase begins by bringing the issue to the attention of the international community and ends with the decision on the type of international action required to address the issue. Hampson's prenegotiation phase is similar to this. Gulliver (1979) has two phases in his model that would fit into a more general prenegotiation or diagnosis phase. These phases, "search for an arena" and "defining agenda and issues," assume that the decision to negotiate has already been taken. Yet, at the same time these two phases define the structure of the upcoming negotiation by assuring a common perception of the major issues to be negotiated and determining where the negotiations will take place, who will participate, and what the agenda will be.

Formula phase

During this phase the parties negotiate a formula or common definition of the conflict in terms of a framework for agreement. Negotiators narrow their divergence of interpretations of the problems to be negotiated, select negotiable issues, and define broad principles, which are apt to become the basis for possible workable solutions (Dupont and Faure 1991, 43). Although the formula phase usually lasts for a shorter period of time than the prenegotiation or diagnosis phase, it is a time of intense negotiation involving direct confrontations at formal sessions. During this phase the tactics of the parties are concentrated on finding a favorable and agreeable framework and making it stick. In addition, the problem is most likely to be undergoing some changes of its own. The longer the negotiations go on, the more likely there will be changes. Whether produced by the problem itself or manipulated by the parties, the changes in the conflict provide arguments for one side or the other, supporting or undermining the formulas under discussion (Zartman and Berman 1982, 143).

Touval (1991) and Rittberger (1983) do not specifically refer to formula-building in their analyses. Touval calls this the "formal negotiation phase." Here the participants explore various alternatives, exchange information, and may reach some tentative understandings. Rittberger calls this the "conference preparation" phase, where a general framework for negotiation is developed and, possibly, negotiation of a draft text is completed.

Three of Gulliver's (1979) phases fit into the broader notion of formula-building. "Establishing maximal limits to issues in dispute" represents the presentation of initial positions, a prerequisite to formula-building. "Narrowing the differences" marks a shift towards coordination and cooperation and could be considered the first part of formula-building. Gulliver's "preliminaries to final bargaining" phase includes the search for a viable bargaining range and the construction of a bargaining formula.

Two of Friedheim's (1987) phases also can be placed into the overall formula-building phase. The "first statement of formal proposals," like Gulliver's "establishing maximal limits," involves the presentation of initial positions. During Friedheim's "informal drafting groups" phase, patterns of agreement on some issues emerge. Although this phase is more inductive (to put an agreement together through mutual compromise or exchanged concessions) than deductive (to establish the formula first and then work out the implementing details), it fits into the overall theme of finding an agreeable framework. Similarly, Williams' (1992) phase "reaching an agreement" is more inductive than deductive. He describes this phase as the one where the parties present drafts and make initial compromises.

Porter et al.'s (2000) "fact-finding" phase could be interpreted as formula-building as well. It involves arriving at a mutual understanding of the problem and bringing forward possible policy options. Their "bargaining" phase straddles both the formula and the details phases since it involves both advancing a proposal and trying to build a consensus around it as well as negotiating the final details. Hampson's (1995) negotiation phase includes both formula-building and working out the details to an agreement.

Detail phase

According to Zartman and Berman (1982, 147), once the formula has been established it can provide guidelines and referents for the solution of more precise problems and, thus, the search for detailed agreements can begin. It is during this phase that the final text of the agreement takes shape and the final concessions are made; the result, in theory, is an agreement that all parties can sign.

Touval's (1991) "agreement" phase is similar to Zartman and Berman's details phase in that the participants translate tentative understandings (possibly formulas) into legally phrased agreements. Last-minute problems are also likely during this phase because the participants often have second thoughts about the implications of some aspects of the "formulas" they may have agreed to in the previous phase. Since Rittberger (1983) focuses on conference diplomacy, he describes the detail phase as "conference decision-making" since the details of an agreement are often worked out at the conference itself, rather than during the preparatory period. Williams (1992) calls this phase of the process "endgame," where the final details are often arrived at under significant time pressure.

Gulliver (1979) calls his version of this phase "final bargaining," which includes the exchange of specific, substantive proposals. Although Zartman and Berman do not go into detail about the conclusion of the negotiations, Gulliver elaborates on this sub-phase, the culmination of the negotiations, and calls it "ritual affirmation."

Friedheim (1987) also subdivides this phase into two components. The first, the "single negotiating text," is when the process of refinement takes place. It presupposes that the parties have accepted a conceptual framework, i.e. a formula. He calls the second sub-phase "endgame," for it is here that parties may insist on major revisions or changes at the last minute before the agreement is finally adopted. These two sub-phases are of a more simultaneous than chronological nature as different parties may insist on major revisions of different parts of the overall agreement.

Porter et al. (2000) do not distinguish between a formula phase and a details phase, but rather encompass both in a phase they call "bargaining." Hampson (1995) includes both the formula and the detail phase in a single phase he calls "negotiation."

Implementation

In their model, Zartman and Berman (1982) do not have a phase entitled "implementation." Their model comes to an end after the details have been negotiated and a final agreement is on the table. Gulliver (1979), Rittberger (1983), and Hampson (1995), however, include a final phase in their models that takes into account what happens after the agreement leaves the table. The implementation phase takes place on two inter-related levels – the national level and the international level.

At the national level, according to Rittberger, once an agreement is complete it has to be translated into policy measures by the participating states. Only after a specified number of nations have voluntarily accepted and ratified the agreement does it enter into force.

At the national level, each party is responsible for developing the laws, regulations, and infrastructure necessary to fulfill the provisions of the agreement. This phase often involves a new series of negotiations within governments, because the domestic political environment for the imple-mentation of internationally negotiated policies is not always favorable. At best there is a delay. At worst, the political battles that attend the adoption of any important international agreement affecting domestic economic interests may prevent ratification altogether. When (or if) the new agreement ultimately comes into force, it may be with the adherence of less than all the members of the organization or it may contain unfor-tunate or restrictive reservations (Chayes and Chayes 1991, 283).

Once a state ratifies the agreement and after it enters into force, a designated national authority typically reports to an international secre-tariat on domestic efforts to implement and comply with the terms of the agreement. The more complex, extensive, and unprecedented the agree-ment, the more likely there will be non-compliance with some or all of its provisions by some national governments. The enforcement of compli-ance with international agreements often depends on peer or public pressure on nations because no supranational body with the authority to enforce compliance exists. To some extent, this arrangement reflects nations' belief that, if compliance mechanisms were more stringent, fewer nations would participate and treaty obligations would be weaker (GAO 1992, 12).

At the international level, negotiation can often continue as the regime evolves, rather than ending with the signing of an agreement. Loopholes need to be tightened, new members brought in, obligations strengthened, ambiguities reaffirmed, and coverage extended. Chayes and Chayes (1991, 282) refer to this as the level of legislation or regulation. It involves institutional processes for formulating general rules to meet new needs or changed circumstances, without the requirement of concluding a new treaty or amending the original one. In some cases this involves the negotiation of one or more protocols that elaborate the details of imple-mentation of the parent treaty.

Summary

In the UN system, the complexities brought about by multiple issues, parties, and roles as well as the use of consensus decision-making have led to the development of practices and procedures that are quite different from those used in bilateral negotiation. Some of the characteristics of multilateral negotiation in general, as well as specific cases of multilateral environmental negotiation, are as follows:

- *Multiple parties.* Each participant has interests that require accommodation. The larger the number of participants, the greater the likelihood of conflicting interests and positions, and the more complex the interconnections among the parties.
- *Multiple issues.* Although multilateral negotiations can focus on a single issue, a multiplicity of issues is the norm. In addition to complicating the negotiations, multiple issues provide the means as well as the subject of agreement, since they allow for trade-offs that can lead to a successful outcome.
- *Multiple roles.* Parties can play a number of different kinds of roles in the negotiations. They can Drive, Conduct, Defend, Brake, or Cruise. Role diversity can allow the issue and party complexities to be combined in an agreeable outcome.
- *Consensus decision-making.* Most multilateral agreements are reached by consensus. This involves the continuation of negotiations in an endeavor to reach a compromise that will be reasonably acceptable to all.
- *Rule-making.* The main goal of most multilateral negotiations is to harmonize national legislation or establish rules that can be applied by and to states.
- *Coalition formation.* The formation of coalitions or groups based on common goals, ideologies, interests, or geography is one of the many ways in which parties in multilateral negotiations handle their own large number by reducing it to a manageable size.
- *Length of negotiation process.* Multilateral environmental negotiations usually take a long time from the analysis and understanding of issues to decision-making and the development of plans for implementation and monitoring.
- *Interpersonal relationships.* Particularly within the UN system, interpersonal relationships, involving reputation, trust, credibility, and friendships outside the conference room, can have an impact on the process and outcome of the negotiations.
- *Multiplicity of types of participants.* Multilateral environmental negotiations typically involve five types of participants: governments, the scientific community, secretariats, non-governmental organizations, and the public/media.

- *Ongoing nature.* Complex multilateral environmental negotiations are usually ongoing and, thus, their outcomes are rarely final. Agreements are often reopened either to include new controls in existing regimes or to expand these control measures quantitatively.

A number of methods are used to analyze negotiations. One of these methods, which is particularly useful in explaining process and outcome in bilateral and multilateral negotiation, is phased process analysis. By viewing the negotiation process as a succession of phases and turning points, it is possible to manage the complexities inherent in multilateral negotiation and identify relationships between variations in process and outcome.

A number of different examples of phased process analysis were examined in this chapter. Some of them are based on studies of bilateral negotiation and non-environmental multilateral negotiations. Yet their definition of phases can be applied to environmental negotiation and can facilitate its analysis. By comparing each of the approaches, four main categories of phases were identified: diagnosis or prenegotiation, formula, details, and implementation. Using these categories as a general framework, it is possible to examine the actions of the negotiating parties to determine how international environmental agreements are arrived at, from the decision by the international community to address a particular issue to the ratification and implementation of the final agreement.

Notes

1. For a discussion of political leadership as a form of entrepreneurship, see Norman Frohlich, Joe A. Oppenheimer, and Oran R. Young, *Political Leadership and Collective Goods* (Princeton, NJ: Princeton University Press, 1971).
2. For more information about these two negotiating processes, see Chapter 4.
3. For more information on applying decision analysis to negotiation see J. Ulvila and R. Brown, "Decision Analysis Comes of Age," *Harvard Business Review*, 1982, 60(5), 130–141; J. Ulvila and W. Snider, "Negotiation of International Oil Tanker Standards: An Application of Multiattribute Value Theory," *Operations Research*, 1980, 28, 81–96; and D. Kahneman and A. Tversky, "Choices, Values and Frames," in H. Arkes and K. Hammond (eds.), *Judgement and Decision Making: An Interdisciplinary Reader* (New York: Cambridge University Press, 1986).
4. For examples, see S. J. Brams, *Negotiation Games: Applying Game Theory to Bargaining and Arbitration* (New York: Routledge & Kegan Paul, 1990) and H. Raiffa, *The Art and Science of Negotiation* (Cambridge, MA: Harvard University Press, 1982).
5. For more information on the dimensions of organization theory, see H. Mintzberg, *The Structuring Organizations* (Englewood Cliffs, NJ: Prentice Hall, 1979); J. G. March and H. A. Simon, *Organizations* (New York: Wiley, 1958); and D. M. Kolb and J. M. Bartunek (eds.), *Hidden Conflict in Organizations: Uncovering Behind the Scenes Disputes* (Newbury Park, CA: Sage, 1992).

6. Although small group research is often not applied to international negotiation, see Galtung (1968) and Druckman (1990) for a review of the relevant literature that does exist.
7. For good descriptions of coalition analysis, see W. B. Stevenson, J. L. Pearce, and L. W. Porter, "The Concept of Coalition in Organization Theory and Research," *Academy of Management Review,* 1985, 10(2), 256–268; S. B. Bacharach and E. J. Lawler, *Power and Politics in Organizations: The Social Psychology of Conflict, Coalitions, and Bargaining* (San Francisco: Jossey-Bass, 1981).
8. For some examples of how leadership theory is used to explain international negotiations, see Young (1989, 1991), Winham and Kizer (1993), and Benedick (1991).
9. Zartman and Berman (1982) do not include an implementation phase in their use of the phased process method of analysis.

4

Eleven cases of multilateral environmental negotiation

The first step in developing the model of the multilateral environmental negotiation process was to select and examine the negotiations of a representative sample of environmental agreements. From the list of international environmental treaties in the United Nations Environment Programme's *Register of International Treaties and Other Agreements in the Field of the Environment*, 11 cases were chosen because: (a) they represent the range of different environmental issues; (b) they represent negotiations on both the global and regional levels; and (c) sufficient primary and secondary sources of information are available about the negotiations themselves.

The cases of multilateral environmental negotiations that were chosen are:

- 1972 Convention on the Prevention of Marine Pollution by Dumping of Wastes and Other Matters (London Convention);
- 1973 International Convention for the Prevention of Pollution from Ships (MARPOL) as modified by the 1978 Protocol;
- 1973 Washington Convention on International Trade in Endangered Species (CITES);
- 1976 Barcelona Convention for the Protection of the Mediterranean Sea against Pollution;
- 1979 Geneva Convention on Long-Range Transboundary Air Pollution (LRTAP);

Table 4.1 International agreements in the field of the environment

Topic	No. of agreements
Ocean/sea pollution	29
Marine life/fish	18
Ocean/sea general	14
Rivers	9
Wildlife/plants/biodiversity	25
Insects/pests/plant disease	5
Timber	1
Antarctica	4
Air pollution	4
Ozone layer	3
Climate change	1
Hazardous waste/toxic substances	4
Wetlands	2
Deserts/drought	1
Regional environment	3
Nuclear	14
Military	2
Space	1
Occupational hazards	5
Miscellaneous	9
TOTAL	154

- 1980 Convention on the Conservation of Antarctic Marine Living Resources (CCAMLR);
- 1983 International Tropical Timber Agreement (ITTA);
- 1987 Montreal Protocol to the Vienna Convention for the Protection of the Ozone Layer on Substances that Deplete the Ozone Layer;
- 1989 Basel Convention on the Control of Transboundary Movements of Hazardous Wastes and Their Disposal;
- 1992 Convention on Biological Diversity; and
- 1992 Framework Convention on Climate Change.

This sample reflects most of the categories of environmental issues that have been the subject of international treaties (see table 4.1). The London Convention, MARPOL, and the Mediterranean Convention all address ocean issues. Since 61 (40 percent) of the treaties on record deal with ocean-related issues, it was imperative that more than one ocean-related treaty be analyzed so that the case studies are more reflective of the subject matter of the complete list of treaties. CCAMLR, CITES, and the Biodiversity Convention address plant and animal resources – the subject of 30 (20 percent) of the treaties on record. The Convention on Long-Range Transboundary Air Pollution, the Montreal Protocol, and the Climate Change Convention all address atmospheric issues. CCAMLR deals with Antarctic issues, ITTA addresses timber/forestry issues, and the Basel Convention focuses on hazardous waste issues. CITES and ITTA also focus on international trade in natural resources.

Negotiations on rivers and other regional environmental issues were not analyzed since they are often bilateral or have a limited number of participants, and little information about the negotiations is readily available. Although the United Nations considers agreements on occupational health hazards and space, and on military, nuclear, and several miscellaneous topics to fall under the category of environmental agreements, and these are all important agreements, there is a large available body of literature for each of these topics. To distill the environmental aspects of these topics for incorporation in this analysis would not add much in the way of substance.

The case studies are representative of both regional and global environmental problems and negotiations, as well as those conventions negotiated under UN auspices and those that were not. The Mediterranean and transboundary air pollution conventions are both regional conventions aimed at regional pollution issues. CCAMLR also addresses a regional issue – Antarctic living marine resources – and was negotiated by the countries that are parties to the Antarctic Treaty. The negotiating processes for the rest of the agreements were open to all states, although the number of participants in the negotiations differed based on the issue and level of interest. For example, ITTA was negotiated primarily by states that export or import tropical timber.

The sample also reflects a balance between negotiations that resulted in framework conventions, "stand-alone" conventions, and protocols. For the purposes of this analysis, a convention is defined as an agreement between states for the regulation of matters affecting all of them. A "stand-alone" convention is one that lays down clear, detailed or specific rules capable of being enacted into municipal law. A framework convention lays down general requirements for states "to take measure" or enact "all practicable measures." These require further action by states to prescribe the precise measures to be taken, which can include concluding more specific conventions, adding protocols to existing conventions, or enacting national legislation. Protocols are discrete actions directed at achieving concrete objectives (or technical standards) consistent with a convention. Whereas the convention develops a general statement of the problem and a possible solution, protocols typically deal with the details of implementation. Although there is a conceptual difference between conventions and protocols, the negotiating processes are similar enough not to merit different treatment in this analysis.

The Mediterranean, transboundary air pollution, hazardous wastes, and climate change conventions are all framework conventions and it was expected almost from the outset that protocols to implement these conventions would be negotiated subsequently. This is often referred to as the "Convention–Protocol" approach to international treaty-making. The London Convention, CITES, CCAMLR, ITTA, and the Biodiversity Convention are conventions that do not depend on implementing protocols. The 1978 MARPOL Protocol and the Montreal Protocol are both aimed at improving or implementing existing conventions – the 1973 Convention for the Prevention of Pollution from Ships and the 1975 Vienna Convention for the Protection of the Ozone Layer.

The negotiations resulting in the 1982 UN Convention on the Law of the Sea were not included in this sample because their length and complexity make this negotiation process difficult to compare with the other negotiations on environmental issues. The UN Conference on the Law of the Sea met in session between December 1973 and December 1982 for a total of over 90 weeks and held extensive intersessional consultations, producing ultimately a text containing 320 articles, with 9 technical annexes and 4 resolutions. Other environmental negotiations have lasted on average for two to three years and the resulting treaties have an average of 20 articles.

Finally, no failed negotiations were included in this sample. Unlike many bilateral negotiations, multilateral environmental negotiations are not characterized by parties walking away from the table, leading to a breakdown in the talks. This is due to the subject matter of the negotiations, the large number of participating countries, and the use of consensus decision-making. Environmental negotiations that move beyond issue definition tend to be "successfully" concluded, although many would argue that the quality of environmental treaties often suffers from the participants' desire to reach an agreed outcome. Consensus decision-making usually ensures that treaties based on "least common denominator" agreements are adopted and the negotiations rarely, if ever, end in stalemate or failure.

Both primary and secondary source materials as well as personal interviews were used in researching the cases. The main purpose of this research was to determine what phases the negotiations passed through from the time the decision was taken to negotiate a treaty to the time that the treaty was adopted. As a result, rather than focusing in detail on the issues being negotiated, these 11 case studies focus on the process. By applying the theoretical aspects of phased process analysis to these cases, it became clear that each of the cases had six loosely defined phases in common: precipitants; issue definition; statement of initial positions; drafting/formula-building; final bargaining/details; and ratification/implementation. The characteristics of each of these phases will be examined in detail in

Chapter 5, together with the turning points that allowed progress from one phase to the next.

The following summaries of the case studies are not intended to provide a complete picture of the issues under negotiation, the positions taken by different states or groups of states, or the numerous problems that may have been encountered along the way. Nor are they intended to provide a detailed analysis of any one aspect of the negotiations. Instead they have been presented to provide background information in the form of a summary of the major phases and turning points of the negotiations, and how they were influenced by specific internal or external events or activities.

1972 Convention on the Prevention of Marine Pollution by Dumping of Wastes and Other Matters (the London Convention)

Objectives of the negotiations

The aim was to prevent indiscriminate disposal at sea of wastes liable to create hazards to human health, harm living resources and marine life, damage amenities, or interfere with other legitimate uses of the sea.

Precipitants

The London Convention had its origins on 15 April 1970 when US President Richard M. Nixon stated in a message to Congress that he was directing the Council on Environmental Quality (CEQ) and several other federal agencies to study the problems and alternatives to ocean dumping, and to "recommend further actions" (Caldwell 1984). The CEQ responded by issuing a report entitled "Ocean Dumping: A National Policy," which led to the enactment of the Marine Mammal Protection, Research, and Sanctuaries Act of 23 October 1972. Meanwhile, Nixon instructed the Secretary of State, in coordination with the chairman of the CEQ, to develop and pursue international initiatives directed toward banning unregulated ocean dumping on a global basis (Leitzell 1973).

Meanwhile, in the international arena, preparations for the 1972 United Nations Conference on the Human Environment (UNCHE) were underway. In the area of marine policy, efforts concentrated on a number of environmentally destructive activities, including ocean dumping. As part of the preparatory process for the UNCHE, a number of intergovernmental working groups were formed. One of these groups, the Intergovernmental Working Group on Marine Pollution (IWGMP), became the major forum for the discussion of ocean dumping.

Turning point 1

The United States initiated the negotiating process for a convention when it tabled the first draft of a convention on ocean dumping in June 1971, at the first meeting of the IWGMP in London.

Issue definition and statement of initial positions

At the London meeting of the IWGMP in 1971, there was general support for the idea of adopting a convention. Nevertheless, the US draft Convention for the Regulation of Transportation for Ocean Dumping was criticized for leaving too much discretion to the states and was even called "a license to pollute" (McManus 1983). The definition of issues continued at the second session of the IWGMP, held in Ottawa in November 1971. During this meeting, two working groups were established. One of these groups, under the chairmanship of C. Calenda of Italy, considered the convention on dumping. By this point, Spain and Sweden had submitted their own drafts of a convention.

Turning point 2/3

With three drafts on the table (from the United States, Spain, and Sweden), the working group decided to establish a drafting group to prepare a single text to serve as the basis for further negotiations.

Drafting/formula-building

By the end of the November 1971 meeting, the IWGMP as a whole approved the "Draft Articles on Ocean Dumping." Since the draft articles did not constitute a complete convention (there were no institutional provisions), they were not included in the documentation of the UNCHE. Negotiations took place in a series of ad hoc meetings of interested governments up until the Stockholm Conference in June 1972. The Intergovernmental Meeting on Ocean Dumping, convened by the government of Iceland, with the co-sponsorship of the United States and Sweden, was attended by representatives from 29 states. The Reykjavik meeting examined a revised draft convention submitted by the United States, the draft articles prepared by IWGMP, the text of the 1972 Oslo Convention on Ships and Aircraft Dumping, and draft articles submitted by Canada (McManus 1983). The participants could not agree on a complete text.

Turning point 4

By the end of the Reykjavik meeting delegates had agreed on a single negotiating text and most of the provisions contained therein.

Final bargaining/details

In May 1972, representatives from 17 states attended a two-day meeting in London in an attempt to resolve the issues outstanding from Reykjavik. They were still unable to resolve such issues as alternative methods of waste disposal and an effective monitoring system.

In June 1972, the Stockholm Conference recommended that governments refer the draft articles to an intergovernmental conference to be convened by the United Kingdom before November 1972, with the purpose of completing a convention and opening it for signature before the end of 1972 (UNCHE 1972).

Representatives from 91 countries met in London from 30 October to 13 November 1972 at the Intergovernmental Conference on the Convention on the Dumping of Wastes at Sea. Under the chairmanship of Martin W. Holdgate of the United Kingdom, negotiations began on the Reykjavik draft together with the suggestions from the London meeting in May. One of the most difficult issues to be resolved was the question of the jurisdiction of states over water adjacent to their coasts – a political issue not related to the question of pollution. A block of about 30 nations, led by Canada and India, insisted that the convention establish a "pollution zone" extending between 50 miles and 200 miles from the shores of coastal states. Under this plan, the signatories would have jurisdiction – for the purposes of preventing pollution – over waters extending considerably beyond traditional territorial limits (*New York Times*, 11 November 1972).

Turning point 5

The delegates ultimately agreed to shelve the issue of the jurisdiction of states over water adjacent to their coasts, upon the understanding that it would be taken up again by the United Nations Law of the Sea Conference (Arbose 1972). Once this obstacle was overcome, the negotiations came to a close and the Convention was adopted and opened for signature on 29 December 1972.

Ratification/implementation

The Convention entered into force on 30 August 1975. As of 30 April 2000, 78 states had become parties to the Convention.[1] The Convention recognizes the ongoing need not only to evaluate reporting, but also to be amended in light of the evolution of scientific knowledge. Thus, each year the Scientific Group on Dumping provides a forum for government scientists to meet. Expert groups have also been established on radioactive dumping, review of the Annexes, legal aspects, and future development of the Convention (Stairs and Taylor 1992). The Consultative Meeting allows all contracting parties to consider each other's activities as reported to the Convention.

The Convention has been amended several times. On 12 October 1978, Annex I of the Convention was amended to deal with the incineration of wastes and other matter at sea. The amendment entered into force on 11 March 1979. New procedures for the settlement of disputes were also adopted at that time; however, this amendment will not enter into force until it has been accepted by two-thirds of the contracting parties. As of 30 April 2000, only 20 states had accepted the amendment, which, after 22 years, had still not entered into force.

On 24 September 1980, the Convention was amended with a list of substances that require special care when being incinerated. These amendments entered into force on 11 March 1981. On 3 November 1989, delegates adopted amendments that qualify the procedures to be followed when issuing permits under Annex III. Before this is done, consideration has to be given to whether there is sufficient scientific information available to assess the impact of dumping. These amendments entered into force on 19 May 1990.

On 12 November 1993, the delegates adopted amendments that ban the dumping into the sea of low-level radioactive wastes. In addition, the amendments phase out the dumping of industrial wastes by 31 December 1995 and ban the incineration at sea of industrial wastes. These amendments entered into force on 20 February 1994.

On 7 November 1996, the parties adopted a protocol that prohibits the dumping of wastes or other matter with the exception of those listed in Annex I, including dredged material, sewage sludge, fish waste, vessels and platforms or other man-made structures at sea; inert, inorganic geological material; organic material of natural origin; and bulky items primarily comprising iron, steel, concrete, and similar unharmful materials for which the concern is physical impact and limited to circumstances where such wastes are generated at locations, such as small islands with isolated communities, having no practicable access to disposal options other than dumping. The protocol will enter into force 30 days after ratification by 26 countries, 15 of which must be contracting parties to the 1972 treaty. As of 30 April 2000, only 9 countries had ratified the protocol.

Summary of the Convention

The Convention, which has a global character, represents a step towards the international control and prevention of marine pollution. It prohibits the dumping of certain hazardous materials, requires a prior special permit for the dumping of a number of other identified materials, and a prior general permit for other wastes or matter. Dumping has been defined as the deliberate disposal at sea of wastes or other matter from vessels, aircraft, platforms, or other man-made structures, as well as the deliberate disposal of these vessels or platforms themselves. Wastes derived from the exploration and exploitation of seabed mineral resources are, however, excluded from the definition.

The provisions of the Convention shall also not apply when it is necessary to secure the safety of human life or of vessels in cases of *force majeure*. Among other requirements, contracting parties undertake to designate an authority to deal with permits, keep records, and monitor the condition of the sea. Other articles are designed to promote regional cooperation, particularly in the fields of monitoring and scientific research. Annexes list wastes that cannot be dumped and others for which a special dumping permit is required. The criteria governing the issuing of these permits are laid down in a third Annex, which deals with the nature of the waste material, the characteristics of the dumping site, and the method of disposal (IMO 2000).

The 1973 International Convention for the Prevention of Pollution from Ships as modified by the 1978 Protocol

Objective

Governments negotiated and adopted the 1973 International Convention for the Prevention of Pollution from Ships (MARPOL) and its 1978 Protocol in order to preserve the marine environment by achieving the complete elimination of international pollution by oil and other harmful substances and the minimization of accidental discharge of such substances.

Precipitants

Although oil pollution from ships had been addressed by the international community since the 1920s, conventions negotiated in 1926 and 1935 never entered into force. The 1954 International Convention for the

Prevention of Pollution of the Sea by Oil was not considered to be particularly effective. The growing environmental interest of the late 1960s
increased in 1972 with the UN Conference on the Human Environment
and the adoption of the London Convention. The oil pollution problem
also continued to grow as the amount of oil transported by sea increased.
The 1967 *Torrey Canyon* oil spill and the resulting public awareness and
outcry forced the international community to address the issue of marine
pollution from ships.

The 1973 Convention can be traced back to 1968 when the United
Nations General Assembly adopted a resolution to this effect. In October
1969, the Assembly of the Intergovernmental Maritime Consultative
Organization (IMCO) decided to convene an international conference on
marine pollution in 1973. The 1972 UN Conference on the Human Environment recommended that governments participate fully in the marine
pollution conference. The preparation for the conference was delegated
to the Maritime Safety Committee and its technical sub-committees.
After a series of meetings between 1971 and 1973, representatives from
71 countries negotiated and adopted the International Convention for the
Prevention of Pollution from Ships (MARPOL).

By the winter of 1976, the Convention had been ratified by only three
states. Some of the necessary technologies still had not been developed
and others were viewed by many as too expensive. Furthermore, Annex
I, dealing with oil pollution, was legally linked to that for hazardous
chemicals (Annex II). This further deterred ratification, because Annex
II imposed additional onerous burdens (Mitchell 1993, 213; M'Gonigle
and Zacher 1979, 122).

A series of tanker accidents in or near US waters during the winter
of 1976–77 (the *Argo Merchant*, *Sansinena*, *Oswego Peace*, and *Olympic
Games* in December 1976 and the *Grand Zenith*, *Barcola*, *Universal
Leader*, and *Irens Challenger* in January 1977) further underscored the
dangers of transporting oil at sea. This resulted in a unique high-level
intervention by US President Jimmy Carter who detailed a comprehensive program to combat vessel pollution.

Turning point 1

In January 1977, US President Jimmy Carter established an inter-agency
task force to develop new legislative and administrative initiatives to improve federal action in the area of pollution from ships. The recommendations from this task force served as the basis for President Carter's
17 March 1977 message to Congress on a comprehensive program to
combat pollution of the sea by ships. The "Carter Initiatives" promised

action to prevent further accidents by requiring collision avoidance aids, inert gas systems, improved steering standards, and double bottoms on all tankers over 20,000 tons within five years. Rules for liability for pollution damage, enforcement, and certification were also to be improved. To prevent operational pollution, President Carter endorsed the installation of segregated ballast tanks on new and existing tankers over 20,000 tons and the ratification of the MARPOL Convention (M'Gonigle and Zacher 1979, 129).

After President Carter's message to Congress, work to persuade the international maritime community to consider the global adoption of the US recommendations moved rapidly. At the 36th session of IMCO's Maritime Safety Committee in April 1977, the United States proposed its initiatives to improve tanker safety and pollution prevention.

Issue definition

At that April 1977 meeting, it was agreed to convene an International Conference on Tanker Safety and Pollution Prevention (TSPP) from 6 to 17 February 1978. To prepare a basic working document for the conference, an intersessional working group met in May, June, and July 1977. A joint meeting of the Maritime Safety Committee (MSC) and the Marine Environment Protection Committee (MEPC) was held in October 1977.

During these sessions it was agreed that all new regulations would be formulated as protocols to the 1973 MARPOL and the 1974 SOLAS (Safety of Life at Sea) conventions. After reviewing the American proposals to control accidental pollution, the October meeting gave tentative approval to all but two of the proposals. Although the desirability of collision avoidance aids was accepted, the dearth of specifications for them led most countries to recommend that the issue be handled through the regular IMCO committees for future acceptance by the Assembly. The second proposal that was rejected was double bottoms. This was replaced with a suggestion that all future segregated ballast tanks would be "protectively located" to provide for maximum protection against the breaching of cargo tanks in the event of an accident (M'Gonigle and Zacher 1979, 130).

TSPP Conference proposals focused on new structural and operational remedies to control pollution from existing ships. At the time of IMCO's 1973 Conference on Marine Pollution, a requirement for segregated ballast on new ships was generally accepted as the answer to operational pollution. A similar requirement for existing ships was not seen as warranted, nor had equivalent alternative methods for reducing discharges been sufficiently developed to challenge the primacy of segregated ballast. But, as the problem persisted and as the economic incentives to conserve oil increased in the mid-1970s, work on the emerging technology of crude-oil washing accelerated. Thus, the major proposals on the reduction of operational discharges centered on segregated ballast tanks (SBT), clean ballast tanks, crude-oil washing (COW), and inert gas systems.[2] The three package proposals that emerged from the MSC/MEPC preparatory meeting presented alternatives on the extent of application of these four technologies to new or existing oil tankers or product carriers of various sizes, effective as of various dates.

Turning point 2

The MSC/MEPC preparatory meeting was unable to make any more progress on determining which of these technologies to advocate in the protocol because participants were largely technical experts rather than political decision makers. Furthermore, preparation time ran out as the date for the conference approached.

Statement of initial positions

The TSPP Conference opened in London on 6 February 1978. As state after state spoke out against retrofitting, it was soon apparent that the United States and its three key allies – Greece, Norway, and Sweden – were becoming increasingly isolated. Some states with heavy coastal pollution (such as Portugal, Spain, and Morocco) supported the American position, as did a few other countries, such as Cyprus and Venezuela. Most, however, strongly preferred COW (M'Gonigle and Zacher 1979, 136).

The United Kingdom, supported by the oil industry, proposed requiring existing tankers over 70,000 tons to install a tank-cleaning system that used crude oil to wash tanks (COW). A few states with very heavy pollution supported the US proposal, but most states, including the Soviet bloc and developing countries, preferred the less expensive UK proposal (Mitchell 1994, 101).

The Nordic countries supported a mandatory clean ballast tanks (CBT) requirement. This concept is, in effect, segregated ballast on the honor system, since it entails no structural modifications and is, thus, the least costly of the primary methods considered at the conference for effecting a rapid reduction in operational discharge. Maritime nations opposed this because it would reduce cargo-carrying capacity by 10–20 percent. From an economic standpoint, such a requirement was an important objective for Nordic and other states severely affected by laid-up tonnage (Sielen and McManus 1983, 163–164).

Turning point 3

On the second day of discussions, the chairman of Committee II (which dealt with the alternative packages),[3] L. Spinelli of Italy, sought to break the growing stalemate and channel the discussions into considering a compromise. France and Italy suggested compromise proposals. For two days each side met separately to consider what elements they could accept in a compromise (M'Gonigle and Zacher 1979, 138).

Drafting/formula-building

By the fourth day, discussions between the opposing sides began in earnest. Spinelli exerted strong pressure on the negotiators to achieve a single package.

The United States introduced a paper at the preparatory meetings for the conference which identified several fundamental and unanswered questions concerning the feasibility and effectiveness of COW as an alternative to SBT.[4] At the conference, the United Kingdom offered responses to the questions raised by the United States. These responses apparently had the effect of answering some of the more serious objections to the use of COW, and helped confer a certain amount of legitimacy on COW as a serious alternative to SBT. Thus, a major obstacle was overcome and the way was cleared for in-depth technical consideration of COW. A working group was then convened to develop technical guidelines for the use of COW, and criteria, personnel qualifications, and detailed operating procedures were subsequently formulated.

On the CBT issue, a working group started to negotiate design standards and operating procedures for CBT, in case the conference should adopt the concept in any form.

As negotiations continued, Canada surfaced as a mediator in the COW working group. The developing countries also played a constructive role. In large measure, they opposed the high costs of the American initiatives but were also convinced of the necessity of achieving a compromise acceptable to the United States (M'Gonigle and Zacher 1979, 139).

Turning point 4

After four days of negotiations, a compromise was ready for submission to the conference. The package agreement that was agreed to represented a compromise between the original US proposal and the preferences of the United Kingdom and other maritime and developing states. The final compromise distinguished between new and existing vessels, crude- and product-carrying vessels, and ship size. The consideration of ship size played a large part in the final stages of the negotiations. According to Sielen and McManus (1983, 163), the package's most glaring deficiency was its failure to incorporate a mandatory CBT requirement, an important objective for the Nordic states. The Norwegian delegation's decision to abstain rather than vote against the package represented only a diplomatic nod (although a gracious one) to the goal of consensus.

Final bargaining/details

Once agreement was reached on the major issue of tanker standards, agreement was reached on a number of other, less controversial issues. The conference also agreed to merge the new agreement with the parent Convention (MARPOL 1973) so that each country need ratify only one instrument. This was hoped to speed up the ratification process. The delegates agreed to an added incentive to ratification. Article II allows states to delay entry into force of Annex II of MARPOL 1973 for three years after acceptance of the new Protocol. By applying the equipment requirements to ships delivered after June 1982 (regardless of the entry into force date), the delegates removed incentives for countries to delay ratification to slow the rule's impact (Mitchell 1994, 102–103). The conference also adopted resolutions recommending a target date for entry into force of the Protocol (June 1981).

Turning point 5

On the final day of the conference, delegates voted to approve the final text and the Protocol was adopted on 17 February 1978. The vote on the final composite package was 41 votes in favor, no votes against, and 9 abstentions (Sielen and McManus 1983, 163).

Ratification/implementation

MARPOL entered into force on 2 October 1983. As of 30 April 2000, 110 countries have become parties to the Convention and Annexes I and II, representing 94.23 percent of world tonnage. Of the three "optional" annexes, Annex III (Regulations for the Prevention of Pollution by Harmful Substances Carried by Sea in Packaged Form, or in Freight Containers, Portable Tanks or Road and Rail Tank Wagons) entered into force on 1 July 1992 and has 93 parties; Annex IV (Regulations for the Prevention of Pollution by Sewage from Ships) has not yet entered into force but has been ratified by 77 countries; Annex V (Regulations for the Prevention of Pollution by Garbage from Ships) entered into force on 31 December 1988 and has 96 parties.[5]

The long delay in ratification meant that several amendments were proposed before the Convention and Protocol even entered into force. These amendments were agreed to during regular meetings of the IMO's Marine Environment Protection Committee in 1981, 1982, and 1983 and adopted in 1984.

In 1985, Protocol I was adopted. This Protocol, which entered into force in April 1987, makes it an explicit requirement to report incidents involving discharge into the sea of harmful substances in packaged form. A second Protocol addresses arbitration procedures. Since 1984, the IMO has adopted several other amendments to MARPOL. In 1987 and 1990, respectively, the Gulf of Aden and Antarctica were designated as special areas deserving greater environmental protection. In 1990 the guidelines for MARPOL surveys were harmonized with those for other IMO conventions. In 1991 and 1992 US pressures in the wake of the *Exxon Valdez* spill resulted in amendments requiring new tankers to be built with double hulls or equivalent spill protection construction and all tankers to carry plans for dealing with any oil pollution emergency (Mitchell 1994, 104).

In 1994, the Convention was amended so that ships can be inspected when in the ports of other parties to the Convention to ensure that crews are able to carry out essential shipboard procedures relating to marine pollution prevention. In July 1996, Protocol I to the Convention, which contains provisions for reporting incidents involving harmful substances, was amended to include more precise requirements for the sending of such reports (IMO 2000). These amendments entered into force in January 1998.

In September 1997, the Convention was amended to specify intact stability criteria for double hull tankers. Another amendment makes the north-west European waters a "special area." These amendments entered into force in February 1999. Parties also adopted the Protocol of 1997 (Annex VI) on Regulations for the Prevention of Air Pollution from Ships to the Convention. The rules will set limits on sulfur oxide and nitrogen oxide emissions from ship exhausts and prohibit deliberate emissions of ozone-depleting substances. The Protocol will enter into force 12 months after being accepted by at least 15 states with not less than 50 percent of world merchant shipping tonnage. As of 30 April 2000, four states had ratified the Protocol.

Summary of the Convention

Annex I of the Convention states that the maximum quantity of oil which is permitted to be discharged on a ballast voyage of new oil tankers is no more than 1/30,000 of the amount of cargo carried. These criteria apply equally to both persistent (black) and non-persistent (white) oils. An important feature of the 1973 Convention is the concept of "special areas" which are considered to be so vulnerable to pollution by oil that oil discharges within them have been completely prohibited, with minor and well-defined exceptions. The main special areas are the Mediterranean Sea, the Black Sea, the Baltic Sea, the Red Sea, and the Gulfs area. All oil-carrying ships are required to be capable of operating the method of retaining oily wastes on board through the "load on top" system or for discharge to shore reception facilities. This involves the fitting of appropriate equipment, including an oil-discharge monitoring and control system, oily-water separating equipment and a filtering system, slop tanks, sludge tanks, piping, and pumping arrangements.

New oil tankers (i.e. those for which the building contract was placed after 31 December 1975) of 70,000 tons deadweight and above must be fitted with segregated ballast tanks large enough to provide adequate operating draught without the need to carry ballast water in cargo oil tanks. Secondly, new oil tankers are required to meet certain subdivision and damage stability requirements so that, in any loading conditions, they can survive after damage by collision or stranding.

Annex II details the discharge criteria and measures for the control of pollution by noxious liquid substances carried in bulk. Some 250 substances were evaluated and included in the list appended to the Convention. The discharge of their residues is allowed only to reception facilities until certain concentrations and conditions (which vary with the category of substances) are complied with. In any case, no discharge of residues containing noxious substances is permitted within 12 miles of the nearest land. More stringent restrictions apply to the Baltic and Black Sea areas.

Annex III on the prevention of pollution by harmful substances carried in packaged form, or in freight containers or portable tanks or road and rail tank wagons, is the first of the Convention's optional annexes. States ratifying the Convention must accept Annexes I and II but can choose not to accept Annexes III–V. Consequently, the latter have all taken much longer to meet the requirements for entry into force. Annex III contains general requirements for the issuing of detailed standards on packing, marking, labeling, documentation, stowage, quantity limitations, exceptions and notifications for preventing pollution by harmful substances.

Annex IV contains requirements to control pollution of the sea by sewage. Annex V deals with different types of garbage and specifies the distances from land and the manner in which they may be disposed of. The requirements are much stricter in a number of "special areas" but perhaps the most important feature of the Annex is the complete ban imposed on the dumping into the sea of all forms of plastic (IMO 2000).

Annex VI sets regulations for the prevention of air pollution from ships. The rules will set limits on sulfur oxide and nitrogen oxide emissions from ship exhausts and prohibit deliberate emissions of ozone-depleting substances.

1973 Convention on International Trade in Endangered Species

Objectives of the negotiations

The objective was to protect certain endangered species from over-exploitation by means of a system of import/export permits.

Precipitants

Events that led to the negotiation of the Convention on International Trade in Endangered Species (CITES) began with the realization that damage and extinction in the natural world were occurring at an unprecedented rate in human history, with a truly global scope and impact. Biologists also realized that, unlike previous incidents of species extinction, the contemporary problems were the result of human activity, not of processes such as natural selection. Initial efforts made little progress in controlling overexploitative international trade, as domestic measures were generally directed only at internal problems. Most of the world's exporting nations did little to regulate wildlife taken from their territories until the economic yield that these states derived from the export of native wildlife dwindled as desired species became increasingly less obtainable. Eventually, many of the nations that depended upon wildlife trade were forced to re-evaluate their conservation policies and concluded that concerted action was necessary to correct what had become an economically self-defeating situation (Schonfeld 1985).

The IUCN–World Conservation Union was concerned with the role of international trade in threatening some prominent species as early as 1951, when it passed the first of a series of resolutions urging prohibitions on the importation of protected species. In 1961 at an IUCN-sponsored meeting on African wildlife conservation, several African countries expressed frustration over their inability to control poaching and urged that an international convention be considered to address the problem of the illegal wildlife trade (Trexler 1990, 22).

Turning point 1

At its Eighth General Assembly in 1963, the IUCN resolved to undertake the drafting of an international convention on the regulation of the export, transit, and import of rare or threatened wildlife species or their skins and trophies.

Issue definition/statement of initial positions

Most of the preparatory work for CITES took place away from the negotiating table. The phases of issue definition and statement of initial positions actually overlapped during the period 1963–1972. During the 1960s, the international community began to coalesce into two distinct blocs that were unified by their common desire to control wildlife trade, although distinguished by differing motives (Schonfeld 1985). Both the economic-oriented and the conservation-oriented nations recognized the necessity of international cooperation. Some had already enacted domestic legislation to protect endangered wildlife within their own territories, but it was clear that legislation of this nature was insufficient to control a problem of international dimensions.

The IUCN produced a first draft of the proposed convention in 1964, but it was not until the third draft in September 1967 that it was circulated to governments; 39 countries and 18 international organizations responded with comments (Boardman 1981, 89). Further drafting was undertaken to address the problem of differing national approaches to trade regulation and wildlife conservation, differences over the meaning of "endangered species," and the fact that discussions over the proposed convention involved government agencies not normally concerned with species conservation issues (Trexler 1990, 23). Two more drafts were circulated to governments in August 1969 and March 1971.

A number of countries were not satisfied with the March 1971 draft. Many, including those that had been involved in the drafting process, believed that the draft treaty was too weak to achieve species conservation aims and others thought that the draft predominantly reflected the views of the European wildlife-importing countries (Trexler 1990, 23). The United States, for one, felt that this draft failed to apply the convention to endangered species in the high seas. Nor did it provide import controls to ensure that specimens subject to protection in the state of export had been obtained legally. In preparing its position, the United States began to develop its own draft (Train 1973). Similarly, Kenya was not satisfied with the IUCN draft and in April 1972 circulated its own proposed draft. This draft called for a quota system whereby each state could continue trading in wildlife based on the amount of trade currently underway.

Turning point 2/3

In its response to the IUCN March 1971 draft, the United States noted that it had a congressional mandate (the Endangered Species Conservation Act of 1969) to convene a ministerial conference and proposed that the IUCN collaborate with it in both the organization and the conduct of such a conference. At Stockholm in June 1972, the UN Conference on the Human Environment recommended that a plenipotentiary conference be held as soon as possible to prepare and adopt a convention on the export, import, and transit of certain species of wild animals and plants. In response, the Eleventh General Assembly of the IUCN in September 1972 followed up with a recommendation urging all governments to participate in the proposed meeting to be held in Washington, DC, with a target date of February 1973.

Drafting/formula-building

After the announcement of the plenipotentiary conference, drafting of the treaty in Kenya and the United States accelerated. The United States was aware of its coming responsibility as host government to offer a Working Paper to the conference and recognized that the conference would be severely impeded should it be faced with three competing drafts, so a meeting was held in July 1972 between the IUCN, the United States, and Kenya to develop a Unified Working Paper. The paper was distributed to governments in November 1972. The final drafting process was largely dominated by conservation interests. Wildlife trading interests were not represented during this drafting process, and are generally perceived to have been "caught napping" (Trexler 1990, 25).

Turning point 4

In November 1972, upon the conclusion of negotiations between the United States, the IUCN, and Kenya, the Unified Working Paper was circulated along with invitations from the US government to attend a Plenipotentiary Conference to Conclude an International Convention on Trade of Certain Species of Wildlife to be held in Washington DC, from 12 February to 2 March 1973.

Final bargaining/details

On 12 February 1973, delegates from 80 countries began negotiations based on the Unified Working Paper. Significant issues still remained unresolved. These included the definition of "specimen," the concept of introduction from the sea, and provisions for the international enforcement of domestic conservation legislation.

The question of defining "specimen" for purposes of treaty application produced a confrontation between nations whose primary objective was preservation of the endangered species and nations determined to adopt only customs procedures that could be fully implemented. Several delegations did not want the concept of "product" to go beyond primary products such as animal skins. If the concept was to be more inclusive, these delegations advocated that the affected parts of products, such as fur coats or alligator-skin handbags, consist only of those specifically listed in the Appendices. They also urged that parts and products should not be subject to re-export controls. On the other side, the United States advocated that the definition of "specimen" include as broad a definition of "product" as possible (Train 1973).

Another difficult issue was the application of the treaty to endangered species taken in the marine environment not under the jurisdiction of any state. This concept was not included in any of the IUCN drafts and appeared for the first time in the Unified Working Paper distributed shortly before the conference. Many delegations believed that this concept raised very serious questions as to its practicality (would a member nation have to police catches by its own fishing vessels?), and as to its effect on their positions relative to the territorial sea and to other conservation agreements (such as the International Whaling Convention) dealing with species that the current convention might list. One delegation proposed an amendment to delete all provisions relating to "introduction from the sea," and, as the conference progressed, several delegations had repeatedly to seek instructions from their capitals on this matter. The United States argued (a) that endangered species in the high seas have particular need of international protection against trade because they enjoy no such national protection; (b) that the convention should not disregard endangered species in 70 percent of the world's area; (c) that the convention could extend them protection with no prejudice to the participating state's position relative to the extent of the territorial sea and to other conventions; and (d) that the protection could be administered easily since it would involve only a limited number of readily identifiable marine species (Train 1973).

Most difficult were issues related to the scope of the appendices, even though the IUCN had developed a list of proposed covered species back in 1967 (Boardman 1981, 89). The committees considering flora and fauna proposals initially called for "hard data" to support the listing of species, but quickly lowered their standards as the scope of the informational inadequacy became obvious (Trexler 1990, 25). It was agreed that Appendices I and II should include threatened species by the parties' common, explicit agreement. For inclusion in Appendix III, however, any party may propose a species that it identifies as subject to conservation regulation within its jurisdiction and as needing the cooperation of other parties in the control of trade. This concept, originally advanced by Kenya and supported by the United States, met with wide resistance because it would have enabled any one party unilaterally to obligate other parties in relation to its Appendix III species. Major importing nations also opposed this concept on the grounds of customs impracticality (Train 1973).

Finally, the question of determining the procedure for amending the appendices – for the purpose of adding, subtracting, or transferring species – posed a conflict between the sovereign will of the parties to have the fullest possible voice in the procedure and the need for all possible flexibility to permit rapid adjustment to the changing conditions of various species. The importing nations initially favored amendment only by the active response of the majority of the parties. The United States advocated greater use of the passive procedure that permits changes to be adopted in the absence of explicit objection (Train 1973).

Turning point 5

Time pressure as well as creative compromise enabled the delegations to resolve these four difficult issues. With regard to the definition of specimen, a compromise was reached so that in Appendix III the definition of specimen includes only those recognizable parts or derivatives listed specifically in that appendix. The more comprehensive view prevailed in the case of animals in Appendices I and II. Here the definition of specimen includes "any readily recognizable part or derivative thereof."

On the issue of endangered species taken from the marine environment, the concept was finally adopted after intensive negotiations in the Ad Hoc Committee on Introduction from the Sea. The conference agreed to include in Appendix I the five species of whales not subject to a moratorium against harvesting under the International Whaling Convention. The United States, as a compromise, announced that it would not at this time press for the inclusion of "non-moratorium" whales in the appendices.

The two problems with regard to Appendix III were also resolved. The objection to individual nations proposing a species for inclusion in Appendix III was obviated through a special amendment procedure permitting parties to enter reservations to specific Appendix III specimens at any time. The objection on the grounds of customs impracticality was met by tailoring the definition of "specimen" so as to reduce customs obligations for Appendix III species.

Finally, a compromise was reached on amending the appendices. The procedure would commence with the passive system and fall back on the active in the event that a party were to object to the proposed amendment. With these compromises, the Convention was adopted on 2 March 1973.

Ratification/implementation

The Convention entered into force on 1 July 1975. As of April 2000, 151 countries had ratified the Convention. The annexes to the Convention have been amended multiple times and two specific amendments to other sections of the treaty have been adopted. The first, which relates to financial provisions and amends Article XI, was adopted in Bonn in 1979 and entered into force on 13 April 1987. The second, which is related to accession to the Convention by regional economic integration organizations and amends Article XXI, was adopted in Gaborone in 1983, but is not yet in force. It will enter into force when it has been formally accepted by 54 of the 80 states that were parties to the Convention on 30 April 1983. The Conference of the Parties meets every two to three years and places species on and removes species from the CITES appendices. Over 30,000 species of plants and animals are currently listed in the three CITES appendices. The eleventh meeting of the Conference of the Parties was held in Nairobi, Kenya, from 10 to 20 April 2000.[6]

Summary of the Convention

CITES has three conservation objectives. First, it aims to end commercial trade in endangered species. Second, it intends to maintain species' ecological roles in the face of commercial exploitation, a goal normally associated with national wildlife management programs. Third, it tries to assist countries in implementing their own species conservation programs if assistance is requested in the form of an Appendix II listing.

CITES is charged with regulating wildlife trade through controls on species listed in three appendices, which form the scientific core of the Convention. The criteria for inclusion in the appendices are set out in the treaty text as follows:

Appendix I: to include all species "threatened with extinction which are or may be affected by trade." Particularly strict regulation is to be employed to prevent further endangerment, with trade authorized "only in exceptional circumstances." Commercial trade in wild specimens of these species is generally prohibited (CITES, Article III).

Appendix II: to include all species for which strict regulation of trade flows is required to prevent unsustainable utilization, as well as look-alike species. Controls are intended "to maintain that species throughout its range at a level consistent with its role in the ecosystems in which it occurs and well above the level at which that species might become eligible for inclusion in Appendix I" (CITES, Article IV).

Appendix III: to include "all species which any Party identifies as being subject to regulation within its jurisdiction for the purpose of preventing or restricting exploitation, and as needing the cooperation of other parties in the control of trade" (CITES, Article V).

1976 Convention for the Protection of the Mediterranean Sea against Pollution

Objectives of the negotiations

The aim was to achieve international cooperation for a coordinated and comprehensive approach to the protection and enhancement of the marine environment in the Mediterranean Sea.

Precipitants

Oil spills and beach closures had led to several piecemeal and limited measures that controlled maritime safety, oil spills, and pollutants that might harm fisheries. Concern about the implications of Mediterranean pollution mounted between the late 1960s and 1974. Initial concern was focused on oil pollution resulting from tanker traffic. Subsequent studies and conferences demonstrated the need for managing a more comprehensive range of sources and channels of pollution, including land-based sources, agricultural runoff, and marine dumping, as well as pollution transmitted by rivers and through the atmosphere.

Turning point 1

At the first meeting of the International Maritime Consultative Organization (IMCO) in June 1971, 10 northern and southern Mediterranean coastal nations (Algeria, Cyprus, Egypt, France, Italy, Malta, Morocco, Spain, Turkey, and Yugoslavia) first discussed a regional approach to identifying and controlling pollutants entering the Mediterranean.

Issue definition

The idea for a framework convention to cover all pollution sources, along with technical protocols on dumping, emergency cooperation, vessel-source pollution, land-based pollution, and pollution from offshore and seabed exploration, originated with the Food and Agriculture Organization (FAO). FAO, however, had little choice but to respond positively in the summer of 1974 to the United Nations Environment Programme's suggestion that UNEP assume responsibility for convening an intergovernmental conference to endorse the idea of a convention.

At its first meeting in early 1973, the UNEP Governing Council asked the executive director to stimulate regional agreements with a policy objective "to detect and prevent serious threats to the health of the oceans through controlling both ocean-based and land-based sources of pollution." A year later, the council decided that "in view of the many activities of numerous other agencies in the field, UNEP should concentrate on the coordination of these activities and on the protection of the marine environment," with priority given to "regional activities ... in the Mediterranean" (Thacher 1993, 122).

Although UNEP recognized the global scope of the environmental problems of the oceans, political and financial realism dictated a regional approach to their solution (Bliss-Guest 1981, 263). UNEP collaborated with other organizations involved in Mediterranean issues (the United Nations and others) and non-governmental organizations (NGOs).

UNEP held a series of task force meetings leading up to the first Intergovernmental Meeting on the Protection of the Mediterranean. In October 1974, UNEP held its first Task Force Meeting on the Mediterranean Action Plan (MAP) in Madrid. The second Task Force Meeting took place in Geneva. At these two meetings, the Task Force developed four papers describing proposed activities related to the protection of the Mediterranean:

(1) Integrated Planning of the Development and Management of the Resources of the Mediterranean Basin.
(2) A Coordinated Program for Research, Monitoring, and Exchange of Information and Assessment of the State of Pollution and of Protection Measures.
(3) A Framework Convention and Related Protocols with Their Technical Annexes for the Protection of the Mediterranean Environment.
(4) Institutional and Financial Implications of the Plan of Action.

On 28 January 1975, the first Intergovernmental Meeting on the Protection of the Mediterranean opened in Barcelona, Spain. The meeting was hosted by UNEP, FAO, and IMCO. Representatives of 16 of the 18 coastal states attended the meeting.[7] From the start it was clear that the earlier meetings had helped participants from around the Mediterranean understand their common problems. "The earlier meetings had contributed to the ease (despite conditions of near hostility between nations at both ends of that sea) with which governments and nongovernment[al] organizations collaborated" (Thacher 1993, 128). After only seven days, on 4 February 1975, the Mediterranean Action Plan was approved.

Turning point 2

Governments requested UNEP to convene working groups of governmental legal and technical experts, with the eventual collaboration of other concerned international organizations, to put into definitive form the draft legal instruments enumerated, with a view to their adoption by a Conference of Plenipotentiaries.

Statement of initial positions

UNEP, in conjunction with other UN agencies, held a number of working group and other meetings in 1975 to draft the convention. In April 1975, the UNEP Working Group on Draft Legal Instruments for the Protection of the Mediterranean met in Geneva. In July 1975, the UNEP/FAO Expert Consultation on the Joint Coordinated Project on Pollution in the Mediterranean met in Rome. In September 1975, the International Oceanographic Commission/World Meteorological Organization/UNEP Expert Consultation on the Joint Coordinated Project on Pollution in the Mediterranean met in Malta.

During these meetings, the common concern of governments about Mediterranean degradation was overwhelmed by specific disagreements over which pollutants to control and who would have to bear the costs for their control.[8] The pollutants that individual countries hoped to control correlated closely to their stage of development. The more industrialized states with energy-intensive production suffered from industrial pollution (metals, phenols). States at lower levels of development and with large populations faced problems of untreated municipal wastes (organic matter, detergents, and nutrients), as did many developed states with old cities without sewerage systems. All states faced the problems of agricultural runoff and oil on beaches.

Political antipathies also exacerbated the problem. Foreign ministries had other objectives besides cleaning up pollution. French and Italian delegates sought to promote regional environmental legislation compatible with international law, particularly EC directives. Developing countries hoped to receive equipment to monitor pollution and get training in oceanography and pollution control. More profoundly, however, developing countries were concerned that attempts to control pollution would divert resources from economic development. Finally, industrialized and developing countries differed on how rapidly to develop pollution controls and on how strong these controls should be. Developed countries, suffering more from pollution, hoped to introduce strong pollution controls immediately. Developing countries still industrializing and with relatively cleaner coasts, preferred waiting until they had industrialized and the problem was more noticeable.

Turning point 3

UNEP decided to sponsor three meetings to draft a framework convention and two protocols on oil pollution and tanker traffic in preparation for the conference.

Drafting/formula-building

UNEP held these three meetings in September and December 1975 and January 1976, in preparation for the Conference of Plenipotentiaries. Negotiating the convention was difficult. Countries disagreed about which pollutants to control. Industrialized countries wanted to control all sources of pollution, whereas many of the developing countries perceived this as a thinly veiled attempt to control their industrialization practices and, thus, opted for control of only municipal and tanker wastes (Haas 1989).

Turning point 4

At the third UNEP-sponsored drafting group meeting, delegates agreed on the framework and most of the elements in the draft convention.

Final bargaining/details

The final draft convention, along with two draft protocols, was presented at the conference in Barcelona in February 1976. A number of difficult issues still needed to be resolved, although the conference was characterized as "amicable" (Haas 1990, 108). Morocco proposed the creation of an Interstate Guarantee Fund to compensate states for the costs of cleaning up in case of emergencies. France fiercely opposed this proposal, maintaining that it would be difficult to determine whether countries would deserve to be compensated for deliberate, accidental, or background cases of pollution. Rather than being included in the framework convention, the Interstate Guarantee Fund was adopted by the conference as a resolution, with the reservation of France (Haas 1990, 109). The European Community was accepted as a signatory state after a long contentious debate between EC members France and Italy, and Yugoslavia and the Arab states. The developing countries did not want the European Community to participate as a supranational actor.

Turning point 5

Once these last two details were resolved, the Barcelona Convention for the Protection of the Mediterranean Sea against Pollution and two protocols, the Protocol for the Prevention of Pollution of the Mediterranean Sea by Dumping from Ships and Aircraft and the Protocol Concerning Cooperation in Combatting Pollution of the Mediterranean Sea by Oil and Other Harmful Substances in Cases of Emergency were adopted on 16 February 1976.

Ratification/implementation

The Convention and the first two Protocols came into force on 12 February 1978; 20 Mediterranean nations and the European Community have ratified the Convention and the Protocols. Additional protocols have since been negotiated. The 1980 Athens Protocol for the Protection of the Mediterranean Sea against Pollution from Land-Based Sources, which entered into force in July 1983, was amended in March 1996 and is now called the Protocol for the Protection of the Mediterranean Sea against Pollution from Land-Based Sources and Activities. As of February 2000, five parties had accepted the amendments. The 1982 Geneva Protocol Concerning Mediterranean Specially Protected Areas entered into force in March 1986. The Protocol was amended in June 1995 and annexes to this Protocol were adopted in 1996. It entered into force on 12 December 1999. The new title is the Protocol Concerning Specially Protected Areas and Biological Diversity in the Mediterranean. As of February 2000, six parties had ratified the new Protocol. In October 1994 the Madrid Protocol for the Protection of the Mediterranean Sea against Pollution Resulting from Exploration and Exploitation of the Continental Shelf and the Seabed and its Subsoil was adopted. As of February 2000, only two parties had ratified the Protocol.

In June 1995, the Action Plan for the Protection of the Marine Environment and the Sustainable Development of the Coastal Areas of the Mediterranean (MAP Phase II) was adopted by the parties at the Conference of Plenipotentiaries held in Barcelona, Spain, from 9 to 10 June 1995. The Conference also adopted the Barcelona Resolution on the Environment and Sustainable Development and Priority Fields of Activities for the period to the year 2005. The new title is the Convention for the Protection of the Marine Environment and the Coastal Region of the Mediterranean. As of February 2000, six parties had accepted the amended Convention.

In October 1996 the Izmir Protocol on the Prevention of Pollution of the Mediterranean Sea by Transboundary Movements of Hazardous Wastes and Their Disposal was adopted. Three parties had ratified it by February 2000.[9]

Summary of the Convention

The core of the Convention is that parties should take all appropriate measures to prevent and abate pollution of the Mediterranean caused by dumping from ships and aircraft, or by discharges from ships, or resulting from exploration and exploitation of the seabed and subsoil, or from discharges from rivers, coastal establishments, or other land-based sources within their territories.

Parties are also required to cooperate in: taking measures to deal with pollution emergencies, whatever their cause; establishing programs for monitoring pollution in the area; scientific and technical research relating to all types of marine pollution; and establishing procedures for the determination of liability and compensation for damage resulting from violations of the Convention and Protocols.

Since its adoption by all Mediterranean states and the European Community, the Action Plan has served as the basis for the development of a comprehensive environment and development program in the region involving the Mediterranean coastal states, specialized organizations of the United Nations system, and intergovernmental and non-governmental programmes and organizations. MAP covers coastal zone management, pollution assessment and control, protection of ecosystems, and preservation of biodiversity. In 1995, it was revised to become more action oriented and an instrument for sustainable development in the region.

1979 Convention on Long-Range Transboundary Air Pollution

Objectives of the negotiations

The objectives were to protect humans and the environment against air pollution and to endeavor to limit and, as far as possible, gradually reduce and prevent air pollution, including long-range transboundary air pollution.

Precipitants

In the 1960s, industrialized countries raised the heights of their industrial chimneys by as much as six times in order to disperse pollutants into the atmosphere. As a result, emissions of sulfur dioxide (SO_2) and nitrogen oxides (NOx) quickly became an international problem. The issue of defining transboundary air pollution as a matter of global environmental politics began in the late 1960s with Sweden as the primary actor. In 1972, Sweden and the other Nordic countries succeeded in getting the Organisation for Economic Co-operation and Development (OECD) to monitor transboundary air pollution in Europe. The measurements and findings of the OECD Program on the Long-Range Transport of Air Pollutants were first published in 1977. The report offered the first independent international verification of Scandinavian charges that, in southern Norway and Sweden, imported sulfur pollution was primarily responsible for acidification of lakes (Wetstone and Rosencranz 1983).

The opportunity for an international agreement on transboundary air pollution grew out of a statement by President Leonid Brezhnev of the Soviet Union at the 1975 East–West meeting of the Conference on Security and Co-operation in Europe in Helsinki. Brezhnev challenged his fellow conferees to reach multilateral solutions on three pressing problems affecting all of Europe: energy, transport, and the environment (Wetstone and Rosencranz 1983). Swedish and Norwegian officials saw in this speech an opportunity for international discussion, negotiation, and possibly resolution of a problem that was very important to them: transboundary air pollution and acid rain. Norway and Sweden recognized that the OECD, the only international organization that had shown any interest in acid rain, did not have the power to enforce its policy recommendations and was unlikely to serve as the center for negotiation of a multilateral treaty.

Turning point 1

In February 1977, at the fifth session of the Senior Advisors to ECE Governments on Environmental Protection (SAEP), Norway, with the support of Sweden and Finland, proposed an international convention on the reduction of air pollutants causing transboundary air pollution. At the thirty-third session of the Economic Commission for Europe (ECE) in April 1978, the Commission decided to hold a high-level meeting in 1979 to focus on environmental issues, especially long-range transboundary air pollution (Topic A) and low- and non-waste technology (Topic B) (Chossudovsky 1989).

Issue definition

The first meeting of the Special Group on Topic A took place in July 1978. The Group's first task was to decide how to clarify the points in Commission Resolution 1 (XXXIII) concerning the content and form of an agreement on transboundary air pollution. The Group decided to ask the governments and the international organizations for elaboration of proposals concerning areas of possible international cooperation. Two working papers were submitted to the Special Group on behalf of the Nordic Group (Denmark, Finland, Iceland, Norway and Sweden), consisting of a draft convention on "Reduction of Emissions Causing Transboundary Air Pollution" and a memorandum on major elements to be considered for inclusion in an annex on emission of sulfur compounds.

Turning point 2

In the absence of other proposals, the Special Group agreed to invite governments, prior to the Group's second meeting, to submit comments or alternative proposals related to what became known as the "Nordic Proposal" (Chossudovsky 1989, 74).

Statement of initial positions

The second meeting of the Special Group took place in September 1978. In response to the Special Group's request for information, 22 governments and 3 international organizations sent replies. To facilitate matters, the secretariat prepared a summary of the specific proposals for international cooperation contained in the replies from the governments and international organizations. Thus, a solid database was established that facilitated the identification of the main components and problems of long-range transboundary air pollution, evaluated and defined those elements that required concentration at the international level, and clarified possible approaches (Chossudovsky 1989, 75).

At the third meeting of the Special Group in early November 1978, attention was focused on defining the areas of the mandate where agreement could be reached and also where further discussion and negotiation were needed. Delegates from Sweden and Norway pressed for a "tough" agreement which, even if not enforceable, would call on signatories to hold the line against further increases in sulfur dioxide emissions (the "standstill" clause) and begin to abate sulfur dioxide pollution levels by fixed, across-the-board percentages (the "rollback" clause). The "Nordic Proposal" made special provision for countries that had already put strict control and abatement measures into effect (the Netherlands) and also for countries at a relatively early stage of industrial development (Ireland) (Wetstone and Rosencranz 1983).

Resistance to the Nordic Proposal came primarily from West Germany and Great Britain. Since the European Community had "competence" in the area of international environmental controls, the Community had to speak with a single voice in ECE deliberations. As two of the Community's most influential members, West Germany and Great Britain easily made their views "Community" views, even though some of the member states – notably the Netherlands and Denmark – might have been willing to accept the Nordic Proposal (Wetstone and Rosencranz 1983). By this time, the European Community and the East European nations had also tabled proposals.

Turning point 3

By the end of the third session, the French and West German delegations declared their willingness to discuss the Nordic Proposal, but stressed again that this did not in any way prejudice their eventual position regarding the form of a possible agreement.

Drafting/formula-building

At the fourth meeting of the Special Group, which was held in late November 1978, the authors of the three principal negotiating texts (the Nordic countries, the European Community, and the East European countries) tabled revised versions of their proposals. During the course of the meeting, various elements of the three texts were fit together to produce the final proposal, "Elements for a document on long-range transboundary air pollution." Although considerable headway was made on the structure and content of the document, a number of gaps remained. Several of the draft paragraphs were not discussed, including the text on procedures aimed at settling disputes concerning damage caused to the environment by atmospheric pollution. The appropriate form that the agreement would finally assume also remained to be considered (Chossudovsky 1989, 77–78).

The fifth and final meeting of the Special Group took place in January 1979. Canada and the United States presented the Group with two additional documents. After reviewing the available documentation, the Group agreed to focus the discussion on the overall draft text. In the course of the paragraph-by-paragraph reading of the "document" a number of important points emerged. Much attention was devoted to the problems connected with the crucial aspect of the follow-up mechanism of a possible agreement. Differences of opinion persisted as to the need for mandatory conciliation and arbitration procedures and pointed to the need for further examination of this aspect at governmental level (Chossudovsky 1989, 79).

At this point, the British had already agreed to go along with the convention, in the belief that their plans for an increased reliance on nuclear power to generate electricity would bring about a net reduction in sulfur emissions. The West Germans, however, still resisted the standstill and rollback positions of the Nordic Proposal, and managed to require that the words "economically feasible" be added to the Nordic provision that the "best available technology" be used to reduce sulfur emissions. The West Germans also expressed concern that the proposed coordinating function of the ECE secretariat could give the secretariat authority to intervene in the internal (pollution control) affairs of member states (Wetstone and Rosencranz 1983).

Turning point 4

In February 1979, the Senior Advisors to the ECE held their seventh session to review the progress of the Special Groups. They realized that the negotiations on transboundary air pollution were falling behind schedule. The Finnish delegation, on behalf of the Nordic group, stated that although "the original ... proposal for a framework convention was still the preferred concept of an agreement ... the Nordic countries had taken a flexible attitude in the preceding negotiations and discussions." The representative of Finland then announced that, as a new major concession with a view to reaching an acceptable solution, the Nordic governments were ready to accept that concrete measures to control transboundary air pollution caused by sulfur compounds could be taken later than originally proposed; and that these measures could be implemented progressively, following a timetable established by common agreement.

This change was helpful in that it opened up new avenues for moving forward in the negotiations on the difficult point of accepting a firm commitment on a precise timetable. France declared that the EC governments were ready to assume a strong and serious political commitment to make substantial efforts to combat air pollution and limit and possibly reduce emissions. The European Community was not ready to pronounce on the form of the agreement. The USSR, on behalf of the East European countries, supported the Nordic Proposal and the concept of a legally binding instrument, but sought compromise to encourage EC support (Chossudovsky 1989, 80).

Final bargaining/details

Three diplomatic maneuvers were undertaken to gain West German and, thus, EC concurrence. During the first half of 1979, France, which held the presidency of the EC, put pressure on the West German government to come on board so that, if the negotiations were to fail, the Community would not be responsible. Simultaneously, the Norwegian Foreign Minister contacted his counterpart in West Germany and the Swedish Prime Minister contacted West German Prime Minister Helmut Schmidt urging the Germans to support the prospective agreement, whose terms the Germans had already successfully watered down. Eventually the West German government expressed its willingness to support the draft (Wetstone and Rosencranz 1983). By the end of the March 1979 special session of the Senior Advisors, the Convention on Long-Range Transboundary Air Pollution (LRTAP) was in draft form.

By the thirty-fourth session of the ECE, which met from 27 March to 7 April 1979, the objections to adopting a legally binding instrument had been removed, the work of finalizing the text of the draft Convention had been essentially completed, and the agenda for the High-level Meeting had been drawn up. But a new problem suddenly emerged: the Eastern bloc countries resisted the European Community's claim to represent its member states in negotiating the agreement and to be a signatory to the agreement. The EC and its member states, which had no heavy investment in concluding the Convention, were adamant that, if the Community itself was not a signatory to such an agreement, none of the member states would sign it (Wetstone and Rosencranz 1983). The meeting was adjourned and all further work on the Convention was suspended.

Turning point 5

This last obstacle was resolved when the Eastern bloc expressed willingness to accept a compromise offered by the European Community. This compromise was an amendment to Article 14 of the Convention, entitling regional economic integration organizations to sign the Convention if, and only if, they had been granted authority to act internationally on behalf of their constituent states. The Convention was adopted by acclamation at the ECE High-level Meeting in Geneva in November 1979.

Ratification/implementation

The Convention entered into force on 16 March 1983. As of 30 May 2000, 45 countries and the European Community had ratified the Convention. Since then, the following eight protocols have been negotiated.

The 1984 Geneva Protocol on Long-Term Financing of the Cooperative Programme for Monitoring and Evaluation of the Long-Range Transmission of Air Pollutants in Europe entered into force on 28 January 1988. This Protocol is an instrument for international cost-sharing of a monitoring program which forms the backbone for review and assessment of relevant air pollution in Europe in the light of agreements on emission reduction. EMEP, as it is known, has three main components: collection of emission data for SO_2, NOx, volatile organic compounds (VOCs), and other air pollutants; measurement of air and precipitation quality; and modeling of atmospheric dispersion. At present, about 100 monitoring stations in 24 ECE countries participate in the program.

The 1985 Helsinki Protocol on the Reduction of Sulphur Emissions or Their Transboundary Fluxes by at Least 30 Percent entered into force on 2 September 1987. The 1988 Sofia Protocol Concerning the Control of Emissions of Nitrogen Oxides or Their Transboundary Fluxes entered into force on 2 February 1991. This Protocol requires, as a first step, to freeze emissions of nitrogen oxides or their transboundary fluxes. The general reference year is 1987 (with the exception of the United States, which chose to relate its emission target to 1978).

The 1991 Geneva Protocol Concerning the Control of Emissions of Volatile Organic Compounds or Their Transboundary Fluxes entered into force on 29 September 1997. Volatile organic compounds (i.e. hydrocarbons) are the second major air pollutant responsible for the formation of ground-level ozone. This Protocol specifies three options for emission reduction targets that have to be chosen upon signature: (a) 30 percent reduction in emissions of volatile organic compounds (VOCs) by 1999, using a year between 1984 and 1990 as a basis; (b) the same reduction as for (a) within a Tropospheric Ozone Management Area (TOMA) specified in Annex I to the Protocol and ensuring that by 1999 total national emissions do not exceed 1988 levels; or (c) where emissions in 1988 did not exceed certain specified levels, parties may opt for stabilization at that level of emission by 1999.

The 1994 Oslo Protocol on Further Reduction of Sulphur Emissions entered into force on 5 August 1998. This Protocol has a differentiation of emission reduction obligations of parties. The effects-based approach, which aims at gradually attaining critical loads, sets long-term targets for reductions in sulfur emissions, although it has been recognized that critical loads will not be reached in one single step. An important new feature was introduced in connection with the adoption of this Protocol: the establishment of an Implementation Committee to review compliance.

The 1998 Aarhus Protocol on Heavy Metals was adopted on 24 June 1998. It targets three particularly harmful metals: cadmium, lead, and mercury. According to one of the basic obligations, parties will have to reduce their emissions of these three metals below their levels in 1990 (or an alternative year between 1985 and 1995). The Protocol aims to cut emissions from industrial sources (iron and steel industry, non-ferrous metal industry), combustion processes (power generation, road transport), and waste incineration. The Protocol also requires parties to phase out leaded petrol. In addition, it introduces measures to lower heavy metal emissions from other products. As of 30 May 2000, the Protocol had been ratified by four parties.

The 1998 Aarhus Protocol on Persistent Organic Pollutants (POPs) was adopted on 24 June 1998. It focuses on a list of 16 substances that have been singled out according to agreed risk criteria. The substances comprise 11 pesticides, 2 industrial chemicals, and 3 by-products/contaminants. The ultimate objective is to eliminate any discharges, emissions, and losses of POPs. The Protocol bans the production and use of some products outright and others are scheduled for elimination at a later stage. As of 30 May 2000, four parties had ratified the Protocol.

The 1999 Gothenburg Protocol to Abate Acidification, Eutrophication and Ground-level Ozone was adopted on 30 November 1999. The Protocol sets emission ceilings for 2010 for four pollutants: sulfur, NOx, VOCs, and ammonia. Parties whose emissions have a more severe environmental or health impact and whose emissions are relatively cheap to reduce will have to make the biggest cuts. Once the Protocol is fully implemented, Europe's sulfur emissions should be cut by at least 63 percent, its NOx emissions by 41 percent, its VOC emissions by 40 percent, and its ammonia emissions by 17 percent compared with 1990. No parties had ratified the Protocol as of 30 May 2000.[10]

Summary of the Convention

The Convention on Long-Range Transboundary Air Pollution calls for the development of exchange of information, consultation, research and monitoring, policies, and strategies to serve as a means of combating the discharge of air pollutants. Parties are required to cooperate in the conduct of research into and/or development of: (i) existing and proposed technologies for reducing emissions of sulfur compounds and other major air pollutants, including technical and economic feasibility, and their environmental consequences; (ii) instrumentation and other techniques for monitoring and measuring emission rates and ambient concentrations of air pollutants; (iii) improved models for better understanding of the transmission of long-range transboundary air pollutants; (iv) the effects of sulfur compounds and other major air pollutants on human health and the environment, including agriculture, forestry, materials, aquatic and other natural ecosystems, and visibility, with a view to establishing a scientific basis for dose/effect relationships designed to protect the environment; and (v) education and training programs related to the environmental aspects of pollution by sulfur compounds and other major air pollutants.

1980 Convention on the Conservation of Antarctic Marine Living Resources

Objectives of the negotiations

The objectives were to safeguard the environment and protect the integrity of the ecosystem of the seas surrounding Antarctica and to conserve Antarctic marine living resources.

Precipitants

The Antarctic Treaty proved relatively silent on the subject of natural resources, mainly because of an appreciation of the need to avoid divisive issues related to the ownership of resources. In practice, the consultative parties found it difficult to ignore resource questions, and the occasional pressures of the 1960s were succeeded in the 1970s by a greater sense of urgency regarding the need for action.

A number of factors led the consultative parties to place the topic of Antarctic marine living resources on the agenda of their 1975 meeting: growing attention to the living resources potential of Antarctic waters, especially krill – small shrimp-like crustaceans that are the primary food for the great whales and that are found in Antarctic waters in very large quantities; the prospects of commercial harvesting of krill; the realization that uncontrolled harvesting of krill or of other Antarctic marine living resources could have unforeseen and perhaps irreversible impacts; and the recognition that there are major gaps in the data necessary to manage Antarctic marine living resources (US Congress 1978, 9). Two additional issues played a role in this decision. The consultative parties were keen to demonstrate their continued authority over all Antarctic-related issues. The issue of marine living resources was also a test of the parties' ability to negotiate rules and procedures on a resource issue with sovereignty implications (Elliott 1994, 87–88).

Turning point 1

At the Eighth Consultative Meeting in 1975, the parties agreed on Recommendation VIII-10, which urged expanded scientific research on the subject of the marine resources of Antarctica.

Issue definition

As more scientific evidence became available and the Antarctic Treaty parties began to pay greater attention to the issue of conservation of marine living resources, there was greater consensus on the need to promote and achieve within the framework of the Antarctic Treaty the objectives of protection, scientific study, and rational use of Antarctic marine living resources. As the technology for harvesting and processing krill developed, several factors related to the ecosystem's vulnerability to krill exploitation became apparent. First, the ecosystem is characterized by short, simple food chains. Second, many intermediate and higher trophic-level species are dependent on krill, and the ecosystem has little chance for diversification or substitution of food sources. Third, many higher trophic-level species have relatively slow growth rates. Fourth, over-exploitation of krill will inhibit the recovery of protected whale and seal species. Fifth, the possibility of local pollution from maritime accidents presents a very real danger. Sixth, krill must be harvested continuously with processing facilities nearby because, once removed from the ocean, krill spoil in about four hours. Finally, whales feed on krill at the same times and in the same longitudes as are most practicable for human harvesting of krill (Frank 1983, 295).

Turning point 2

At the Ninth Consultative Meeting in 1977, the parties unanimously agreed to negotiate a convention for the conservation of Antarctic marine living resources, based on an "ecosystem" approach that would not be limited to commercially exploitable species (Barnes 1982, 248). Part I of Recommendation IX-2 reiterated the Treaty spirit of cooperation in scientific investigations and in the exchange of information, and extended a new mandate to intensify research relating to Antarctic marine living resources. Part II established interim conservation guidelines to prevent the depletion of stocks of any species or endangerment of the ecosystem as a whole. Part III stated that the consultative parties would establish a definitive conservation regime by the end of 1978 (Frank 1983, 299).

Statement of initial positions

The first Special Meeting of Antarctic Treaty Consultative Parties (Argentina, Australia, Belgium, Chile, France, Japan, New Zealand, Norway, Poland, South Africa, the Soviet Union, the United Kingdom, and the United States) took place in Canberra, Australia, from 27 February to 16 March 1978. The parties concentrated on the elaboration of a draft regime and determination of the form of the regime and of arrangements for a subsequent decisive meeting to conclude the regime. The participants agreed that the conservation regime would take the form of an international convention. The convention would be separate from the Antarctic Treaty but consistent with and supportive of it.

In all, nine draft conventions were tabled by Argentina, South Africa, Poland, Japan, Australia, Chile, France, the United States, and the USSR (Elliott 1994, 90; Barnes 1982, 250). Several combined innovative ideas and were oriented to some degree toward conservation. With strong support from the United Kingdom, Norway, and New Zealand, the United States urged that the convention had to define the "Antarctic marine ecosystem" on scientific and biological grounds. These countries stated their commitment to a conservation standard that included protection for dependent and related species.

Japan and the USSR strongly objected to this approach and proposed texts that were variations on normal fishing agreements, complete with maximum sustainable yield language to cover krill harvest. It was evident from these drafts that there was going to be no immediate agreement on what an "ecosystem approach" to conservation meant (Barnes 1982, 250).

Turning point 3

The chair of the Special Consultative Meeting, Ambassador John Rowland of Australia, prepared an informal draft convention based on the nine drafts submitted by the parties.

Drafting/formula-building

The chair's draft text then became the focus of discussion. After days of discussions among the scientists and preparation of numerous versions of a "conservation objective," the chair prepared a formulation of the article along the lines proposed by the United States and the United Kingdom. But it was clear that more negotiation would be required to convince the fishing countries (Barnes 1982, 250).

The chair's text was twice revised following intensive comment and debate. The representatives at the Canberra meeting agreed that the chair's second revised draft was a good basis for further negotiation and agreed to forward it to their governments for further study (US Congress 1978, 10). Upon the close of the Canberra meeting, the major unresolved issues included:

- The voting procedures in the Commission. There were differences between those supporting a qualified majority system and those supporting a unanimity system.
- The conservation standard. Should the convention take an ecosystem approach?
- The jurisdictional question. There remained divergences as to the degree of Commission competence to set conservation measures in areas covered by the convention where contracting parties assert maritime jurisdiction.
- The observer system. There were varying perceptions over whether detailed provisions on this point should be included or a simple commitment made to create such a system.
- Financing the regime. There was no consensus on a formula for apportioning contributions to the regime's budget.
- Interim arrangements. The question of possible interim conservation measures before the regime entered into force remained to be discussed (US Congress 1978, 11).

The 13 Treaty parties resumed their Special Consultative Meeting in Buenos Aires from 17 to 28 July 1978. The purpose of the meeting was to reach agreement on the key issues in the chair's draft prepared at Canberra and to make final arrangements for an international conference to adopt the agreement. Delegates agreed to create an ad hoc scientific working group that would deal first with the conservation standard and possible conservation measures (Articles II and VIII), with its future work plan open. The juridical and decision-making issues would be discussed at meetings of delegation heads accompanied by a few advisers (Barnes 1982, 252).

Negotiations almost broke down in Buenos Aires because of intransigence on a number of issues, including sovereignty and jurisdiction, conservation standards, and decision-making rules (Barnes 1982, 251–255). The meeting was not a total loss as there was substantial consensus on the draft articles dealing with the objectives of the convention, the conservation measures, and the principles of a system of inspection and observation, and on a number of other matters of less significance (Antarctic Treaty 1980). However, the session did conclude on a somewhat negative note, with the chair, Argentine Ambassador Munoz, merely identifying a number of working papers for governments to study on the same basis as the Canberra text. These included the agreed changes to the conservation articles on the system of observation and inspection, financing, and supply of information. Thus, the Buenos Aires meeting did not achieve its major objectives. Delegates could not even reach agreement on whether or not to hold another Special Consultative Meeting (Barnes 1982, 255).

Turning point 4

After the near-breakdown of negotiations at Buenos Aires, the United States offered to host a small "informal" session in Washington, DC, that would coincide with the resumed Law of the Sea Conference in New York from 18 to 26 September 1978. Although the mood at this meeting was sober, there were none of the assertions of various special rights for claimants that had produced earlier difficulty. Under the chairmanship of John Negroponte from the United States, a new draft of the convention was produced and most delegates thought that this draft provided a sound basis on which to hold an international conference (Barnes 1982, 255).

Final bargaining/details

After the Washington session there were several months of bilateral talks regarding the suitability of the Washington draft for presentation at an international conference. During this time, France repeatedly indicated that it was not prepared to attend such a conference (Barnes 1982, 255). French objections related to its concerns about coastal state jurisdiction over undisputed islands lying just outside the Treaty area but within the area covered by the draft convention (Elliott 1994, 90). It was not possible to conclude a definitive regime by the end of 1978 as Recommendation IX-2 had anticipated.

Two more sessions of informal consultations were held. The first, convened by Australia, was held in Berne from 9 to 13 March 1979. The second was held in Washington at the preparatory session for the Tenth Antarctic Consultative Meeting in June 1979. The two sessions focused on two outstanding issues: participation of the European Community, and French control over the waters around the islands of Kerguelen and Crozet. The parties reached agreement on the first, namely "agreement in principle on the participation of the European Economic Community in the future Convention." However, they did not work out the precise details of EC participation at the international conference (Barnes 1982, 256). Nor did the parties find an acceptable solution on the second question, which arose from the French concern to exclude the Crozet and Kerguelen Islands from the area of application of the convention. An attempt was made to reach agreement on the protection of the rights of coastal states, including France. Several new versions of an annex to the convention that would address this issue were prepared by various countries, but none of them was acceptable to the entire group (Barnes 1982, 257).

The Tenth Consultative Meeting of the Antarctic Treaty parties took place in Washington in September–October 1979. Informal negotiating sessions were held to develop a version of an annex to be attached to the final act of the international conference. By the end of the meeting, several countries were unwilling to agree formally to the new version. Nevertheless, delegates took home the new version of the annex for their governments to study (Barnes 1982, 257).

On 5 May 1980, Australia convened a two-day Consultative Meeting in Canberra to complete preparations for the international conference. This meeting was principally concerned with procedural matters, including the preparation of a draft agenda and of rules of procedure for the diplomatic conference. The meeting concluded by recommending that the draft text of the convention, the draft rules of procedure, and the text of the annex regarding the application of the convention to Kerguelen and Crozet be referred to the diplomatic conference.

The diplomatic Conference on the Conservation of Antarctic Marine Living Resources opened on 7 May 1980 in Canberra. Delegates from the governments of Argentina, Australia, Belgium, Chile, France, the German Democratic Republic, the Federal Republic of Germany, Japan, New Zealand, Norway, Poland, the Republic of South Africa, the Union of Soviet Socialist Republics, the United Kingdom of Great Britain and Northern Ireland, and the United States of America attended. The following international organizations participated as observers: the European Communities, the Food and Agriculture Organization, the Inter-Governmental Oceanographic Commission, the IUCN–World Conservation Union, the International Whaling Commission, the Scientific Committee on Antarctic Research, and the Scientific Committee on Oceanic Research.

Turning point 5

After 10 days of largely fruitless negotiations, a consensus package was produced at a late-night weekend session. It left all of the key articles as they were in the Washington draft, with the notable exception of the article on amendments (Article XXVIII). The European Community was not permitted to sign the Convention on the Conservation of Antarctic Marine Living Resources (CCAMLR), but was given a right to automatic membership of the Commission immediately after entry into force.

The issue of the area of application of the Convention was resolved by adopting the "coordinates" approach and, by its own terms, the Convention "applies to the Antarctic marine living resources of the area south of 60 degrees South latitude and to the Antarctic marine living resources of the area between that latitude and to the Antarctic Convergence which form part of the Antarctic marine ecosystem." This language signaled the consensus finally achieved, accommodating the interests of Argentina by redrawing the boundary farther away from the Drake Passage, of France by balancing its interests in the Kerguelen and Crozet Islands, and of the United States by specifying an ecosystem scope of application (Frank 1983, 302).

The conferees finally decided to sidestep the sovereignty issue, adopting a so-called "bifocal" approach, which permitted all interested states to participate in the Convention. This approach was essentially a gamble by conservationist states that neither claimants nor non-claimants would take assertive action regarding coastal state jurisdiction, since such action would undermine the force of the Convention and perhaps the viability of the Antarctic Treaty as well (Frank 1983, 307).

Another issue that was not resolved was how to monitor harvesting levels and provide for conservation measures during the interim period between signature and the Convention's entry into force. Instead, the signatory states informally indicated their commitment to ratify the Convention quickly, to harvest marine living resources conservatively, to share scientific and fishery data actively, and to convene a meeting during the interim period to facilitate operation of the institutions of the Convention (Frank 1983, 312). The Convention was adopted on 20 May 1980 in Canberra.

Ratification/implementation

The Convention entered into force on 7 April 1982. The Secretariat is located in Hobart (Tasmania), Australia. Any state that has acceded to the Convention is entitled to become a member of the Commission if it is actively conducting research or harvesting in the Convention area. The Convention also provides for regional economic integration organizations, subject to certain conditions, to be members of the Commission. There are 23 members of the Commission: Argentina, Australia, Belgium, Brazil, Chile, the European Community, France, Germany, India, Italy, Japan, Republic of Korea, New Zealand, Norway, Poland, the Russian Federation, South Africa, Spain, Sweden, Ukraine, the United Kingdom, the United States, and Uruguay. States that have ratified the Convention but are not members of the Commission are: Bulgaria, Canada, Finland, Greece, the Netherlands, and Peru.

The Commission meets annually to receive reports of the activities of members over the past year and their plans for the coming year, to review compliance with conservation measures in force, and, on the basis of advice from the Scientific Committee, to review existing conservation measures and adopt new ones as necessary. At these meetings the Commission also attends to matters related to the annual administration and financing of Commission activities. The eighteenth meeting of the Commission was held in November 1999 in Hobart, Australia.[11]

Summary of the Convention

The objective of the Convention is to conserve marine life. It does not exclude harvesting as long as such harvesting is carried out in a rational manner. The Convention defines a Commission and a Scientific Committee to work together to manage marine living resources in the Southern Ocean. The resources specifically exclude seals and whales, as these are covered by other conventions. However, there is full cooperation with the operating bodies of these other conventions.

The Commission for the Conservation of Antarctic Marine Living Resources has the following functions:
(a) to facilitate research into and comprehensive studies of Antarctic marine living resources and the Antarctic marine ecosystems;
(b) to compile data on the status of and changes in populations of Antarctic marine living resources, and on factors affecting the distribution, abundance, and productivity of harvested species and dependent or related species or populations;
(c) to ensure the acquisition of catch and effort statistics on harvested populations;

(d) to analyze, disseminate, and publish the information referred to in subparagraphs (b) and (c) above, and the reports of the Scientific Committee;

(e) to identify conservation needs and analyze the effectiveness of conservation measures;

(f) to formulate, adopt, and revise conservation measures on the basis of the best scientific evidence available;

(g) to implement a system of observation and inspection; and

(h) to carry out such other activities as are necessary to fulfill the objective of the Convention.

1983 International Tropical Timber Agreement

Objectives of the negotiations

The objectives were: (a) to provide an effective framework for cooperation and consultation between countries producing and consuming tropical timber; (b) to promote the expansion and diversification of international trade in tropical timber and the improvement of structural conditions in the tropical timber market; (c) to promote and support research and development with a view to improving forest management and wood utilization; and (d) to encourage the development of national policies aimed at sustainable utilization and conservation of tropical forests and their genetic resources, and at maintaining the ecological balance in the regions concerned.

Precipitants

Between 1974 and 1979, the Integrated Programme for Commodities (IPC) of the United Nations Conference on Trade and Development (UNCTAD) attempted to restructure the entire commodity order so that the mutual benefits of producer–consumer cooperation could be realized and developing countries could earn a greater share of the income and wealth derived from commodity production and trade. UNCTAD had been dealing with various commodity issues since 1964 but had not had any substantive results. Giving fresh impetus to the effort to restructure the entire commodity order, however, were the events of 1973–74: the OPEC phenomenon and the euphoria it induced in much of the Third World (in spite of the damage OPEC inflicted on the Third World); the evident disarray among the developed countries; and the new perceptions of the resource universe that were emerging in response to the "limits-to-growth" debate. An end to the post-1972 commodity boom was also of some significance, as it motivated commodity producers. UNCTAD and the Group of 77 clearly hoped that these factors would change developed country attitudes toward commodity agreements and international regulation (Rothstein 1987, 24).

Turning point 1

UNCTAD resolution 93(IV) of 30 May 1976 on the Integrated Programme for Commodities requested the UNCTAD Secretary-General to convene preparatory meetings on individual products and, as required, commodity negotiating conferences as soon as possible after the completion of such preparatory meetings (UNCTAD 1983c).

Issue definition

The first preparatory meeting on tropical timber (23–27 March 1977) focused on issue definition.[12] The participants agreed that one of the objectives should be to promote investment for regeneration of forest resources in order to achieve continuity of supplies of tropical timber on a long-term basis. Other main objectives agreed to at this meeting were: to develop and sustain a comprehensive and purposeful program of research and development aimed at improving forest management, reinvestment, and maintenance, and the quality of tropical timber and products thereof; to accomplish stable market conditions in the trade in tropical timber, including avoidance of excessive price fluctuations, at levels that would be remunerative and just to producers and equitable to consumers; and to improve and sustain the real income of countries producing tropical timber through increased export earnings.

Further objectives related to measures to be taken. One was to accomplish greater accessibility to and continuity of information relating to supply and market structure, conditions, and behavior in producing and consuming countries. Another was to overcome infrastructural, technological, and other structural deficiencies within the timber industry of the tropical timber producing countries. A third was to achieve the expansion and development of processing and manufacturing of timber-based products in the producing countries with the aim of improving and increasing their export earnings. Other objectives included improving access to markets in consuming countries and achieving international standardization of nomenclature of species, qualities, grades, and specifications in the tropical timber trade.

Turning point 2

At the conclusion of the first meeting, the participants had reached agreement on the objectives and the general content of the new agreement. They also agreed that the next session should examine appropriate measures and techniques, and prepare and recommend a work program directed to achieve the various objectives.

Statement of initial positions

At the second preparatory meeting (24–28 October 1977), the producing countries tabled a position paper in which they outlined a series of measures that would have to be taken to minimize market and price instability. Consumers did not believe that sufficient time remained to do full justice to all the points raised in the producers' paper, yet they agreed that they would further study the specific measures as suggested by the producers and they would be prepared to enter into a preliminary discussion of these and other possible measures at the next preparatory meeting (UNCTAD 1977). At the third preparatory meeting (23–27 January 1978), the producing and consuming countries exchanged views on the preliminary position paper tabled by the producing countries at the previous meeting (UNCTAD 1978).

Turning point 3

At the fourth preparatory meeting (31 July – 4 August 1978), participants agreed that the following possible elements could be considered as a basis for an international arrangement on tropical timber: reforestation and forest management, increased and further processing in the producing countries, research and development, and market fluctuation. The meeting suggested that the secretariats of UNCTAD and FAO, with the assistance of governments, competent international organizations, and private experts and other relevant bodies, prepare a document to be submitted at the fifth preparatory meeting showing how a scheme covering the above elements might be organized and operated (UNCTAD 1993).

Drafting/formula-building

At the fifth preparatory meeting (22–26 October 1979), the secretariats of UNCTAD and FAO presented their report, which elaborated further on the four basic elements. In preparation of the report it had become evident that extensive technical work was still required before a realistic scheme could be designed. This was particularly the case with respect to the financial and institutional requirements. The delegates discussed the UNCTAD/FAO report and continued to express their positions on the four basic elements. By the end of the meeting, the delegates decided that, owing to lack of time, they were unable to complete their consideration of the draft conclusions. Accordingly, they decided to reconvene the fifth preparatory meeting during the first half of 1980 and annex the following to the report of the meeting: the draft conclusions submitted by the chair; the draft conclusions submitted by the producing countries; and the draft conclusions and recommendations submitted by the United States on behalf of some consuming countries. The Nordic countries did not associate themselves with the US draft conclusions and recommendations (UNCTAD 1979).

At the second part of the fifth preparatory meeting (7–18 July 1980), the chair commented that the three sets of draft conclusions submitted at the conclusion of the first part of the meeting reflected a large degree of agreement on substance and this had encouraged the secretariats of UNCTAD and FAO to prepare five studies on three of the four elements that had been identified as a possible basis for an international arrangement on tropical timber. During the intersessional period, parallel negotiations on the Common Fund had been successfully concluded. This removed one barrier from the tropical timber negotiations, as the Common Fund provided an additional source of finance for commodity development measures, and it was now possible to move from general discussions on tropical timber to the formulation of a more concrete and specific program of international action. By the end of the meeting, delegates had agreed on the following (UNCTAD 1980):

Research and development. They agreed on the criteria for the selection of projects and gave the task of proposing a list of specific research and development projects to an intergovernmental group of experts.

Improvement of market intelligence. They recognized the need to identify and endeavor to achieve comparability on the types of trade-related data on tropical timber required for the improvement of market intelligence and the need to make such data available from producing and consuming countries. They asked the secretariats of UNCTAD and FAO to prepare a report on this and submit it to an intergovernmental group of experts, who would suggest proposals for the sixth preparatory meeting.

Reforestation and forest management. Supplementary financing would be needed to support reforestation efforts. They requested the secretariats of UNCTAD, FAO, and the World Bank to submit a paper on this at the next meeting.

At the sixth preparatory meeting (1–11 June 1982), a package of the basic elements for an international agreement to be negotiated was broadly agreed upon and the preparatory phase was completed after nearly five years of discussion. The delegates were able to reach consensus and adopt text on the following:

Research and development. Individual research and development projects prepared on the basis of the 42 project profiles already considered (on wood utilization, forest development, harvesting, manpower development, etc.) should be selected for implementation by a responsible producer/consumer body within the framework of the agreement in accordance with the criteria agreed on at the fifth preparatory meeting.

Market intelligence. Various proposals on market intelligence submitted by the expert meeting of November 1981, notably the proposal for a mechanism that would feature monitoring, evaluating data, and holding producer/consumer meetings on the market situation and short-term prospects, met the requirements of an international agreement.

Further and increased processing in developing producing countries. Cooperation between producing and consuming countries should cover the transfer of technology, training, product nomenclature and specification, standardization, and encouragement of investment and joint ventures. A responsible producer/consumer body within the framework of an international agreement would be entrusted with monitoring ongoing activities and with identifying and considering problems and possible solutions to them in cooperation with the competent organizations.

Reforestation and forest management. Producers and consumers should cooperate to keep under regular review the support and assistance being provided at national and international levels; encourage increased technical assistance to national reforestation and forest resource management programmes; assess the requirements and identify all possible sources of financing; and regularly review the future needs of the international trade in industrial tropical timber and on this basis identify and consider possible schemes and measures aimed at satisfying such needs (Kunugi 1982).

There was not time for the sixth preparatory meeting to discuss the institutional issues relating to the agreement. Thus, a meeting was convened from 29 November to 3 December 1982 to consider these and related issues to facilitate the task of the negotiating conference. The government of Japan had proposed a set of draft articles for an international agreement at the sixth preparatory meeting and, although governments had been invited to submit their own draft articles, no such communications had been received. At the conclusion of the meeting, delegates agreed on the following:

• To establish an autonomous International Tropical Timber Organization (ITTO) to administer the provisions of the agreement and supervise its operation. They also agreed on the structure and organs of the ITTO, the frequency of meetings, voting procedures, cooperation with other organizations, and finance and contributions.

• There should be two categories of membership in the ITTO – producers and consumers. There was no agreement on the definition of membership categories.

- They also agreed on the definition of tropical timber (UNCTAD 1983a).

Turning point 4

Based on the agreement on the package of elements to be included in the agreement and the institutional issues, by February 1983 drafts were submitted by the tropical timber producing countries, Japan, the Nordic countries, and the United States. The Conference on Tropical Timber convened on 14 March 1983 in Geneva.

Final bargaining/details

By the conclusion of the first session of the UN Conference on Tropical Timber on 31 March 1983, delegates from 64 countries had reached consensus on all but 6 of the 43 articles. Outstanding issues included the location of the headquarters of the new International Tropical Timber Organization, for which Belgium, France, Greece, Japan, the Netherlands, and the United Kingdom had offered cities. Another issue was the number of committees that the organization should have. The chair proposed three: Economic Information and Market Intelligence; Reforestation and Forest Management; and Processing. The consumers thought only two were necessary. Differences on other broader points, such as objectives and definitions of what should be regarded as tropical timber for the purposes of the agreement, reflected a major divergence on the concept of the agreement, with producers stressing production and resource management, while most consumers focused on the trade aspects (UNCTAD 1983a).

Turning point 5

Between the two sessions, the conference requested that the chair undertake consultations on outstanding issues and that the UNCTAD Secretary-General arrange to reconvene the conference. The conference reconvened from 7 to 18 November 1983 in Geneva. The decision on the location of the International Tropical Timber Organization (ITTO) headquarters was postponed for decision by the ITTO at its first meeting (Wasserman 1984). The International Tropical Timber Agreement was adopted on 18 November 1983, in Geneva.

Ratification/implementation

The Agreement entered into force on 1 April 1985. The headquarters of the ITTO is in Yokohama, Japan. The Agreement remained in force for an initial period of five years and was extended twice for two-year periods by decisions of the Council.

The Agreement was renegotiated during a series of meetings in April, June, and October 1993 and January 1994. On 26 January 1994, the Successor Agreement to the International Tropical Timber Agreement was adopted. The Agreement was opened for signature on 1 April 1994 and entered into force on 1 January 1997.

In June 1991, the ITTO Council committed itself by Decision 3(X) to what is now known as the Year 2000 Objective, which is the goal of having all tropical timber entering international trade come from sustainably managed sources by 2000. Since then, the Council has approved policy studies and project financing for a number of activities to help member countries move toward this Objective.

The 1994 ITTA established a fund for sustainable management of tropical producing forests, the Bali Partnership Fund (BPF). The BPF has been established to assist producing members to make the investments necessary to enhance their capacity to implement a strategy for achievin exports of tropical timber and timber products from sustainably manage sources by the Year 2000.

As of November 1999, ITTO's membership consisted of the following 29 producing countries: Bolivia, Brazil, Cambodia, Cameroon, Central African Republic, Colombia, Congo, Côte d'Ivoire, Democratic Republic of the Congo, Ecuador, Fiji, Gabon, Ghana, Guyana, Honduras, India, Indonesia, Liberia, Malaysia, Myanmar, Panama, Papua New Guinea, Peru, the Philippines, Suriname, Thailand, Togo, Trinidad and Tobago, and Venezuela; and the following 25 consuming countries: Australia, Canada, China, Egypt, the European Union (Austria, Belgium/Luxembourg, Denmark, Finland, France, Germany, Greece, Italy, the Netherlands, Portugal, Spain, Sweden, the United Kingdom), Japan, Nepal, New Zealand, Norway, Republic of Korea, Switzerland, and the United States. The members together represent 95 percent of world trade in tropical timber and 75 percent of the world's tropical forests.[13]

Summary of the Convention

The ITTA establishes the International Tropical Timber Organization to administer the provisions and supervise the operation of the Agreement, functioning through the International Tropical Timber Council established under Article 6 of the Agreement. The Council makes arrangements for consultation or cooperation with the United Nations and its organs such as UNCTAD, UNDP, UNEP, and the UN Industrial Development Organization, and with FAO and other United Nations specialized agencies and intergovernmental, governmental, and non-governmental organizations. The Agreement also establishes permanent committees on economic information and markets, intelligence, reforestation and forest management, and the forest industry. The Council meets twice a year, in the spring and the fall. The twenty-ninth session is scheduled for November 2000.

Unlike some other commodity agreements, the ITTA has no price regulation mechanisms or market intervention provisions, and accords equal importance to trade and conservation. ITTO's underlying concept is to promote sustainable development of tropical forests by encouraging and assisting the tropical timber industry and trade to manage and thus conserve the resource basis upon which they depend.

The Successor Agreement to the ITTA continues to focus on the world tropical timber economy. In addition, it contains broader provisions for information sharing, including non-tropical timber trade data, and allows for consideration of non-tropical timber issues as they relate to tropical timber.

ITTO's objectives, as set forth in the 1994 International Tropical Timber Agreement, include:

- to provide an effective framework for consultation, international cooperation, and policy development among all members with regard to all relevant aspects of the world timber economy;
- to provide a forum for consultation to promote non-discriminatory timber trade practices;
- to contribute to the process of sustainable development;
- to enhance the capacity of members to implement a strategy for achieving exports of tropical timber and timber products from sustainably managed sources by the Year 2000;
- to promote the expansion and diversification of international trade in tropical timber from sustainable sources by improving the structural conditions in international markets, by taking into account, on the one hand, a long-term increase in consumption and continuity of supplies, and, on the other, prices which reflect the costs of sustainable forest management and which are remunerative and equitable for members, and the improvement of market access;
- to promote and support research and development with a view to improving forest management and the efficiency of wood utilization as well as increasing the capacity to conserve and enhance other forest values in timber producing tropical forests;
- to develop and contribute towards mechanisms for the provision of new and additional financial resources and expertise needed to enhance the capacity of producing members to attain the objectives of this Agreement;
- to improve market intelligence with a view to ensuring greater trans-

parency in the international timber market, including the gathering, compilation, and dissemination of trade-related data, including data related to species being traded;

• to promote increased and further processing of tropical timber from sustainable sources in producing member countries with a view to promoting their industrialization and thereby increasing their employment opportunities and export earnings; and

• to encourage members to support and develop industrial tropical timber reforestation and forest management activities as well as rehabilitation of degraded forest land, with due regard for the interests of local communities dependent on forest resources.

1987 Montreal Protocol on Substances that Deplete the Ozone Layer

Objectives of the negotiations

The objective was to protect the ozone layer by taking precautionary measures to control global emissions of substances that deplete it.

Precipitants

In 1974, Mario Molina and Sherwood Rowland at the University of California, Irvine, discovered that, unlike most other gases, chlorofluorocarbons (CFCs) are not chemically broken down or rained out quickly in the lower atmosphere, but rather, because of their exceptionally stable chemical structure, persist and migrate slowly up to the stratosphere (Benedick 1991, 10). They argued that the chlorine in CFC emissions reacts with and breaks down ozone molecules in the thin layer of stratospheric ozone and thus hinders the ozone layer's ability to prevent harmful ultraviolet rays from reaching the earth (Molina and Rowland 1974, 810–812).

In 1975, UNEP first introduced the issue of ozone depletion to the international arena when it funded a study by the World Meteorological Society on the Molina/Rowland theory that the depletion of the ozone layer was caused by CFCs. In 1977, the United States, Canada, Finland, Norway, and Sweden urged UNEP to consider the international regulation of ozone, a move based on the same Molina/Rowland theory. In March 1977, UNEP held a conference with experts from 32 countries who adopted a World Plan of Action on the Ozone Layer. Although international action to regulate CFC use was suggested as a policy option, there was still much scientific uncertainty and the idea was dropped.

UNEP also established the Coordinating Committee on the Ozone Layer, consisting of representatives from governmental agencies and non-governmental organizations, to determine the extent of the problem as a guide to international action (Porter, Brown, and Chasek 2000, 88).

In May 1981, the UNEP Governing Council authorized UNEP to begin work toward an international agreement on protecting the ozone layer. The Ad Hoc Working Group of Legal and Technical Experts for the Elaboration of a Global Framework Convention for the Protection of the Ozone Layer, which included representatives from 24 nations, began meeting in January 1982. Although the Toronto Group (the United States, Canada, Australia, and the Nordic states) called for binding obligations to reduce CFC use, the European Community and Japan preferred less stringent restrictions. The group met four times, but by March 1985, when representatives from 43 nations convened in Vienna to complete work on the agreement, the only agreement that could be forged was a framework convention. The 1985 Vienna Convention for the Protection of the Ozone Layer was essentially an agreement to cooperate on monitoring, research, and data exchanges. It imposed no specific obligations on the signatories to reduce production of ozone-depleting chemicals and did not even specify what chemicals were the cause of ozone depletion (Porter, Brown, and Chasek 2000, 89; Benedick 1991, 44–46).

Turning point 1

At the last minute in Vienna, the United States and other members of the Toronto Group introduced a resolution authorizing UNEP to reopen diplomatic negotiations with a 1987 target for arriving at a legally binding control protocol. The resolution further provided that, before the formal negotiations, UNEP would convene a workshop to develop a "more common understanding" of factors affecting the ozone layer, including the costs and effects of possible control measures (Benedick 1991, 45; Tolba 1998, 61).

Issue definition

Two workshops were held in 1986 that enabled the negotiators to re-assess the whole situation. The first workshop, sponsored by the European Community in May 1986 in Rome, examined CFC production and consumption trends, the effects of existing regulations, and possible alternatives to CFCs. The second workshop, sponsored by the United States in September 1986 in Leesburg, Virginia, evaluated alternative regulatory strategies in terms of their implications for the environment, demand for CFCs, trade, equity, cost effectiveness, and ease of implementation.

According to Richard Benedick, these informal workshops established a framework for the difficult formal negotiations ahead. "The process was characterized by breaking down the problems into smaller components, developing consensus by incremental stages, and, as important as any other factor, establishing a degree of rapport and mutual confidence among future participants in the diplomatic negotiations" (Benedick 1991, 49).

Turning point 2

Manifestations of growing scientific consensus contributed to greater open-mindedness among the participants at Leesburg. There was also a growing general belief that some kind of international regime was required, that past national positions would have to be modified, and that every country would have to make concessions (Benedick 1991, 49).

Statement of initial positions

The first round of negotiations took place in Geneva in December 1986.[14] The week-long session was attended by 19 industrialized countries and 6 relatively advanced developing nations. The negotiating parties appeared to be divided into three major camps, basically unchanged from the Vienna Conference 20 months earlier. Officially, the European Community, negotiating as a bloc, followed the industry line and reflected the views of France, Italy, and the United Kingdom. The European Community continued to advocate some form of production capacity cap, but argued that there was time to delay actual production cuts and wait for more scientific evidence. This perspective was shared by Japan and the Soviet Union. The Soviet Union was concerned by the lack of substitutes for CFCs in air conditioning and refrigeration, both essential in the Soviet south, fearing that CFC controls would lead to unrest there. The Japanese worried that no substitutes had been developed for the CFCs used as solvents in their electronics industry, the backbone of their economy (Tolba 1998, 65).

In contrast, Canada, Finland, New Zealand, Norway, Sweden, Switzerland, and the United States publicly endorsed strong new controls. Despite the gaps in knowledge, these governments were convinced that further delay would increase health and environmental risks to an unacceptable degree. A third group of active participants, including Australia, Austria, and a number of developing countries, was initially uncommitted.

Canada, the United States, and the Soviet Union each proposed texts that were incompatible with one another. The United States called for an initial freeze followed by cutbacks until CFCs were eliminated by the year 2000. Canada proposed national emissions quotas based on a formula incorporating gross national product and population. The Soviet Union suggested national allocations based rather vaguely on population and CFC production capacity, with a complete exemption for developing countries. The European Community claimed that it could have no position until its Council of Environmental Ministers convened in late March 1987 (Benedick 1991, 70).

Turning point 3

At the beginning of the second round of negotiations, the United States proposed that, rather than argue over which text should serve as the basis for negotiation, four separate working groups should be established to deal with the issues of science, trade, developing countries, and control measures.

Drafting/formula-building

At the second session, which met in Vienna from 23 to 27 February 1987, representatives from 31 countries, a number of international organizations, and non-governmental organizations debated the issues. Canada, the Nordic countries, Egypt, Mexico, New Zealand, and Switzerland supported the US text. Important gaps continued to separate the United States and the European Community on virtually every substantive issue. Four difficult issues presented themselves: agreement on the status of science; control measures; trade provisions; and the special situation of developing countries. Added to these issues was the debate over the transfer of financial resources from the North to the South (Tolba 1998, 69).

An important step forward was the setting of a firm September date for the final plenipotentiaries' conference in Montreal. "This both turned up the pressure and eradicated any lingering doubts or wishful thinking about the seriousness of the intent to push forward to a protocol" (Benedick 1991, 71).

The February session produced a sixth draft protocol. The third negotiating session took place in Geneva in April 1987, when 33 nations participated, including 11 developing countries. By this time, scientists had agreed almost unanimously that ozone was in the process of being depleted; the NGOs had begun to take a major interest in the issue; the media were demanding action; and much of industry, having seen that international controls were inevitable on ozone-depleting substances, had decided to cooperate (Tolba 1998, 70).

Turning point 4

UNEP Executive Director Mostafa Tolba attended the April 1987 meeting and organized a series of closed meetings of key delegation heads, away from the formality of the large plenary sessions, and focused on the crucial control measures. This group (heads of delegation of Canada, Japan, New Zealand, Norway, the Soviet Union, the United States, and the European Commission, plus Belgium, Denmark, and the United Kingdom – the EC presidential troika) was able to produce an unofficial draft by the end of the session (Benedick 1991, 72; Tolba 1998, 70–71).

Final bargaining/details

In June 1987, Tolba reconvened his group of key delegation heads in Brussels to consider the controls and other major provisions. In July a small number of legal experts met in The Hague to analyze the entire protocol text as it had emerged from various working groups, in order to produce a relatively uncluttered and internally consistent draft for the final negotiating session in Montreal (Benedick 1991, 73).

During this nine-month period, the points of debate included: what chemicals would be included; whether production or consumption of these substances would be controlled; the base year from which reductions would be calculated; the timing and sizing of cutbacks; how the treaty could enter into force and be revised, including the question of weighted voting; restrictions on trade with countries not participating in the protocol; treatment of developing countries with low levels of CFC consumption; and special provisions for the European Community (Benedick 1991, 73).

The parties reconvened in Montreal on 8 September 1987. Sixty governments, of which more than half were developing countries, sent delegations. The first six days were devoted to attempts in various working groups to reach greater convergence on the many bracketed portions of the protocol text. On 14 September, the plenipotentiary conference was convened to complete the negotiations. Some of the issues were not fully resolved until the last day of the Montreal meeting, when the heads of the US and EC delegations met through the early hours of the morning (Benedick 1991, 74–76).

Turning point 5

A number of factors have been credited with forging the final compromise, including disunity within the European Community (with the

Federal Republic of Germany, Denmark, Belgium, and the Netherlands all urging stronger regulation), the personal role played by UNEP Executive Director Mostafa Tolba, relentless diplomatic pressure by the United States, and a certain reluctance to be blamed for the failure of the conference (Porter, Brown, and Chasek 2000, 89). The final compromise included a pledge by industrialized countries to reduce CFC production by 50 percent of 1986 levels by 1999. Developing countries were permitted to increase their use of CFCs substantially for the first decade up to 0.66 pounds (0.3 kilograms) per capita annually. The Montreal Protocol on Substances that Deplete the Ozone Layer was adopted on 16 September 1987.

Ratification/implementation

The Protocol entered into force on 1 January 1989. As of May 2000, the Protocol had been ratified by 173 parties. The Protocol has since been amended several times.

Within months of the Protocol's adoption, British scientists discovered an "ozone hole," that is, springtime decreases of 40 percent of the ozone layer, over Antarctica between 1977 and 1984. Then a 1988 report by 100 leading atmospheric scientists concluded that the northern hemisphere ozone layer had also been reduced up to 3 percent between 1969 and 1986. In London in June 1990 at the second meeting of the parties, the parties agreed to phase out CFCs by 2000 and to add a series of other chemicals to the list of controlled substances, including carbon tetrachloride and methyl chloroform. They also agreed to establish a special fund to help developing countries comply with the Protocol and devised rules for contributions by industrialized countries as well as a management plan. The London amendments entered into force on 10 August 1992. As of May 2000, 139 parties had ratified the London amendments.

In 1992 in Copenhagen, the Protocol was revised again to bring forward the phase-out date to 1996 for CFCs and to 1994 for halons, save for essential uses. The Copenhagen amendments entered into force on 14 June 1994. As of May 2000, 105 parties had ratified the Copenhagen amendments. In November 1993 in Thailand, the parties agreed that there was no longer a need for any exemption on the question of essential uses for halons. Thus, halons were phased out completely at the end of 1993.

The Protocol's control measures were further strengthened by the Montreal amendment, adopted at the ninth Meeting of the Parties in Montreal in September 1997. The Meeting agreed to a phase-out schedule for methyl bromide, a fumigant that was the most important ozone-depleting substance whose phase-out by developing countries had not yet been established. It also set up a licensing system to help governments track international trade in CFCs and other controlled substances and discourage illegal sales. The amendment entered into force on 10 November 1999 and had been ratified by 37 parties as of May 2000.

The Beijing amendment was adopted at the eleventh Meeting of the Parties in Beijing in December 1999. Among other things, the amendment bans trade in hydrochlorofluorocarbons (HCFCs) with countries that have not yet ratified the Protocol's 1992 Copenhagen amendment, requires developed countries to freeze the production of HCFCs in 2004 at 1989 levels and developing countries to do so in 2016 at 2015 levels, and requires the production of bromochloromethane (a recently developed ozone-depleting chemical) to be completely phased out in all countries by 2002. The Beijing amendment will enter into force after it has been ratified by 20 governments. Chile became the first country to ratify the amendment on 3 May 2000.[15]

Summary of the Protocol

The Protocol, as adopted in September 1987, controls eight substances: five CFCs (numbers 11, 12, 113, 114, and 115) and three bromine compounds (halons 1211, 1301, and 2402). Within 10 years, the production and consumption of the CFCs were to be cut back, in three stages, to 50 percent of their 1986 levels. Production and consumption of the halons would be frozen within three years, except for essential uses such as fire retardants, because no satisfactory substitute was yet available. Qualifications to the agreement were built into the Protocol to meet the special circumstances of several nations. Additional controls limiting trade with nonparties were adopted to give these nations an incentive to become parties to the Protocol. Developing countries were given a 10-year grace period before they had to comply with the control measures, provided that their annual consumption of the eight substances during that period did not exceed 0.3 kilograms per capita.

The 1990 London amendments called for a complete phase-out of the five CFCs and the three halons by 2000, as well as a phase-out of 10 other fully halogenated CFCs and carbon tetrachloride by 2000 and methyl chloroform by 2005. The Multilateral Fund for the Implementation of the Montreal Protocol was also established by the London amendments.

The 1992 Copenhagen amendments accelerated the ban on all CFCs by four years and shortened timetables on other ozone-depleting chemicals. They also added HCFCs to the chemicals to be phased out by 35 percent in 2004 and completely banned by 2030.

The 1997 Montreal amendment accelerated the phase-out schedule for methyl bromide. It also set up a licensing system to help governments track international trade in CFCs and other controlled substances and discourage illegal sales.

The 1999 Beijing amendment banned trade in HCFCs with countries that have not yet ratified the Protocol's 1992 Copenhagen amendment, which introduced the HCFC phase-out. It also requires developed countries to freeze the production of HCFCs in 2004 at 1989 levels and developing countries to do so in 2016 with a similar baseline of 2015. Production of 15 percent above baseline will be permitted to meet the "basic domestic needs" of developing countries. In addition, the production of bromochloromethane (a recently developed ozone-depleting chemical) is to be completely phased out in all countries by 2002.

1989 Basel Convention on the Control of Transboundary Movements of Hazardous Wastes and Their Disposal

Objectives of the negotiations

The objectives were to prevent developing countries from becoming repositories for improperly identified and improperly managed hazardous wastes; to pinpoint what constitutes illegal traffic; to ensure mechanisms for redress in case of illegal or inappropriate exports of hazardous wastes to developing countries; and, in general, to ensure environmentally sound management of hazardous wastes subject to transboundary movement.

Precipitants

North–South hazardous waste shipments increased through the 1970s and 1980s, and unsafe and illegal waste dumps were discovered in several developing countries. It was found that an estimated US$3 billion worth of hazardous wastes, representing one-fifth to one-tenth of the total annual global trade in such wastes, is exported from industrialized countries to developing countries, most of which lack the technology or administrative capacity to dispose of them safely. These states, particularly the poorer states in Africa, Central America, and the Caribbean, have been tempted by offers of substantial revenues for accepting the wastes (Porter, Brown, and Chasek 2000, 104). Increased disposal costs owing to stronger environmental and human health regulations in industrialized countries began displacing hazardous wastes to lower-cost areas.

Turning point 1

The UNEP Governing Council agreed to address the issue of the hazardous waste trade and UNEP's legal department began working in 1981 towards an international agreement to control the movement of wastes.

Issue definition

As a first step, UNEP commissioned an international group of experts to draw up wide-ranging guidelines on the environmentally sound management of hazardous wastes. From 1984 to 1985 the working group met to define the issues, examine the facts, and develop the guidelines. On 17 June 1987, the UNEP Governing Council adopted the principles developed by the working group, known as the Cairo Guidelines. These guidelines specified prior notification to the receiving state of any export, consent by the receiving state prior to export, and verification by the exporting state that the receiving state has requirements for disposal at least as stringent as those of the exporting state.

At the same time, the Organisation for Economic Co-operation and Development (OECD) was preparing guidelines for the export and import of hazardous wastes. At the OECD Environment Committee meeting in June 1985, governments declared their intention to "[s]trengthen control of the generation and disposal of hazardous wastes and establish an effective and legally binding system of control of their transfrontier movements, including movements to non-member countries" (OECD 1990). The European Community was also developing a series of recommendations regarding transfrontier shipments of hazardous wastes. A directive on the supervision and control within the European Community of the transfrontier shipment of hazardous waste was adopted in December 1994.

Turning point 2

The decision to begin negotiation of an international convention was motivated by a number of events. First, the problem of hazardous waste shipments from the industrialized to certain developing countries began to receive greater media attention. Armed with the evidence of the hazardous waste trade, a coalition of environmental NGOs and developing countries led by the African states lobbied the UNEP Governing Council to negotiate an international convention. At the June 1987 UNEP Governing Council meeting, UNEP's executive director, Mostafa Tolba, was authorized to convene a Working Group of Legal and Technical Experts with a mandate to prepare a global convention on the control of the transboundary movement of hazardous wastes.

Statement of initial positions

The organizational session of the Ad Hoc Working Group of Legal and Technical Experts took place in Budapest from 17 to 29 October 1987. It was clear from the opening statements that the African states wanted a total ban on such waste exports as well as export-state liability in the event of illegal traffic in wastes. The exporting states demanded an "informed consent" regime – a convention that would require waste exporters to notify their governments of any exports and notify importing countries of any shipments before they arrive (Porter, Brown, and Chasek 2000, 105). There were also fundamental disagreements on how comprehensive the convention should be. Some delegates thought that the treaty should be general in character, leaving technical issues to future protocols or to bilateral and regional accords. Others thought that the treaty should contain comprehensive and detailed controls (Hampson 1995, 283).

Turning point 3

At the conclusion of the organizational session, delegates requested that the UNEP secretariat draft a convention, taking into consideration the Cairo Guidelines, the work done by the OECD and the European Community, as well as statements made by the delegates in Budapest.

Drafting/formula-building

The first substantive session took place from 1 to 5 February 1988, in Geneva. Experts from 31 countries attended the meeting. Since the OECD was scheduled to meet to develop a core list of hazardous wastes during the week of 7 February, many of the discussions at the UNEP meeting were postponed until after the OECD meeting had taken place (Bureau of National Affairs 1988a, 131).

Negotiations were based on a draft text submitted by the secretariat. The meeting addressed a number of key issues, including the question of "prior informed consent" under which both the nation accepting the shipment of wastes and the country shipping them have to agree before a shipment can be made. Developing countries were insistent that the principle of prior informed consent be included in the treaty (Bureau of National Affairs 1988a, 131). It remained open to question how a transit country would handle such permissions and whether it would have the right to require its written consent before a shipment of hazardous wastes crosses its territory. The question of whether exporters should have the obligation to receive hazardous wastes back into their territory was also a matter of continuing discussion. Other hot topics included the definition of hazardous wastes and the issue of disposal and how and where disposal should be handled (Hampson 1995, 284).

The second substantive session was held from 6 to 10 June 1988, in Caracas; 40 governments attended, 22 of them from developing countries, an indication of the concern of the developing countries over the issue of the transboundary movement of hazardous waste (Tolba 1998, 102). Using the secretariat's draft as a starting point, the Working Group agreed to base the definitions of hazardous wastes on a core list of categories and characteristics of wastes, which had been approved in May by the OECD Working Group on international waste shipment. Delegates agreed that the convention would not include nuclear waste because this falls under the jurisdiction of the International Atomic Energy Agency. General agreement was reached on procedures for advance notification of transboundary shipments of such wastes to countries of import and transit, on the establishment of a prior informed consent mechanism for importing countries and on the duty to re-import wastes when a shipment could not be completed as foreseen. The group also decided on the establishment of a secretariat to facilitate the implementation of the proposed convention (UNEP 1991a, 5–7). Disagreements still existed on the shipment of waste to developing countries, what constitutes hazardous waste, and where third parties stand in the shipment of waste (Bureau of National Affairs 1988b, 376).

At the request of the Working Group, a Sub-Working Group of Legal Experts met with experts in transportation to consider selected issues and to review points pertaining to the relationship of the proposed convention with existing international instruments in the field of transport of hazardous goods. This meeting took place in Geneva from 10 to 12 August 1988 (UNEP 1991a, 5–7).

The third meeting of the Working Group took place from 7 to 16 November 1988 in Geneva, where they reviewed a fourth draft of the convention, which consisted of 29 articles and five annexes, one of which contained a list of wastes to be controlled under the convention. Issues that continued to block consensus included the rights of transit states, the status of "offshore" or dependent territories, and territorial waters. Progress was made in other areas of the 36-page draft convention, including the acceptance of a "limited ban" wherein a party to the convention may not export or import hazardous wastes from or to a country which has not ratified the convention. A new article on control of illegal traffic was also accepted (Bureau of National Affairs 1988c, 660).

The fourth meeting, attended by 50 countries, took place in Luxembourg from 31 January to 4 February 1989. There was still no agreement on the question of prior informed consent on the transhipment of hazardous wastes between countries. Developing countries continued to say that they would block any convention that did not give them the right to disapprove the import or transhipment of wastes through their territory. Delegates at the Luxembourg meeting, however, agreed to drop the question of offshore territories such as the British Channel Islands or the US Virgin Islands from the proposed text. Earlier negotiations had revolved around including these territories as controversial points on the grounds that, while controlled by a major power, they are not governed by its environmental law (Bureau of National Affairs 1989a, 49).

Informal consultations conducted by UNEP Executive Director Tolba immediately followed this meeting in Geneva and again from 8 to 10 March. No progress was made and when the Working Group met for its final session in Basel in March 1989, prior to the Conference of Plenipotentiaries, there were still three major difficulties: the position of a group of African governments that were leading resistance to the adoption of the convention; the position of the United States, especially regarding the relation of municipal waste to hazardous waste, as well as the problem of national legislation and regulations that might be difficult to change if they contradicted the text of the convention; and a number of reservations on issues that needed final clarification by various countries (Tolba 1998, 111).

Turning point 4

Negotiations were at a stalemate and the plenipotentiary conference was to begin in one week's time.

Final bargaining/details

Seventy-six governments were represented at the 13 March meeting. The list of outstanding issues included: the desire of some developing countries for a complete ban on hazardous waste exports; developing countries' desire to make the exporter responsible for "illegal" shipments and for the exporting country to take back or assume responsibility for the disposal of wastes that had been shipped illegally; developing country interests in strong liability and compensation rules; monitoring and enforcement provisions; the secretariat; and provisions for technical assistance and technology exchange. Compromise proposals were finally accepted for most of these issues, just in time for the plenipotentiary conference.

When delegates representing 116 countries (including 41 African states) assembled in Basel on 20 March 1989, however, it still looked as though the convention would not be ready for their signature. The Organization of African Unity (OAU) expressed concern that, because of the limited technical capabilities of developing countries, it would be difficult for them to use the Basel Convention to prevent unscrupulous individuals from engaging in illegal dumping activities, and that African countries could still be used as dumping grounds for foreign waste (Tolba 1998, 113). The OAU presented some 24 different amendments to the draft convention, including amendments to prevent the export of wastes to developing countries, as well as to any other countries that lack the same level of facilities and technology as the exporting nations. The OAU also proposed required inspection of disposal sites by UN inspectors, but the industrialized countries rejected the amendments (Porter, Brown, and Chasek 2000, 105; Bureau of National Affairs 1989b, 160; Tolba 1998, 114).

Turning point 5

After a 10-hour marathon session of informal consultations, all issues were resolved, guaranteeing that the African states present would not object to the adoption of the Convention. The issue of exporting-state liability was not resolved and it was agreed to leave this for a future protocol to the Convention. The Basel Convention was adopted by 116 states participating in a Conference of Plenipotentiaries on 22 March 1989.

Ratification/implementation

As of February 1992, 20 parties had ratified the Convention, and it entered into force on 5 May 1992. As of May 2000, 134 counties had ratified the Convention. In late 1989, after extended negotiations, the European Community reached agreement with 68 former colonial states to ban hazardous waste shipments to these countries. A number of African states were not satisfied with the Basel Convention and in January 1991 they adopted the Bamako Convention, banning the import of hazardous wastes from any country to Africa.

At the second meeting of the Conference of the Parties in March 1994, the parties agreed to an immediate ban on the export from OECD to non-OECD countries of hazardous wastes intended for final disposal. They also agreed to ban, by 31 December 1997, the export of wastes intended for recovery and recycling (Decision II/12). However, because Decision II/12 was not incorporated in the text of the Convention itself, the question arose as to whether or not it was legally binding. Therefore, at the third Conference of the Parties in 1995, it was proposed that the ban be formally incorporated in the Basel Convention as an amendment (Decision III/1). However, Decision III/1 does not use the distinction OECD/non-OECD countries. Rather, it bans hazardous wastes exports for final disposal and recycling from what are known as Annex VII countries (Basel Convention parties that are members of the European Union or the OECD, and Liechtenstein) to non-Annex VII countries (all other parties to the Convention). The ban amendment has to be ratified by three-fourths of the parties present at the time of the adoption of the amendment in order to enter into force (62 parties). As of May 2000, 20 countries had ratified the amendment.

Negotiations towards a liability regime or protocol to the Basel Convention began in September 1993, in response to the concerns of developing countries about their lack of funds and technologies for coping with illegal dumping or accidental spills. These negotiations were completed in December 1999 and the Protocol on Liability and Compensation for Damage Resulting from the Transboundary Movement of Hazardous Wastes and Their Disposal was adopted by the fifth meeting of the Conference of the Parties on 10 December 1999. The objective of the Protocol is to provide for a comprehensive regime for liability as well as adequate and prompt compensation for damage resulting from the transboundary movement of hazardous wastes and other wastes, including incidents occurring because of illegal traffic in those wastes. The Protocol will enter into force 90 days after receipt of the twentieth instrument of ratification.[16]

Summary of the Convention

The Basel Convention strictly regulates the transboundary movements of hazardous wastes and provides obligations to its parties to ensure that such wastes are managed and disposed of in an environmentally sound manner. The main principles of the Basel Convention are:
- Transboundary movements of hazardous wastes should be reduced to a minimum consistent with their environmentally sound management.
- Hazardous wastes should be treated and disposed of as close as possible to their source of generation.
- Hazardous waste generation should be reduced and minimized at source.

In order to achieve these principles, the Convention aims through its secretariat to control the transboundary movement of hazardous wastes, to monitor and prevent illegal traffic, to provide assistance for the environmentally sound management of hazardous wastes, to promote cooperation between parties in this field, and to develop Technical Guidelines for the management of hazardous wastes.

1992 Convention on Biological Diversity

Objectives of the negotiations

The 1992 Convention on Biological Diversity addresses the conservation of biological diversity, the sustainable use of its components, and the fair and equitable sharing of the benefits arising out of the utilization of genetic resources, including by appropriate access to genetic resources, by appropriate transfer of relevant technologies, taking into account all rights over those resources and to technologies, and by appropriate funding.

Precipitants

Although actual negotiation of the convention did not get underway until 1990, international concern about the loss of the earth's biological diversity crystallized in the 1980s. For hundreds of years the extinction of plant and animal species occurred entirely by natural processes, but now human activity – mainly the destruction of tropical rainforests, wetlands, and marine ecosystems – was recognized as the cause of the overwhelming majority of species losses. Scientists and NGOs began publishing a greater number of reports and studies that pointed to the need for decisive action to conserve and maintain genes, species, and ecosystems.

In its decisions 14/26 and 15/34, the UNEP Governing Council formally recognized and emphasized the need for concerted international action to protect biological diversity on earth, including the implementation of existing legal instruments and agreements in a coordinated and effective way and the adoption of a further appropriate international legal instrument, possibly in the form of a framework convention (UNEP 1991a, 25).

Turning point 1

The first concrete step towards the negotiation of a convention took place at the 1987 UNEP Governing Council. The United States came to the Governing Council with an initiative calling for work on a global convention on biological diversity. The purpose would be to rationalize arrangements under existing international conservation agreements and their variously located secretariats, with a view to bringing everything together under an "umbrella" convention (McConnell 1996, 5). The Governing Council took up the US proposal and, in decision 14/26, adopted on 17 June 1987, requested UNEP Executive Director Mostafa Tolba to establish an Ad Hoc Working Group of Experts on Biological Diversity. This Working Group would investigate, in close cooperation with the Ecosystem Conservation Group and other international organizations, the desirability and possible form of an umbrella convention to coordinate activities in this field and address other areas that might fall under such a convention (UNEP 1991a).

Issue definition

In response to decision 14/26, UNEP prepared a draft inventory of existing legally binding international agreements, other international instruments, and principal intergovernmental and non-governmental activities in the field of biological diversity, identifying gaps and overlaps among them. This draft was discussed at a meeting of Senior Advisers to the Executive Director of UNEP. The Senior Advisers recommended that efforts to develop a new convention should focus on habitat preservation. The advisers emphasized that special attention should be paid to, and probably even a separate study undertaken in, the area of genetic resources of plants and biotechnology. A further meeting of Senior Advisers to the Executive Director in this field was held in Nairobi from 29 August to 1 September 1988 (UNEP 1991a).

During its meeting from 16 to 18 November 1988 in Geneva, the Ad Hoc Working Group concluded that the existing conventions addressed specific questions of biodiversity conservation but, because of their piecemeal nature, did not adequately meet the needs of conserving biodiversity worldwide. The Group recommended the preparation of a new convention on biological diversity that would close the gaps between existing conventions.

When discussion of this issue resumed at the 1989 UNEP Governing Council, there was still some concern among countries, including the United Kingdom, about duplicating or contradicting existing agreements. The United States was still a firm champion of an umbrella convention, but reacted strongly against proposals to include biotechnology in the convention. Developing countries made it clear that, if biotechnology was excluded, they would oppose any new convention (McConnell 1996, 11).

Turning point 2

In decision 15/34, the UNEP Governing Council requested the executive director of UNEP to convene additional working sessions of the Ad Hoc Working Group of Experts on Biological Diversity to consider technical issues within a broad socio-economic context in developing a suitable new international legal instrument, as well as other measures that might be adopted for the conservation of the biological diversity of the planet. In the same decision, the Council also requested that the executive director expedite the work of the Ad Hoc Working Group as a matter of urgency, with the aim of having the proposed new international legal instrument ready for adoption as soon as possible (UNEP 1991a).

Statement of initial positions

Negotiations formally got underway at the second session of the Working Group, which was convened in Geneva from 19 to 23 February 1990. Experts from 41 countries attended the meeting to advise further on the contents of a new international legal instrument, with particular emphasis on its socio-economic context. The Group identified areas of basic conservation and utilization needs, as well as the need for and scope of financing that would lead to measures for implementation and funding through the adoption of a new legal instrument on biodiversity (Tolba 1998, 140). The Group requested the executive director of UNEP to begin a number of studies as a means of responding to specific issues in the process of developing the new legal instrument (UNEP 1991a, 25).

The third session of the Working Group was held in Geneva in July 1990. Representatives from 78 countries agreed that, in dealing with the issues of costs, financial mechanisms, and technology transfer, the broad estimates of the costs involved should be accepted. The Group maintained that the complex issues involved in biotechnology required further expert examination, assisted by a Sub-Working Group on Biotechnology, before the set of elements covering the issues could be agreed upon. This Sub-Working Group met in Nairobi in November 1990 (UNEP 1991a, 25–26).

In a special session in August 1990, the UNEP Governing Council established the Ad Hoc Working Group of Legal and Technical Experts to consider the outcome of the three sessions of the Ad Hoc Working Group of Experts on Biological Diversity, as well as that of the Sub-Working Group on Biotechnology, and prepare for the actual negotiation of draft articles for a convention on biological diversity. The Ad Hoc Working Group held its first session from 19 to 23 November 1990, in Nairobi; it discussed the elements of the future convention, revised them, and proposed the introduction of new elements (UNEP 1991a, 27).

The Nordic countries proposed that the convention should address sustainable development rather than biodiversity. The Group of 77 warned that there would be no negotiations before developed countries committed themselves to fund all conservation action in developing countries (McConnell 1996, 25).

By the end of these meetings, there appeared to be agreement that there was an urgent need for a new international legal instrument, that biological diversity and its related technologies were complementary and this should be reflected in the instrument, and that unless commitments to funding are fulfilled the instrument would be rendered meaningless (United Nations 1991). Developing countries, led by Brazil, India, and

China, demanded that the convention must allow them access to expertise in biotechnology that would enable them to exploit their biological resources. Industrialized countries did not agree, insisting that the convention should concentrate on conserving areas of great biodiversity that are not protected by existing conventions and agreements (Sattaur 1990). At this point, it appeared as though the North–South dispute would be the major problem to be overcome during the negotiations. Of the 70 countries at the meeting, 43 presented the secretariat with written comments on, additions or deletions of, or changes to the elements for inclusion in the draft convention (Tolba 1998, 145).

At the next session of the Ad Hoc Working Group in Nairobi from 25 February to 6 March 1991, UNEP presented a draft convention and draft rules of procedure for the negotiating process. They also agreed on a bureau, the organization of work, and the future meetings to allow, if possible, the adoption of the convention in 1992 (UNEP 1991a, 27). Two sub-working groups were formed to consider the revised draft convention. Sub-Working Group I dealt with objectives, fundamental principles, general obligations, measures, and institutional measures at the national level. Sub-Working Group II considered access to biodiversity and technical information, transfer of technology, technical cooperation, and financial mechanisms (UNEP 1991b).

Turning point 3

The secretariat circulated a revised draft convention which included all of the draft articles. This marked the first real consolidated draft convention and allowed governments to shift from stating positions to negotiating text.

Drafting/formula-building

At UNEP's Governing Council meeting in May 1991, it was agreed to rename the Ad Hoc Working Group, the Intergovernmental Negotiating Committee (INC) for a Convention on Biological Diversity. The third session of the Working Group, now called the INC, met in Madrid from 24 June to 3 July 1991. The fourth session of the INC met in Nairobi from 23 September to 2 October 1991 to consider the second revised draft of the convention. The fifth session met in Geneva from 25 November to 4 December 1991 to consider the third revised draft of the convention. Working Group II established four sub-working groups to deal with the most difficult issues. According to the INC chair, Vincente Sánchez

(1994, 9), during this phase of the negotiations certain questions and issues became the central aspects of the negotiations:

- the cost of taking measures to conserve biodiversity versus the cost of not taking any such measures;
- whether the focus should be only on wild species or whether it should include both wild and domesticated species;
- access to and transfer of technology – including biotechnology – which must be considered for conservation and rational use of the components of biodiversity;
- eventual sources and methods of funding the costs of the measures that would have to be agreed upon;
- the consequences and impact of biodiversity conservation on trade and development.

The sixth session of the INC took place in Nairobi from 6 to 15 February 1992. Most of the outstanding issues were discussed, but agreement was not reached on all of them. At the conclusion of the session, delegates could still not agree on the relationship between *ex situ* conservation and *in situ* conservation, the establishment of global lists of threatened and/or otherwise important species and ecosystems, rights of the country-of-origin, and financial support (Bilderbeek 1992). By the end of the session it was becoming clear that governments were still very far from reaching agreement. With but a single session left before the date set for signing the convention, the situation appeared "bleak" (Tolba 1998, 156).

The final session of the INC took place in Nairobi from 11 to 22 May 1992. With the UN Conference on Environment and Development due to begin on 3 June 1992 (the convention was due to be signed at the conference in Rio), there was little time left for negotiation. In spite of the time pressure, old animosities and tensions resurfaced and very little progress was made in reaching agreement on the final details in the text.

Turning point 4

With negotiations at a stalemate and only three days left at the seventh session, Mostafa Tolba stepped in. In a "carefully thought out but passionate speech" he described the participants as paralyzed mice. He announced that the working groups would be disbanded, final decisions would be taken in Plenary beginning that afternoon, and he and Ambassador Sanchez would meet with the heads of 20 key delegations to reach agreement on the outstanding issues (McConnell 1996, 90).

Final bargaining/details

Until the very last moment it was uncertain whether there would actually be a convention on biodiversity to be signed at UNCED, especially owing to North–South polarization over whether the Global Environment Facility (GEF) would become the financial mechanism for the convention, France's preoccupation with the question of global lists of endangered species, principles, and links to other conventions, and the US problems with intellectual property rights and biosafety.

When the Plenary reconvened, Sanchez announced that the Plenary would meet around the clock and go through the text of the convention article-by-article until there was agreement. Any difficult issues would be given to small contact groups to resolve. If the contact groups were unable to reach agreement, the text in question was sent to the core group of the heads of 20 key delegations, under Tolba's leadership. Thus, with Tolba's assistance and increased time pressure, the convention was concluded by 6:00 pm on the last day of the negotiations.

Turning point 5

The Convention on Biological Diversity was adopted on 22 May 1992, and opened for signature during the United Nations Conference on Environment and Development in Rio de Janeiro in June 1992. Delegates also agreed to establish an Intergovernmental Committee for the Convention on Biological Diversity to operate until the first meeting of the Conference of the Parties (COP) in order to prepare for the operational phase of the implementation process.

Ratification/implementation

The Convention entered into force on 29 December 1993. As of February 2000, 174 countries had ratified the Convention. The Conference of the Parties to the Convention met five times between November 1994 and May 2000.

The Second Conference of the Parties, which took place in November 1995 in Jakarta, Indonesia, established an ad hoc working group to negotiate a protocol on biosafety. The biosafety protocol was negotiated during a series of five meetings from 1996 to 1998. In February 1999, delegates convened in Cartagena, Colombia, to complete negotiations in a sixth session and to adopt the protocol at an extraordinary session of the COP. But the world's major grain exporters minus the European Union (Argentina, Australia, Canada, Chile, the United States, and Uruguay) – called the "Miami Group" – successfully thwarted efforts to complete the protocol on schedule. The Miami Group was concerned that the draft protocol, particularly the requirement to obtain advance informed consent from the importer prior to exporting living modified organisms (LMOs) or LMO-related foodstuffs, would harm the multi-billion dollar agricultural export business. It took another year of informal consultations before the Cartagena Protocol was finally adopted in January 2000, in Montreal. The Protocol will enter into force 90 days after receipt of the fiftieth instrument of ratification.[17]

Summary of the Convention

The objectives of this Convention are the conservation of biological diversity, the sustainable use of its components, and the fair and equitable sharing of the benefits arising out of the utilization of genetic resources, including by appropriate access to genetic resources, by appropriate transfer of relevant technologies, taking into account all rights over those resources and to technologies, and by appropriate funding.

The Convention on Biological Diversity restates the principle of national sovereignty over domestic natural resources, subject to respect for the rights of other states. The Convention, however, places a duty on States Parties to conserve biological diversity within their jurisdiction, as well as outside their jurisdiction in certain cases. Parties are required to cooperate in the preservation of biological diversity in areas out of national jurisdiction. Parties are also given the responsibility to:
- formulate and implement strategies, plans, or programmes for the conservation and sustainable use of biological diversity;
- monitor the elements of biological diversity, determining the nature of the urgency required in the protection of each category, and in sampling them, in terms of the risks to which they are exposed;
- conserve both *in situ* and *ex situ* biological diversity;
- provide for research, training, general education, and the fostering of awareness in relation to measures for the identification, conservation, and sustainable use of biological diversity;
- provide for environmental impact assessment of projects that are likely to have significant adverse effects on biological diversity;
- exchange information and undertake consultation with other states in all cases where proposed national projects are likely to have adverse effects on biological diversity in other states.

There are also provisions concerning access to genetic resources as well as access to transfer of technology for application in the conservation and sustainable use of biological diversity. The Convention also places a duty on States Parties to provide, in accordance with their individual capabilities, financial support for the fulfillment of the objectives of conservation and sustainable use of biological diversity.

1992 United Nations Framework Convention on Climate Change

Objectives of the negotiations

The aim was to achieve stabilization of carbon dioxide and other greenhouse gas concentrations in the atmosphere at a level that would prevent dangerous anthropogenic interference with the climate system.

Precipitants

Popular and scientific concern had been rising about the possibility that human activities would result in damaging global climate change. Along with weather extremes in the mid-1980s, a number of computer models suggested that global warming could change weather and crop patterns, cause sea-level rise that would inundate low-lying areas, and have other unprecedented and adverse consequences. Scientists began to devote more attention to the possibility of climate change, and reports from a series of scientific conferences and workshops held in the mid-1980s argued that, if present trends continued, climate change would be more rapid in the future than it had been for thousands of years.

Although climate change had been on the scientific agenda for a number of years, the issue first hit the political agenda of governments and policy makers at the Toronto Conference on "The Changing Atmosphere: Implications for Global Security," held from 27 to 30 June 1988. More than 300 scientists and policy makers from 48 countries, UN organizations, other international organizations, and NGOs participated in the sessions. It was at this meeting where ideas about the kind of international response that was necessary became strongly expressed (Thomas 1992, 177).

Turning point 1

After the Toronto meeting, the climate change issue continued to attract substantial attention. Increasingly, however, the discussions moved onto an intergovernmental track. The World Meteorological Organization (WMO) and UNEP established the Intergovernmental Panel on Climate Change (IPCC). The Panel was given three tasks: to assess the scientific information related to the various aspects of climate change; to evaluate the environmental and socio-economic impacts of climate change; and to formulate realistic response strategies.

Issue definition

The first meeting of the IPCC was held in November 1988. The Panel agreed to establish three working groups to prepare timely assessments of the situation regarding human-induced climate change and the formulation of response strategies. The first working group was to conduct reviews of the state of knowledge of the science of climate change; the second was to review programs and conduct studies of the social and economic impacts of climate change; and the third was to develop and evaluate possible policy responses by governments to delay or mitigate the adverse impacts of climate change.

The increasing governmental interest in climate change was also reflected in the UN General Assembly, where the issue was raised for the first time in September 1988. In its Resolution 43/53, "Protection of Global Climate for Present and Future Generations of Mankind" of 6 December 1988, the UN General Assembly endorsed the establishment of the IPCC, and urged governments, intergovernmental and non-governmental organizations, and scientific institutions to treat climate change as a priority issue (Bodansky 1994, 52).

In May 1989, UNEP Governing Council Decision 15/36 requested UNEP's executive director, in cooperation with the secretary-general of WMO, to prepare for negotiations on a framework convention on climate, taking into account the work of the IPCC, as well as the outcome of recent and forthcoming international meetings on the subject. To meet this request, UNEP and WMO formed a Task Force consisting of representatives of both organizations and experts serving in their personal capacity. The Task Force met in Nairobi in June 1989 to draw up possible elements for a climate convention and plans for the negotiation process (UNEP 1991a).

At its forty-fourth session in 1989, the UN General Assembly adopted Resolution 44/207 on protection of the global climate. The resolution recommended that negotiations on a framework convention on climate change begin as soon as possible after the adoption of the interim report of the IPCC (UNEP 1991a, 22).

While the IPCC continued to meet during 1990, international meetings on climate change took place around the world. From 15 to 19 January, the Soviet government organized the Global Forum on Environment and Development in Moscow. Also in January, the small island states held a conference in the Maldives to discuss their position. Additional conferences were held in Washington DC, 17–18 April, in Nairobi, 2–4 May, and in Bergen, 8–16 May (Thomas 1992, 179–180).

After two years of research, the IPCC's reports were tabled at the Second World Climate Conference in Geneva in October 1990. Although there was much disagreement over the findings of the IPCC, delegates agreed that negotiations on a framework convention on climate change should begin as soon as possible. Meanwhile, the heads of UNEP and WMO called for an ad hoc working group of government representatives to prepare for negotiations on a framework convention. The Working Group met in Geneva in September 1990 and adopted several recommendations and identified options regarding the organization of the negotiating process for a convention. These recommendations and options were submitted to the UN General Assembly for consideration.

Turning point 2

Based on the recommendations of the IPCC, on 11 December 1990 the forty-fifth session of the UN General Assembly adopted a resolution recognizing the continuing need for scientific research into the sources and effects of climate change. This resolution unexpectedly took control of the negotiating process away from UNEP/WMO and put it under the direct control of the General Assembly (Thomas 1992, 180). The resolution established a single intergovernmental negotiating process (Intergovernmental Negotiating Committee) under the auspices of the General Assembly, supported by UNEP and WMO, open to all member states of the United Nations and specialized agencies of the UN system, and with the participation of observers, for preparation of an effective framework convention on climate change. It was also decided that the negotiations should try to be completed prior to the UN Conference on Environment and Development in Rio de Janeiro in June 1992.

Statement of initial positions

The first negotiating session of the Intergovernmental Negotiating Committee (INC) took place in Chantilly, Virginia, from 4 to 14 February 1991. Delegates from 107 states, with a host of observers from international organizations and environmental NGOs, attended the opening meeting. The discussions at this session revealed a number of differences in approach among the industrialized countries themselves as well as between North and South. A number of informal papers and texts were circulated at the session, including drafts of the convention prepared by the United States and the United Kingdom (Bodansky 1994, 73). There were basic differences between those who wanted no more than a framework convention of general principles and obligations and others who wanted a framework convention with firm commitments (Raghavan 1991).

Much of the first meeting was spent on procedural matters, including the formation of working groups. According to Tony Brenton (1994, 186), even this early in the negotiations it was clear in most delegations' minds that the three big substantive issues were what commitments developed countries should make to limit their greenhouse gas emissions, what commitments developing countries should make in this area, and what arrangements, in terms of aid and technology, would be made to help the developing countries.

By the conclusion of the meeting, it was clear that numerous groups were forming. Developing countries appeared to be split into three camps: minor greenhouse gas emitters that were concerned about climate change and wanted the developed world to act quickly (the small island states and some of the African nations); major greenhouse gas emitters that saw climate change as a long-term threat, were willing to help mitigate it, but needed financial and technical assistance to do so (China, India, Brazil); and a small but vocal group that was concerned that efforts to cut greenhouse emissions (particularly carbon dioxide) would damage their economies (Saudi Arabia and other fossil fuel exporting countries) (Hurley 1991). Developed countries were also split. The United Kingdom initially opposed a fiscal instrument (such as an energy tax) in order to achieve the necessary carbon cuts equitably. France departed from the common European position by talking about carbon cuts based on per capita calculations, a similar formula to the ambiguous position adopted by Japan. Whereas Switzerland and Austria were committed to firm policies to reduce carbon dioxide emissions from traffic and other sources, the Nordic countries, normally among environmental leaders, refused to commit themselves to measures to achieve a freeze on the gas by 2000 in line with the EC position (ECO 1991a).

The second session convened in Geneva on 19 June 1991, with over 120 states and an increased number of NGOs and others participating. A number of countries, including the United Kingdom, India, Vanuatu, France, and New Zealand, circulated draft texts or informal "non-papers." After much debate, delegates agreed to establish two working groups and decided who would chair them. Discussions in Working Group I focused on principles, commitments, technology transfer, and financial resources. Working Group II dealt with legal and institutional issues, scientific cooperation, monitoring, information, and mechanisms for the transfer of financial resources and technology.

Two important new ideas emerged during the second session. Although developing countries continued to insist on the establishment of a climate fund, the bulk of developed countries now offered their alternative: use of the newly created World Bank/UNEP/UNDP Global Environment Facility (GEF), which they saw as having the virtue of pulling together funding for all the major global environmental problems in one place and being subject to the "highly competent management" of the World Bank (Brenton 1994, 188). It would also depend on voluntary contributions from developed countries – unlike the proposed climate fund, where contributions would be compulsory. This alternative was rejected by the developing countries.

The second new idea was initially entitled "pledge and review." The idea was that, instead of a quantified target on reduction of greenhouse gas emissions, states should commit themselves to a process. They would establish their own greenhouse gas limitation strategies but would submit those strategies for regular review by other parties to the treaty. This idea, which was proposed separately by the United Kingdom and Japan, was vehemently rejected by India and China, as well as by NGOs. It nevertheless became a mainstream of the negotiation (Brenton 1994, 188; Bodansky 1994, 65).

Turning point 3

At the conclusion of the second session, Working Group II authorized its co-chairs to develop a negotiating text that would serve as the basis for discussions at the next session. This turning point in Working Group I did not occur until the conclusion of the third session (9–20 September 1991 in Nairobi). Rather than narrowing alternatives in order to move towards consensus, Working Group I spent the third session producing even longer compilations of alternative proposals, and governments continued to air their views (Bodansky 1994, 65).

Drafting/formula-building

In Working Group I, discussions on a negotiating text began at the fourth session, which met in Geneva from 9 to 20 December 1991. The main points of disagreement centered on differentiated commitments, targets, and timetables for reducing greenhouse gas emissions and on implementation.

In Working Group II, discussions based on a negotiating text began at the third session in September 1991. This text served to focus the discussions and helped delegates to explore each other's positions and begin to draft specific provisions. North–South differences emerged on matters relating to financial resources and technology, research priorities, information exchange, access to information, institutions, and the role of NGOs.

The issue of financial mechanisms and the role of the Global Environment Facility proved one of the most contentious issues. Industrialized countries supported the GEF, which would use existing expertise at UNDP, UNEP, and the World Bank to fund projects aimed at implementing the provisions contained in the convention. India and China preferred a "dedicated" institution rather than an existing one. India noted that the real issue was the location of the fund, and took exception to the GEF's links with the World Bank (ECO 1991b).

On emissions, most countries repeated previous positions: the European Community, Canada, and some other West European countries favored stabilization at 1990 levels by the year 2000. Japan called for "best efforts" by industrial countries. The United States continued to rebuff any binding limits. Developing nations concentrated their fire on the issues of financial assistance, technology transfer, equity, structural issues such as trade and debt, and overall industrial country responsibility for the climate problem (ECO 1991b).

At the fourth session there was some progress in moving from general discussion of concepts to debate on specific wording. In terms of what commitments countries should make, there was broad support for the concept of "common but differentiated responsibilities," i.e. all countries must be involved in global warming strategies though their approaches will vary greatly in relation to their responsibility for emitting greenhouse gases, their vulnerability to the impacts of climate change, and their economic status. When it came to specific commitments to reduce emissions, the United States, supported by Saudi Arabia and Kuwait, continued to oppose the proposal, supported by almost all other countries, that carbon dioxide emissions of industrialized countries be stabilized at 1990 levels by the year 2000.

By the end of the fourth session, the INC combined the various texts from the two working groups into a "Consolidated Working Document," allowing participants to claim that they finally had succeeded in preparing a negotiating text. According to Bodansky (1994, 67), "the Consolidated Working Document was no different stylistically than the consolidated texts prepared for the session by the working group co-chairs. . . . The main difference was that, by assembling the texts from the two working groups into a single document, the result looked more like a complete convention."

The fifth session, which was considered by many to be the low point in the negotiations, met in New York in February 1992. This was expected to be the final session of the INC; however, by the end of the session these issues still had not been resolved. According to Brenton (1994, 190),

Much of the interest of participants was less in the plenary discussion than in the private meetings where the OECD tried, unsuccessfully, to sort out its position on greenhouse gas targets. Those discussions grew increasingly bitter as the gap between the US and most other OECD countries remained yawningly wide.... The failure to close this gap communicated itself to the wider meeting, contributing to a number of bad-tempered exchanges between developed and developing countries and what looked like a campaign by India and Saudi Arabia to place pressure on the West (or wreck the negotiation) by introducing language which they knew to be unacceptable into already agreed portions of text. This mood of North–South tension was exacerbated by increasingly brutal Northern statements that in the absence of some Southern commitment to action and acceptance of the GEF as the funding channel, there simply would be no funding.

For the first time there was widespread talk in the corridors of the possibility that either there would be no convention ready for Rio or it would be at most the framework convention for which a minority of delegations (including China) had argued throughout (Brenton 1994, 190). As a result, the INC decided to hold a resumed fifth session from 30 April to 8 May 1992 to finalize the convention.

Turning point 4

Time had run out and there was a great deal of international and domestic pressure to complete the convention in time for the UN Conference on Environment and Development. Consciousness of the imminence of Rio and the stakes now riding on the successful conclusion of the convention was beginning to produce movement. The search began in earnest for a compromise on the carbon dioxide target issue. The INC chair, Jean Ripert, used a private April meeting in Paris of key negotiators, and subsequent bilateral contacts, to try to identify generally acceptable compromises on the issues that had plagued the negotiations (Brenton 1994, 191). At the April meeting of this "extended bureau," members urged Ripert to develop his own compromise text for the final meeting, so that the Committee would not have to work its way through the many brackets and alternatives remaining in the revised text under negotiation. Somewhat reluctantly, Riper agreed – a move that most participants believed was crucial to the ultimate success of the negotiations (Bodansky 1994, 68–69).

Final bargaining/details

The fifth session of the INC resumed in New York on 30 April 1992. The chair's draft text helped focus the discussions on the specific details of the convention that still remained to be resolved. The difficult issues included: targets and timetables for stabilizing carbon dioxide emissions, financing the convention, and specific commitments to be made by industrialized countries (Bernstein et al. 1992). Delegates reviewed and debated the chair's revised text. The INC decided to abandon its working group structure and divide instead into three groups to consider various clusters of articles (Bodansky 1994, 69). These groups met informally and worked line-by-line through the new text. Once the delegates had had an opportunity to review the entire text, the chair reconstituted the extended bureau, which met practically around the clock during the final days of the session to hammer out compromises on outstanding issues. In the end, the major sticking point was Article 11 on the financial mechanism, with OECD countries seeking to designate the Global Environment Facility as the mechanism and developing countries pressing either to create a separate fund or to leave the issue to the Conference of the Parties.

Turning point 5

After two days of round-the-clock informal consultations, the Plenary resumed on 8 May to adopt the final text. The financial mechanism issue was not resolved. Rather, delegates agreed to leave the establishment of a financial mechanism for the convention to the first Conference of the Parties. As an interim measure, delegates agreed to allow the Global Environment Facility to operate the fund until other provisions were made. On the matter of commitments, the chair proposed an ongoing review process that would give substance to the political commitments undertaken by the parties to the convention without actually setting targets and timetables.

There was recognition that the revised text represented a carefully crafted package and that any new changes by the Plenary would jeopardize the entire convention. Although some delegates threatened to re-open the package on the grounds that they had been excluded from the extended bureau meetings, the Framework Convention on Climate Change was adopted by the Committee in New York on 9 May 1992 (Bodansky 1994, 70).

Ratification/implementation

The Convention was opened for signature during the UN Conference on Environment and Development in June 1992 in Rio de Janeiro. On 21 December 1993, the Convention received its fiftieth instrument of ratification and entered into force on 21 March 1994. As of 22 May 2000, 181 countries and the European Union had ratified the Convention.

Following the conclusion of the negotiations, the INC met six more times to continue negotiations towards strengthening the Convention, prepare for the first meeting of the Conference of the Parties, and work out numerous implementation details, including those related to the financial mechanism. The Conference of the Parties met six times between 1995 and 2000.

The first Conference of the Parties, which met in Berlin in March 1995, agreed to initiate negotiations on a protocol or other legal instrument that would strengthen commitments under the Convention and address emissions reductions beyond the year 2000. After eight negotiating sessions of the Ad Hoc Group on the Berlin Mandate between 1995 and 1997, the Kyoto Protocol was adopted by the third Conference of the Parties in Kyoto, Japan, in December 1997. The Protocol calls for the industrialized country parties to reduce overall emissions of six greenhouse gases by at least 5.2 percent below their 1992 levels between the years 2008 and 2012. Although no formula for differentiation based on some objective characteristics of the party was adopted, the Protocol does differentiate national targets, based on intense bargaining between and among veto states and the European Union. The national targets vary from a 10 percent increase for Iceland and 8 percent increase for Australia to 8 percent reductions for the European Union and most of Eastern Europe. As of May 2000, there were 84 signatories to the Protocol and 22 countries had ratified it. The Protocol will enter into force on the ninetieth day after the date on which not fewer than 55 parties to the Convention, incorporating Annex I parties which accounted in total for at least 55 percent of the total carbon dioxide emissions for 1990 from that group, have deposited their instruments of ratification, acceptance, approval, or accession.[18]

Summary of the Convention

The Climate Change Convention sets forth a number of commitments for its parties, including the preparation of national inventories on greenhouse gas emissions and on actions taken to remove them. Parties are also required to: formulate and implement programs for the control of climate change; undertake cooperation in technology for the control of change in the climate system; incorporate suitable policies for the control of climate change in national plans; and undertake education and training policies that will enhance public awareness in relation to climate change.

The developed country parties (and other parties listed in Annex I) commit themselves to take special measures to limit their anthropogenic emissions of greenhouse gases and to enhance the capacity of their sinks and reservoirs for the stabilization of such gases. The developed country parties (and other parties listed in Annex II) undertake to accord financial support to developing country parties, to enable the latter to comply with the terms of the Convention. Parties are required to cooperate in the establishment and promotion of networks and programs of research into and systematic observation of climate change.

Notes

1. The latest information about the status of the London Convention can be found on the International Maritime Organization's web site: http://www.imo.org.
2. For more information about these technologies, see Sielen and McManus (1983, 158–163).
3. The other committees were concerned with the legal aspects of the Protocols (Committee I) and with the proposals on safety and accidental pollution (Committee III).
4. This paragraph borrows heavily from Sielen and McManus (1983).
5. The latest information about the status of MARPOL can be found on the International Maritime Organization's web site: http://www.imo.org.
6. The latest information about CITES can be found on the Convention's web site: http://www.cites.org.
7. The 16 attending states were Algeria, Egypt, France, Greece, Israel, Italy, Lebanon, Libya, Malta, Monaco, Morocco, Spain, Syria, Tunisia, Turkey, and Yugoslavia. Albania and Cyprus did not attend.
8. This paragraph is based largely on Haas (1990).
9. The latest information about the status of the Barcelona Convention can be found on the Convention's web site: http://www.unepmap.org/.
10. The latest information about the status of the LRTAP and its Protocols can be found on the Convention's web site: http://www.unece.org/env/lrtap/.
11. The latest information about the status of CCAMLR can be found on the Convention's web site: http://www.ccalmr.org.
12. This section is based on information contained in UNCTAD (1993).
13. The latest information about the status of the ITTA can be found on the ITTO's web site: http://www.itto.or.jp.
14. This section is drawn largely from Benedick (1991, 68–70).
15. The latest information about the status of the Montreal Protocol can be found on the Protocol's web site: http://www.unep.org/ozone/.
16. The latest information about the status of the Basel Convention and the Liability Protocol can be found on the Convention's web site: http://www.basel.int.
17. The latest information about the status of the Convention on Biological Diversity and the Cartagena Protocol on Biosafety can be found on the Convention's web site: http://www.biodiv.org.
18. The latest information about the status of the Framework Convention on Climate Change and the Kyoto Protocol can be found on the Convention's web site: http://www.unfccc.int.

5

Phases and turning points in multilateral environmental negotiations: Developing the model

After selecting and examining the negotiations of a representative sample of environmental agreements, it is time to begin the next step in developing the model. This involves analyzing and explaining the negotiation process through the use of phased process analysis. In this chapter, the concepts of phased process analysis will be used to create a model for multilateral environmental negotiations from the decision to explore negotiation as an option to the signature, adoption, and ratification of the resulting agreement.

It was first necessary to examine the literature on phased process analysis (see Chapter 3) and then apply the theoretical aspects of this type of analysis to the 11 cases of multilateral environmental negotiation described in Chapter 4. During this exercise, I identified six phases: precipitants; issue definition; statement of initial positions; drafting/formula-building; final bargaining/details; and ratification/implementation. I shall examine the characteristics of each of the phases in detail in this chapter.

Although establishing the phases of the multilateral environmental negotiation process is important, it is the understanding of how and why the negotiations move from phase to phase that brings the model to life. To identify the nature of these turning points, three primary questions were asked: (1) when did the negotiations move from one phase to the next? (2) what was the event or activity that led to the turning point? and (3) was this event or activity external to or within the negotiations themselves?

The concept of phases and turning points in any discipline has a degree of artificiality to it and may often seem like trying to fit a square peg into a round hole. However, in spite of its shortcomings, it does provide a road map so that both negotiators and students of negotiations can better understand where they are in the process and how best to proceed. Once again, it is important to realize that these phases are not necessarily sequential and that negotiations having passed through a phase does not rule out the possibility of returning to this phase again as negotiations break down or new elements get introduced into the process.

Phases of the negotiating process

Precipitants

In each of the case studies, there was an event or problem that provoked or precipitated the decision by the international community to take action to combat a particular environmental problem. Brian W. Tomlin (1989) calls this phase of the prenegotiation process the "problem identification" phase and writes that the onset of this phase is:

brought about by an event or change in conditions that (1) causes a restructuring of the values attached to alternative outcomes by one or more of the parties ... and (2) results in the addition of a negotiated solution to the array of outcomes under consideration.... The stage is characterized by an assessment of the problem produced by changing events or conditions and a preliminary evaluation of alternative responses that may or may not add negotiation to the range of policy options.

The cases reflect four major categories of precipitant. The first type can be called "incidents of human-induced pollution." This refers to a situation where specific incidents or crises resulting from human-induced pollution (such as oil spills, hazardous waste disposal, toxic chemical releases, nuclear reactor mishaps, or severe transboundary water pollution) have created the international concern that led to the decision to negotiate an international convention. Sometimes governments are concerned enough to propose negotiation. Other times it is not until the media, the public, or non-governmental organizations start pressuring governments to act that negotiation becomes the preferred option. The 1978 MARPOL negotiations followed a series of oil tanker accidents during the winter of 1976–77, including the *Argo Merchant, Sansinena, Oswego Peace*, and *Olympic Games* in December 1976 and the *Grand Zenith, Barcola, Universal Leader*, and *Irens Challenger* in early 1977, which underscored the lack of international regulation of transporting oil by sea.[1] The decision to address pollution in the Mediterranean resulted from oil spills and beach closures. Although the coastal areas and harbors had been polluted by industrial growth over the years, increasing tanker use of the sea in the 1960s greatly exacerbated the problem. The Basel Convention negotiations commenced as a response to the increase in North–South hazardous waste shipments in the 1970s and 1980s and the public outcry over the discovery of unsafe and illegal waste dumps in several developing countries, which was the subject of significant media attention.

The second type of precipitant involves growing scientific evidence about an environmental problem, where negotiation is often precipitated by the release of a scientific report that galvanizes national or international public opinion. Impetus for the London Convention was the release of a report by the US Council on Environmental Quality, "Ocean Dumping: A National Policy." This report spurred the US Congress to regulate ocean dumping and prompted the US government to lead the call for an international convention to address the issue. The Convention on Long-Range Transboundary Air Pollution (LRTAP) was precipitated by Scandinavian concern that imported sulfur pollution was primarily responsible for acidification of lakes. When the Organisation for Economic Co-operation and Development (OECD) released a report documenting the Scandinavians' concern, the UN Economic Commission for Europe began to take a serious look at negotiating a convention. The Montreal Protocol negotiations were precipitated by increasing scientific evidence that the chlorine in chlorofluorocarbon (CFC) emissions reacts with and breaks down ozone molecules in the earth's stratospheric ozone layer and thus hinders the ozone layer's ability to prevent harmful ultraviolet rays from reaching the earth. The climate change negotiations began as a result of scientific evidence that human activities have been substantially increasing the atmospheric concentrations of carbon dioxide and other "greenhouse" gases that are linked to an increase in the earth's surface temperature and may adversely affect natural ecosystems and humankind.

A third type of precipitant is concern about the overexploitation of biological resources. This concern may result from scientific studies, NGO activities, or media attention about species extinction and its repercussions. The loss of the world's biological diversity, mainly from habitat destruction, over-harvesting, pollution, and the inappropriate introduction of foreign plants and animals, has increased over the past 20 years. The decision to negotiate the Biodiversity Convention was taken as NGOs and scientists started publishing a greater number of reports and studies that pointed to the need for decisive action to conserve and maintain genes, species, and ecosystems. One of the reasons that the parties to the Antarctic Treaty decided to negotiate the CCAMLR was the realization that uncontrolled harvesting of krill and other Antarctic marine living resources could have unforeseen and perhaps irreversible impacts on the ecosystem as a whole.

The fourth type of precipitant is concern about the economic impact of overexploiting natural resources through trade or domestic markets. The CITES negotiations actually had two types of precipitants. On the one hand, the negotiations were triggered by realization that damage and extinction in the natural world were occurring at an unprecedented rate in human history and, unlike previous incidents of species extinction, the contemporary problems were the result of human activity, not processes such as natural selection. On the other hand, countries that had profited by the lucrative international trade in flora and fauna were suddenly suffering from decreased income as many of these species were becoming decimated or extinct. The ITTA was initially negotiated to provide a forum for countries producing and consuming tropical timber to consider a variety of aspects of the tropical timber economy that concerned them, including trade, forest management, and marketing.

The precipitants phase can often be quite drawn out. For example, it took approximately seven years from the time that the Scandinavians first identified acid rain as a problem to the decision to negotiate the Convention on Long-Range Transboundary Air Pollution (approximately 1969–1977). In the London Convention negotiations, however, this phase lasted only 14 months, because it was apparent from the start that some type of international agreement was necessary. This phase continues until governments recognize that the particular issue is global or regional in nature and cannot be solved on a bilateral or unilateral level and agree that multilateral negotiation is the preferred mechanism to address and resolve the problem at hand.

Issue definition

The second phase in the multilateral environmental negotiation process is the issue definition or fact-finding phase. Porter, Brown, and Chasek (2000, 79) explain that the issue definition phase involves "bringing the issue to the attention of the international community and identifying the scope and magnitude of the environmental threat, its primary causes, and the type of international action required to address the issue." This fact-finding process may be well developed or only minimal. Porter et al. (2000, 80) continue:

In the most successful cases, a mediating international organization has brought key policymakers together in an attempt to establish a baseline of facts on which they can agree. In cases where there is no such mediated process of fact-finding and consensus building, the facts may be openly challenged by states that are opposed to international action.

These phases are not as well defined in practice as they are in theory and, as a result, they can overlap with each other. The issue definition phase is one that often overlaps with the next phase, "statement of initial positions." In these cases, meetings that are supposed to be devoted to establishing the scope of the problem also serve to identify positions and elaborate proposals for policy options.

In some cases, the issue definition phase takes place within the framework of discussion on a proposed draft convention. This was the case for the London Convention, where the US draft provided the framework for further elaboration and definition of the issues. During the MARPOL negotiations, the US proposal also provided the framework for issue definition and spurred the development of new proposals by other governments. The same was true for CITES, where the draft prepared by the IUCN–World Conservation Union provided the framework for issue definition. During the early meetings of the negotiating group that elaborated the Convention on Long-Range Transboundary Air Pollution, the Nordic Group (Denmark, Finland, Iceland, Norway, and Sweden) submitted a draft convention and a memorandum on major elements to be considered for inclusion in an annex on the emission of sulfur compounds. These documents served as the framework for initial discussions on transboundary air pollution in Europe.

There are also times when one of the UN specialized agencies provides both the forum and the framework for the definition of issues. Often these agencies will have their technical staff prepare reports that can serve as a basis for discussion by a panel of experts, a task force, or a group of government delegates. For the Mediterranean Convention, both the Food and Agriculture Organization (FAO) and the UN Environment Programme (UNEP) hosted a series of technical meetings to define the issues that should be included in the convention. The UN Conference on Trade and Development (UNCTAD) provided the forum for issue definition on tropical timber. The first preparatory meeting was partially devoted to identifying the issues and agreeing on objectives for the agreement. For the Basel Convention, UNEP commissioned an international group of experts to draw up wide-ranging guidelines on the environmentally sound management of hazardous wastes and this group met to define the issues, examine the facts, and develop guidelines. UNEP also took the lead in issue definition on biological diversity. It prepared a draft inventory of existing legally binding international agreements, other international instruments, and the principal intergovernmental and nongovernmental activities in the field of biological diversity, identifying gaps and overlaps. UNEP's Ad Hoc Working Group of Experts on Biological Diversity then discussed the technical issues. In the early phase of the Montreal Protocol negotiations, UNEP convened two special workshops devoted to issue definition. The first workshop examined CFC production and consumption trends, the effects of existing regulation, and possible alternatives to CFCs. The second workshop evaluated alternative regulatory strategies.

In some cases, the issue definition phase takes place outside of the negotiating chambers, often in the form of independent scientific studies or ad hoc meetings. The Antarctic Treaty parties examined scientific evidence for two years, on an ad hoc basis, before actually convening a special meeting to elaborate the CCAMLR. The Intergovernmental Panel on Climate Change (IPCC) provided the forum for definition of the issue of climate change as it prepared assessments of human-induced climate change and the formulation of response strategies.

By the conclusion of this phase, governments should have a better idea of the nature of the issue(s) under negotiation. Whether this phase takes place within a separate forum or process or within the context of the negotiations themselves, it serves to facilitate and focus the preparation of initial drafts and positions.

Statement of initial positions

In most of the cases the statement of initial positions phase marked the transition from the two prenegotiation phases – precipitants and issue definition – to the negotiations themselves. During this phase, delegates present their initial positions or proposals in the form of opening statements, written proposals, or drafts of the agreement. This is also the time when early alliances or coalitions are formed and initial caucusing begins. The formation of groups or alliances is one of the means of managing the complexities inherent in large-scale multilateral negotiations.

The opening of the 1978 Conference on Tanker Safety and Pollution Prevention served as the forum for the statement of initial positions in the MARPOL negotiations. During the first few days of the conference, the United States, the United Kingdom, and the Nordic countries submitted proposals for consideration. The US proposal to expand the use of segregated ballast tanks to reduce oil pollution from tankers was supported by a few states with heavy pollution problems. The less expensive UK proposal, which endorsed crude-oil washing techniques, received the support of most countries, including the Soviet bloc and developing countries. The Nordic countries did not receive much support from maritime nations for their support of a mandatory clean ballast tanks requirement, as this proposal would reduce cargo-carrying capacity by 10–20 percent.

During the Mediterranean Convention negotiations, countries stated their initial positions during a series of meetings hosted by UNEP, the FAO,

the International Oceanographic Commission, and the World Meteorological Organization. The Mediterranean countries formed initial alliances
along North–South lines. The more industrialized states suffered from
different forms of pollution than the developing states, although they all
faced the problems of agricultural runoff and oil on beaches. Not only did
they disagree on what types of pollution should be controlled, but they
also differed on how rapidly these controls should be developed and how
strong they should be.

In most of the cases, the statement of initial positions phase took place
within the context of a special working group established to negotiate the
agreement. The third session of the negotiations on the Convention on
Long-Range Transboundary Air Pollution focused on statements of
initial positions and defined the areas of the mandate where agreement
could be reached and where further discussion and negotiation were
needed. The Nordics pressed for a "tough" agreement and called for
sulfur dioxide abatement across the board. West Germany and the United Kingdom, as two of the European Community's most influential
members, led the resistance to the Nordic proposal.

At the first Special Meeting of Antarctic Treaty Consultative Parties in
1978, 9 of the 13 parties tabled draft conventions for the conservation of
Antarctic living marine resources. Similarly, at the second preparatory
meeting for the ITTA, the producing countries tabled a position paper in
which they outlined a series of measures that would have to be taken to
minimize market and price instability. The consuming countries then
prepared their initial comments and response to this paper and presented
them at the next meeting. At the first substantive session of the Ad Hoc
Working Group of Legal and Technical Experts on the control of transboundary movement of hazardous wastes, countries stated their initial
positions on the proposed convention and its contents. African states
wanted a total ban on waste exports whereas the exporting states preferred a "prior informed consent" regime – a convention that would
require waste exporters to notify their governments of any exports and
notify importing countries of any shipments before arrival.

After the opening statements at the first round of the Montreal Protocol negotiations, the participants appeared to be divided into three major
camps: the European Community, Japan, and the Soviet Union argued
that there was time to delay actual CFC production cuts and wait for more
scientific evidence. Canada, Finland, New Zealand, Norway, Sweden,
Switzerland, and the United States endorsed strong new controls. Australia,
Austria, and a number of developing countries were initially uncommitted.

The members of the Ad Hoc Working Group of Experts on Biological
Diversity spent most of 1990 exchanging ideas and elaborating their
positions on the contents of a new international legal instrument. The

negotiations were polarized along North–South lines as developing countries demanded that the convention allow them access to expertise in biotechnology that would enable them to exploit their biological resources.
Industrialized countries insisted that the convention should concentrate on
conserving areas of great biodiversity that were not protected by existing
conventions and agreements. Similarly, the first session of the Intergovernmental Negotiating Committee (INC) for a Framework Convention
on Climate Change revealed a number of differences among the industrialized countries as well as between North and South. There were basic
differences between those who wanted no more than a framework convention of general principles and obligations and others who wanted
a framework convention with firm commitments. Developing countries
insisted that there should be common but differentiated responsibilities
under the convention.

By the conclusion of this phase it is usually clear where the different
participants stand on the issues under negotiation and what groups and
alliances have formed as a means to manage the large number of delegations. This phase can also streamline a potentially unmanageable list
of issues to be negotiated into a smaller number – the most contentious
issues.

This phase in the negotiating process often overlaps with the phases
before and after it. Sometimes, if the issue definition phase involves the
same diplomats who will be negotiating the convention or treaty, it is
almost inevitable that different positions will emerge during the course of
discussing and defining the issues. These were the circumstances in which
the London Convention was negotiated. The Convention emerged as part
of the preparations for the UN Conference on the Human Environment
(UNCHE) and many of the diplomats participating in UNCHE's Intergovernmental Working Group on Marine Pollution, which served as the
forum for issue definition, also participated in the early negotiations of
the Convention. During the issue definition phase, some country positions emerged in the form of draft conventions (submitted by Spain,
Sweden, and the United States).

These two phases also overlapped during the CITES prenegotiation
period, 1963–1972. Although the IUCN draft conventions provided the
forum for issue definition, they also gave governments the opportunity to
air their views. Not only did two different blocs emerge – conservation
oriented and economic oriented – but two alternative conventions were
drafted during this period. By 1971, the United States, as one of the
conservation-oriented countries, was not satisfied that the IUCN draft
addressed the issues of endangered species on the high seas and import
controls, and it distributed its own draft. Kenya, as one of the economic-
oriented countries, submitted a draft that called for a quota system

whereby each state could continue trading in wildlife based on the amount of trade currently underway.

Drafting/formula-building

Touval (1991, 354) defines the phase where the actual drafting and negotiation of an agreement begin as the one where the exchange of information and the negotiation proper over the detailed terms of an agreement take place. The participants explore various alternative packages or a draft prepared by the chair or the secretariat, and may reach some tentative, conditional understandings. Sometimes these "conditional understandings" could be in the form of a final draft treaty, with only a few articles or passages still under negotiation. In other cases delegates agree on a formula or general framework and do not elaborate the final provisions or details until the next phase.

Consequently, this phase can take two different routes. The first route is deductive: the delegates first establish the general principles, or formula, governing the issues and then work out the implementing details (Zartman and Berman 1982, 89). For example, in the negotiation of the UN General Assembly resolution that established the UN Conference on Environment and Development, delegates agreed on a formula that pervaded the subsequent two years of negotiations. The formula was that the developing countries would reorient their economic development policies so that they are environmentally sound and the industrialized countries would facilitate this process by assisting with the necessary technology transfer and financial assistance.

Several of the cases used the deductive approach, although the formulas are not always as clear-cut as in the UNCED case. For example, in the case of the Mediterranean negotiations, no drafts of the agreement were presented at the start of the drafting/formula-building phase. During this phase UNEP sponsored three meetings in September and December 1975 and January 1976 to draft the final convention and the first two protocols. The formula that served as the basis for the drafting was the agreement that difficult issues, such as land-based sources of marine pollution, were to be postponed and the less controversial issues, such as oil pollution and dumping, should be addressed immediately.

The ITTA negotiations also followed this approach, using the drafting/formula-building phase to agree on the formula or elements to be contained in the convention, and, with the help of the secretariat, develop a negotiating text. The formula was an agreement to limit the focus of the negotiations to the elaboration of guidelines on research and development, market intelligence, further and increased processing in developing timber-producing countries, and reforestation and forest management.

In the MARPOL negotiations, drafting could not proceed until the delegates were able to reach agreement on a formula for oil tanker standards. Thus, most of this phase was spent trying to build a formula that would allow governments to reach agreement on the contentious issue of tanker standards, in exchange for compromises on some of the other issues, including ratification incentives and provisions for the Protocol's entry into force.

The second route that this phase can take is inductive: the delegates put the agreement together piecemeal, building it primarily through mutual compromise or exchanged concessions on specific items (Zartman and Berman 1982, 89). If the inductive route is used, a number of different methods of work are utilized during this phase. In rare cases the drafting takes place at the plenary level. It is more likely that the Plenary will break down into working groups that focus on different aspects of the treaty. Negotiations can also take place in informal sessions, without the benefit of simultaneous interpretation and closed to NGOs and other observers. These sessions are where the delegates roll up their sleeves and get down to the difficult work of drafting the agreement or discussing principles. These sessions can take place within the United Nations or other conference center, at an embassy or mission, or even in a hotel room or restaurant. The crucial drafting sessions are usually attended by only a few key delegates who represent the major groups and interests.

In some of the case studies, the delegates had a draft text at the beginning of this phase. At the second Special Consultative Meeting to elaborate CCAMLR, the chair's second revised draft text served as the basis for negotiation. Over the course of two formal sessions and three sets of informal consultations, interested delegates achieved consensus on most of the draft articles. Similarly, UNEP submitted a draft text for consideration at the second session of the biodiversity and hazardous wastes negotiations. Delegates then began a paragraph-by-paragraph review of the texts where alternative language was proposed, disagreements aired, and initial compromises made. At the climate change negotiations, delegates focused on draft texts for articles in the convention that had been prepared by the chairs of the two working groups. At the end of each session delegates authorized the chairs to prepare revised drafts for consideration at the next session.

In some cases this phase begins with the drafting of the agreement. Although different states and intergovernmental and non-governmental organizations may have submitted proposals, no one has actually prepared a draft that could serve as the basis for negotiation. In the London Convention negotiations, this phase actually contained two parts. The first part included the negotiations within the UNCHE preparatory process, where the Intergovernmental Working Group on Marine Pollution negotiated the "Draft Articles on Ocean Dumping." The second part took place at a government-hosted meeting where a draft text was constructed based on the "Draft Articles," a revised draft convention submitted by the United States, the text of the 1972 Oslo Convention on Ships and Aircraft Dumping, and draft articles submitted by Canada. By the end of this meeting, government representatives had a single negotiating text and had reached agreement on most of the issues.

The situation in the Long-Range Transboundary Air Pollution negotiations was similar. The delegates were confronted with three principal negotiating texts (tabled by the Nordic countries, the European Community, and the East European countries). During the fourth meeting, the delegates elaborated a single compromise text, entitled "Elements for a document on long-range transboundary air pollution," based on many of the proposals contained in the three aforementioned texts.

In the Montreal Protocol negotiations, there were no drafts at the beginning of this phase. Instead, delegates focused primarily on debating the issues. At the third negotiating session in April 1987, UNEP Executive Director Mostafa Tolba organized a series of closed meetings of key delegation heads. This group, away from the formality of the large plenary sessions, was able to produce an unofficial draft text by the end of the session.

Most of the drafting of the CITES convention took place on an ad hoc basis prior to the conference. During this period the United States spearheaded the negotiations with the IUCN and with Kenya so that the conference would not be faced with three competing draft texts. During a meeting in Nairobi in July 1972, the three parties developed a Unified Working Paper that was submitted to the conference for its consideration.

Final bargaining/details

During the final bargaining phase, final agreement on the entire text is reached. This phase is where some of the major concessions take place, according to Zartman and Berman (1982, 199):

As parties announce positions on details, they can either exchange agreements on different points or they can concede their way to some point in between their initial positions. Wherever possible, it is better to group, package, or exchange concessions rather than to fight it out over separate issues taken individually, since the former allows for greater total payoffs and greater possibility for satisfaction for each side on at least some of the points, and therefore facilitates agreement.

The number of details agreed upon increases greatly as the end of the negotiations approaches. The existence of a specific deadline generally causes parties to hold out until they are ready to establish final positions just before the time runs out.

During this phase delegates concentrate on consensus-building. Where the previous phase concentrated on drafting and reaching agreements on formulas or a framework for agreement, this phase focuses on specific language and provisions in the final agreement. The consensus process is not defined in any general treaty or customary law, but a useful guide is the procedure laid down in Article 161(8)(e) of the UN Convention on the Law of the Sea, which requires negotiation to continue if objections are raised to proposed articles until an article acceptable to all emerges (Birnie, 1992, 55) Most multilateral environmental agreements are forged through the consensus-building process rather than by voting. Those parties that vote against a treaty are not likely to ratify it and thus will not be bound by it, so voting is usually avoided since it is important that as many states as possible support, ratify, and implement the agreement. Consensus-building usually takes a long time, is characterized by a constant exchange of proposals and counter-proposals, and results in deliberate constructive ambiguity in the negotiated text.

At this point, the different states or coalitions examine the range of concessions needed to reach an agreement and acknowledge a commitment to see the negotiations through until the final agreement is adopted. This is when parties examine the text point-by-point to reconcile opposing positions. This process is more like incremental convergence as each party adjusts its expectations in favor of what is needed to get a final agreement (Druckman 1986, 333). Governments often approach this phase from widely divergent viewpoints, and through a series of proposals and counter-proposals usually reach some degree of consensus so that the negotiations can move forward. In some cases, the delegates may reach a stalemate and someone – the chair, a member of the secretariat, or a neutral delegation – steps in to mediate a solution between the opposing factions. In other cases, the only solution may be to weaken a provision to the point where all governments can easily accept it.

In most multilateral environmental negotiations, the final bargaining/details phase takes place at the formal Conference of Plenipotentiaries that is convened to adopt and sign the treaty. Sometimes the participants in this conference are at a higher (usually ministerial) level than those who had been negotiating the agreement all along. These high-level negotiators are often able to make the tough political choices and concessions that the diplomats could not. Another factor that plays a major role in this phase is that the conference has a set deadline that more often than not forces consensus on even the most difficult issues. Finally, the conference usually attracts more governments than did any of the formal or informal consultations that preceded it, so additional views, priorities, and politics enter into and may complicate the picture.

At this point in the process most of the negotiations take place in informal sessions behind closed doors. Usually the chair, a member of his/

her bureau, a member of the secretariat, or an impartial delegation plays the role of mediator and tries to facilitate consensus on the details or the last of the unresolved issues. On the whole, these meetings are attended only by the key states – leaders of regional and/or interest groups and individual delegations that have played a leading role in the negotiations. The states are likely to be represented by their head of delegation or other high-level diplomat or minister, because they have the authority to make the necessary compromises and decisions. While these informal sessions are going on, there are often meetings of the Plenary or the formal working groups where some of the less controversial details are worked out.

This phase of the London Convention took place at the Intergovernmental Conference on the Convention on the Dumping of Wastes at Sea. Representatives from 91 countries gathered for the two-week conference in London in late October 1972 where negotiations were based on the draft text developed by 29 states that met in Reykjavik the previous spring. Although agreement had been reached on most of the provisions, delegates still had to resolve the questions related to jurisdiction. Similarly, delegates from 80 countries met in Washington at the Plenipotentiary Conference to Conclude an International Convention on Trade of Certain Species of Wildlife in February 1973. Negotiations began on the Unified Working Paper, which was the result of consultations between the United States, Kenya, and the IUCN. Among the final details that proved difficult to resolve were questions relating to the definition of "specimens," the application of the treaty to endangered marine species, and the concept of lists of species in appendices.

When the draft Mediterranean Convention was presented at the Barcelona Conference in February 1976, a number of difficult issues still had not been resolved during the months of consultations that preceded the conference, including funding emergency clean-up and the acceptance of the European Community as a signatory. Similarly, it was not until the thirty-fourth session of the Economic Commission for Europe that the final details were worked out on the draft Convention on Long-Range Transboundary Air Pollution, including the acceptance of the European Community as a signatory to the Convention. The diplomatic Conference on the Conservation of Antarctic Marine Living Resources took place in May 1980 in Canberra. The conference had before it the draft convention prepared by the Special Consultative meeting and had only a few difficult issues left to resolve, including the area of application, the sovereignty issue, and monitoring during the interim period. However, unlike CITES and the London Convention, most of the governments that participated in the Mediterranean, air pollution, and Antarctic conferences also participated in the working groups that drafted the conventions. This was largely due to the fact that all three of these negotiations were regional or had a limited number of participants.

At the first session of the UN Conference on Tropical Timber in March 1983, drafts of the agreement had been submitted by UNCTAD, Japan, the Nordic countries, and the United States. By the conclusion of the session, the delegates from 64 countries reached consensus on all but 6 of the 43 articles in the final agreement. The remaining articles were agreed upon at the second session of the conference held in November 1983. This was the only case where a conference held a second session because consensus could not be reached during the scheduled two weeks of the original conference. There was very little public pressure or sense of urgency surrounding these negotiations that would have forced agreement in March. With the knowledge that no one would be blamed for failure and since there was no crucial deadline, governments chose to continue negotiating and conclude the agreement in November, rather than make concessions they might later regret.

In four of the cases that did not use the formula/detail approach, agreement on the core issues had not been reached by the final conference. The ozone negotiations culminated in Montreal in September 1987, when 60 governments attended the Conference of Plenipotentiaries. The final compromise, which was not reached until the last day of the conference, included a pledge by industrialized countries to reduce CFC production by 50 percent of 1986 levels by 1999. Without agreement on CFC reduction targets and timetables, the negotiations would have had to postpone the deadline or end in failure. At the final meeting of the hazardous wastes negotiations in Basel in March 1989, the crucial issues of an informed consent regime versus a ban on hazardous waste exports and of liability provisions were still on the table.

For the biodiversity and climate change conventions there was no final Conference of Plenipotentiaries. Instead, the deadline established for these two conventions was the 1992 UN Conference on Environment and Development. The conference organizers wanted to open these two conventions for signature during the two-week conference in Rio de Janeiro. Thus, the final bargaining/details phase of these two cases took place at the last INC meeting under much public and media pressure as the date of the Earth Summit approached. In both of these negotiations the core issues proved to be contentious right up until the final days. In the biodiversity negotiations, the issues of the financial mechanisms for the convention, the establishment of global lists of threatened species and ecosystems, and the rights of the country of origin had to be resolved. In the climate change negotiations, the remaining issues included the mechanism for the transfer of funds and technology and targets and timetables for stabilizing carbon dioxide emissions.

In some cases, most of the drafting and negotiating takes place at the Conference of Plenipotentiaries, so that the final bargaining/details phase usually occurs during the final days or even hours of the conference. Under often immense time pressure, delegates are forced to soften their positions and reach consensus, to bring the matter to a vote, or to take the responsibility for the failure of the negotiations. This was the case during the MARPOL negotiations. Once agreement was reached on the formula – tanker standards – delegates were able to examine a complete draft of the Protocol and reach agreement on the details.

Ratification/implementation

The final phase in the multilateral environmental negotiating process is the ratification/implementation phase. Rittberger (1983, 180) states that, during this phase, the program that was agreed to as a result of the negotiations has to be translated into policy measures by the participating states and, in most cases, by one or more international organizations. After the treaty is signed, it must still be ratified by the participating states before it can enter into force. So, in a sense, there is still one more turning point in the overall treaty-making process – ratification. During this phase, activities take place at both the national and the international levels. At the national level, another series of negotiations may begin as governments first have to ratify the agreement and then have to determine what national policies must be adopted or adapted to implement the convention.

At the international level, it is often assumed that nothing happens until the treaty enters into force and the Conference of the Parties can meet to review progress made in implementing the convention. However, this is not always the case. Some conventions have incorporated mechanisms to ensure that a forum exists so that the international dialogue can continue before the convention enters into force. At the final session of the Conference on the Conservation of Antarctic Marine Living Resources, the signatory states informally indicated their commitment to convene a meeting during the interim period to facilitate operation of the institutions of the Convention. After the adoption of the Montreal Protocol, UNEP convened a meeting in Paris of about a dozen senior advisers from governments, environmental organizations, and industry to consider the practical details of implementing the Protocol. UNEP also sponsored meetings in Nairobi and The Hague in 1988 to continue to focus the attention of governments and world public opinion on the most recent scientific evidence. The Framework Convention on Climate Change included provisions to enable the INC to continue to meet during the period before the Convention entered into force. The INC met every six months between the fall of 1992 and February 1995.

Once the treaty is ratified by the requisite number of countries and enters into force a new process begins, which may involve the adoption of amendments and/or protocols to the convention. In many cases, the Conference of the Parties holds regular meetings (usually annually or bi-annually) to discuss reporting, implementation, the latest scientific evidence, and means of strengthening or otherwise adjusting the convention or protocol. Sometimes this takes the form of resolutions adopted by the Conference of the Parties and other times it may take the form of an amendment to the convention. CITES has been amended numerous times as different endangered species have been placed on the lists in one of the three appendices. The Montreal Protocol was amended and considerably strengthened in London in June 1990, in Copenhagen in 1992, and in Bangkok in 1993. The amendments added new chemicals to the list of controlled substances, set new timetables for the phase-out of certain chemicals, and established a financial mechanism for implementation.

In some of the cases, new negotiations have begun on one or more protocols that serve as a means for implementing a framework convention. Once adopted, these protocols have to go through their own ratification processes. Protocols have been adopted or are under negotiation within the London Convention, MARPOL, the CITES regime, the Barcelona Convention for the Protection of the Mediterranean Sea against Pollution, the Convention on Long-Range Transboundary Air Pollution, the Basel Convention, the Climate Change Convention, and the Biological Diversity Convention.

The ITTA is the one case where there is actually an expiry date. The ITTA was originally in force for five years. Its mandate was extended twice by decisions of the International Tropical Timber Council and was due to expire on 31 March 1994. Renegotiation of the Agreement was completed in January 1994.

If a treaty is not ratified, one of two things may happen. Either some of the provisions of the treaty are treated as customary international law by some countries regardless of the ratification status (such has been the case with certain provisions of the UN Convention on the Law of the Sea) or the treaty just sits on the shelf gathering dust and is soon forgotten.

Summary

Thus far, six major phases of the environmental negotiating process have been delineated: precipitants, issue definition, statement of initial positions, drafting/formula-building, final bargaining/details, and ratification/implementation. These phases have different characteristics and, based on the nature of the previous phase, can take different directions (see

PHASE	CATEGORY			
PRECIPITANTS	Incidents of human-induced pollution	Growing scientific evidence	Concern about overexploiting biological resources	Economic concerns
ISSUE DEFINITION	Through discussion of a draft convention	Within the framework of a UN agency	Scientific studies or meetings	
STATEMENT OF INITIAL POSITIONS	Opening of a conference	UN agency-sponsored working group meetings	Meetings of a special negotiating group	
DRAFTING/ FORMULA-BUILDING	Negotiations based on prepared text	Initial drafting begins	Competing drafts form basis for negotiation	Drafting on an ad hoc basis
FINAL BARGAINING/ DETAILS	Negotiations at a Conference of Plenipotentiaries	Negotiations during final days of conference	Negotiations during final session of INC	
RATIFICATION/ IMPLEMENTATION	Treaty enters into force/ Conference of the Parties meets	Interim mechanism for meetings	Negotiation of protocols or amendments	Treaty does not enter into force

Fig. 5.1 Phases of multilateral environmental negotiation (Note: These phases may overlap or be repeated during the negotiations. Only some of the variations in the process are indicated; they are not exclusive and more than one option may be used during the negotiations)

figure 5.1). Each phase has a different focus, including exploring the scientific and technical intricacies of the issues, forming coalitions and developing position papers, and looking for areas of consensus and compromise. These phases are not necessarily sequential or chronological and they may be repeated several times during the negotiating process.

The length of the phases can vary quite substantially, as can the length of the negotiations as a whole. The cases bear witness to this (see table 5.1). The precipitants phase can run from as little as 14 months (London Convention) to more than five years (MARPOL, the Convention on Long-Range Transboundary Air Pollution, the Montreal Protocol, and the Convention on Biological Diversity). The length of this phase depends in part on the nature of the issue of concern and the event that precipitated the negotiations. The issue definition phase can last from six months (London Convention) to nine years (CITES). This phase is generally shorter when a deadline has been established early in the process, an external event galvanizes public opinion and puts pressures on governments, or the issues are more concrete and not subject to scientific uncertainty; it is longer when governments are still grappling with the issue and are not convinced that there is a need for an international agreement to address it.

The statement of initial positions phase is generally the shortest phase. With the exception of CITES, the average length of this phase is seven months. The length of the drafting/formula-building phase is also related to the presence of a deadline or external pressure. This phase ran from a mere 12 days in the MARPOL negotiations to more than four years in the ITTA negotiations. The final bargaining/details phase usually takes place either just before or during the final Conference of Plenipotentiaries. This phase lasted for less than one month in seven of the cases. Finally, the ratification part of the ratification/implementation phase, as measured by the length of time between adoption of the agreement and its entry into force, lasted for an average of 31 months (2 years 7 months). The implementation part of the phase lasts until the agreement and its Conference of Parties are dissolved.

In spite of the variations in the nature and length of these phases, they provide a framework from which the process can be examined and analyzed. But how do the negotiations progress from one phase to another? The concept of "turning points" can illuminate the process of transition between phases within the process and complete the model of multilateral environmental negotiations.

The concept of turning points

According to *Webster's Dictionary*, a turning point is a point where a decisive change takes place. Within the framework of negotiation analysis, a turning point is a critical point in the negotiations where a decision is taken, a compromise is agreed upon, or a concession is made that allows the negotiations to proceed from one phase to the next.

Tomlin (1989, 25) says that a turning point "guides the search for the events and conditions that facilitate or impede the movement of the parties through and between the stages." For example, in what Tomlin refers to as "the prenegotiation phase," he identifies a turning point in the relationship between parties that enables them to make the decision to consider negotiation. This turning point could be a change in the relations between the parties, an event, or a change in conditions that prompts a reassessment of alternatives and adds negotiation to the range of options. In Tomlin's case study on North American free trade, he states that the turning point that led to the onset of the prenegotiation phase of the bilateral free trade negotiations between the United States and Canada was

Table 5.1 Length of phases in the negotiating process

Case	Precipitants[a]	Phase Issue definition	Statement of initial positions	Drafting/ formula-building	Final bargaining/ details	Ratification/ implementation[b]
London Convention	Apr. 1970–Jun. 1971 (14 months)	Jun.–Nov. 1971 (6 months)[c]	Jun.–Nov. 1971 (6 months)[c]	Nov. 1971–Jun. 1972 (6 months)	Jun. 1972–Nov. 1972 (6 months)	Nov. 1972–Aug. 1975 (3 years, 9 months)
MARPOL	1968–1977[d] (8.5 years)	Apr. 1977–Feb. 1978 (10 months)	6–8 Feb. 1978 (2 days)	8–14 Feb. 1978 (6 days)	14–17 Feb. 1978 (3 days)	Feb. 1978–Oct. 1983 (5 years, 8 months)
CITES	1960–1963 (3 years)	1963–1972 (9 years)[c]	1963–1972 (9 years)[c]	Jun. 1972–Feb. 1973 (8 months)	Feb.–Mar. 1973 (3 weeks)	Mar. 1973–Jul. 1975 (2 years, 4 months)
Mediterranean Convention	1969–1971 (2 years)	Jun. 1971–Feb. 1975 (3 years, 8 months)	Feb. 1975–Sep. 1975 (7 months)	Sep. 1975–Feb. 1976 (5 months)	2–16 Feb. 1976 (2 weeks)	Feb. 1976–Feb. 1978 (2 years)
Convention on Long-Range Transboundary Air Pollution	1969–1977 (8 years)	Feb. 1977–Sep. 1978 (1 year, 7 months)	Sep.–Nov. 1978 (2 months)	Nov. 1978–Feb. 1979 (3 months)	Feb. 1979–Nov. 1979 (9 months)	Nov. 1979–Mar. 1983 (3 years, 4 months)
Convention on Antarctic Marine Living Resources	1970–1975 (5 years)	1975–1978 (3 years)	Feb.–Mar. 1978 (1 month)	Mar.–Sep. 1978 (6 months)	Oct. 1978–May 1980 (19 months)	May 1980–Apr. 1982 (1 year, 11 months)

International Tropical Timber Agreement	1973–1976 (3 years)	May 1976–Mar. 1977 (10 months)	Mar. 1977–Aug. 1978 (1 year, 5 months)	Aug. 1978–Mar. 1983 (4 years, 7 months)	Mar.–Nov. 1983 (8 months)	Nov. 1983–Apr. 1985 (1 year, 5 months)
Montreal Protocol	1974–1985^d (11 years)	Mar. 1985–Dec. 1986 (1 year, 9 months)	Dec. 1986–Feb. 1987 (2 months)	Feb.–Sep. 1987 (7 months)	8–16 Sep. 1987 (8 days)	Sep. 1987–Jan. 1989 (1 year, 4 months)
Basel Convention	1976–1981 (5 years)	1981–1987 (6 years)	Jun. 1987–Feb. 1988 (8 months)	Feb. 1988–Mar. 1989 (13 months)	8–22 Mar. 1989 (2 weeks)	Mar. 1989–May 1992 (3 years, 2 months)
Convention on Biological Diversity	1981–1987 (6 years)	Jun. 1987–Jun. 1989 (2 years)	Jun. 1989–May 1991 (1 year, 11 months)	May 1991–May 1992 (1 year)	11–22 May 1992 (11 days)	May 1992–Dec. 1993 (1 year, 7 months)
Framework Convention on Climate Change	1984–1988 (4 years)	Nov. 1988–Dec. 1990 (2 years, 1 month)	Dec. 1990–Jun. 1991 (6 months)	Jun. 1991–Apr. 1992 (10 months)	Apr.–May 1992 (2 weeks)	May 1992–Mar. 1994 (1 year, 10 months)

a. All dates for the Precipitants phase are approximate because it is not always possible to determine when the issue first came to the attention of the international community or any national government(s).
b. All dates for the Ratification/Implementation phase represent the amount of time between adoption and entry into force of the agreement.
c. In this case, the Issue Definition phase and the Statement of Initial Positions phase overlapped completely.
d. Since this case deals with the negotiation of protocols, the Precipitants phase includes the negotiation of the framework convention.

an acute bilateral conflict that erupted in 1981 over Canadian energy and investment policies.

Zartman and Berman (1982, 87–88) also discuss the role of a "turning point of seriousness" in moving between the diagnosis and the formula phases of negotiation. They define the turning point of seriousness as "the perception by each side that the other is serious about finding a negotiated solution – that is, that the other is willing to 'lose' a little to 'win' a little rather than win or lose all in a non-negotiated approach." The turning point does not necessarily occur simultaneously for both sides, and it does not have to correspond to any formal moment in the process, such as the beginning or end of a conference. Zartman and Berman (1982, 88) continue:

Depending on the degree of familiarity existing between the parties, the turning point may be achieved through an exchange of communications preceding a conference, through the process of arriving at a formula, or through an actual agreement resolving minor issues in the whole problem area, or anywhere in between. When the talks began in Helsinki in November 1969, the Soviet commitment to SALT was tentative, but after one month of preliminary talks it became clear that the Soviet leadership had given its firm approval to the SALT process, having judged that the United States was indeed interested in serious negotiations.

Druckman (1986, 332–333) describes a number of different types of turning points that can be used to characterize the negotiating process. The first consists of the point at which all sides agree that negotiations are realistic because they perceive each other's expectations to be within range. This may take the form of a declaration of principles, reinforced by repeated statements of agreement to adhere to those principles or to continue to negotiate in good faith. The second turning point in Druckman's analysis occurs when an agreement has been reached on the interpretation of the problem. This leads to an attempt to negotiate a framework from which details can be deduced. The third turning point occurs when there is agreement on a framework.

Druckman (1986, 333) continues:

Two types of turning points are those that occur after a period of no progress and those that occur after a threat to the sustenance of the talks. The former, a period of no progress, is defined as an *impasse,* the latter, a threat to talks, is regarded here as a *crisis.* Both types of turning points are inflections in a trend, or "upturns" that represent either sudden progress or a return to a period of stability. The progress that occurs after an impasse often signals passage to a new stage of the negotiation. However, the recovery that follows a crisis or threatened breakdown usually does not signal a new stage. The new stage occurs during the period of stability *after* the recovery.

The turning points that lead to resolution of these impasses and passage to the next phase of the negotiations are triggered both by decisions or events within the negotiations as well as by events external to the negotiations.

One of the most common types of turning point is a deadline, whether it is internally imposed by the negotiators themselves – such as the decision to complete the negotiations for the Montreal Protocol on Substances that Deplete the Ozone Layer by September 1987 – or imposed on them from the outset – such as the UN General Assembly decision that called for the Framework Convention on Climate Change to be completed before the UN Conference on Environment and Development in June 1992. An approaching deadline will often force compromise or a concession where it might not have been considered before. Other internal turning points can be triggered by the promotion of innovative trade-offs or package deals, the creation of a small, informal working group within a negotiation process, a change in the chairmanship of a working group, the appearance of a mediator, or a breakdown in the negotiations. There are also a number of events that actually occur outside the negotiations yet lead to a turning point within the process, including a change in the political situation within one of the major participating states; intense media coverage of or public pressure on the negotiations; new scientific evidence; a human-induced or natural environmental disaster; and negotiations or conferences covering different, although related, subject matter.

Turning points in multilateral environmental negotiation

Now that the six phases have been outlined, the next step in the development of the model is to analyze the events and the turning points that advanced the negotiations from phase to phase. In other words, what are these critical points in the negotiations where a decision is taken, a compromise is agreed upon, a concession is made, or an external event has an impact that allows the negotiations to proceed from one phase to the next. Alternatively, the absence of one key turning point could lead to the failure of the negotiations as negotiators are unable to make the necessary concessions or compromises that will allow them to move forward. To discover the nature of these turning points, three primary questions were asked: (1) When did the negotiations move from one phase to the next? (2) What was the event or activity that led to the turning point? (3) Was this event or activity external to or from within the negotiations themselves?

Turning point 1: The international community agrees to address the problem

The first turning point occurs when the international community agrees that it must address the problem. This turning point is almost always motivated by one or more of the precipitants described earlier in this chapter. Once the problem is recognized by the international community, however, it does not necessarily mean that governments agree that multilateral negotiation is the proper mechanism to control or manage the situation. Sometimes the time is not ripe for negotiation owing to lack of convincing scientific evidence, a lack of desire among governments to negotiate an international agreement that they may view as being inimical to their interests, or the view that a problem is regional or local in nature and should not be addressed at the global level. For example, during the preparatory process for the UN Conference on Environment and Development the issue of disposal of hazardous and radioactive waste by the military was brought to the attention of the delegates. Since a number of countries felt that this issue had a definite impact on their national security and did not think this was the proper forum for such a discussion, the issue was largely ignored.[2]

If governments decide to negotiate a convention, treaty, agreement, or protocol at this point, this decision may actually be triggered by the initiative of a state, a group of states, a non-governmental organization, or an intergovernmental body. As the precipitants phase can be classified as "prenegotiations" and the actual negotiating process has not begun, this first turning point is always motivated by events outside the process.

One of the cases where a state or small group of states triggered the decision to begin negotiations was the London Convention. The initial turning point took place when the United States tabled a draft convention during the preparatory process for the 1972 UN Conference on the Human Environment. This action forced the other delegates to think about negotiating a convention to control ocean dumping. The United States also took the lead in the MARPOL negotiations, when the Carter administration proposed a set of legally binding actions to improve tanker safety and prevent pollution at a meeting of the Intergovernmental Maritime Consultative Organization's Maritime Safety Committee. The Scandinavians took the lead on transboundary air pollution when they proposed the negotiation of a convention at a meeting of the UN Economic Commission for Europe. In the case of CITES, the activities of a non-governmental organization triggered the turning point: the IUCN's decision to circulate a draft convention forced the international community to consider a convention to control international trade in endangered species.

In other cases, an intergovernmental body takes a decision to begin negotiations. This decision may be proposed by one state, a group of states, or the secretariat of the intergovernmental body. In the case of ITTA, UNCTAD took the decision to convene preparatory meetings on the trade in tropical timber as part of a series of international commodity agreements. UNEP's Governing Council launched the Montreal Protocol, the Basel Convention, and the Biodiversity Convention in response to growing concern about ozone layer depletion, hazardous waste disposal, and species extinction, respectively. The issues of Mediterranean pollution and Antarctic living marine resources were initially addressed at intergovernmental meetings, where delegates agreed that further study was necessary. UNEP and WMO established the Intergovernmental Panel on Climate Change (IPCC) to evaluate scientific research on climate change.

Once the international community has decided that it should address the environmental issue, the next stage – issue definition – begins.

Turning point 2: Agreement to begin negotiations

The second turning point allows the process to progress from the issue definition phase to the statement of initial positions phase. This turning point marks the transition between the prenegotiation segment of the process and the actual negotiations. Up until this point, governments are often still exploring the idea of negotiations, investigating the causes and effects of the environmental problem under discussion, determining their positions and desired outcomes, and, possibly, examining the emerging positions of other states for indications of potential allies and areas where opposition exists.

This turning point tends to be one of the most subtle and in some situations does not even take place if the issue definition and statement of initial positions phases overlap to the point where it is difficult to distinguish between the two. However, in some cases the issue definition phase takes place in a different forum than the rest of the negotiations or government-appointed scientists or technicians participate in the issue definition phase and then the diplomats and lawyers step in for the statement of initial positions phase. In these cases, this turning point is more concrete. To arrive at this turning point, governments can spend months and even years studying the problem to determine what is the best way of managing it without compromising their own country's national sovereignty and other socio-economic concerns. It is only once governments recognize the need to negotiate an international agreement and are ready to begin formal negotiations that this turning point occurs. This turning point can take a number of different forms, both internal and external to the negotiating process. These can include a stalemate in the issue definition phase, agreement on goals, agreement on procedures, and the actions of a major state or a group of states.

During the MARPOL negotiations, the turning point was the result of a stalemate in the issue definition phase. The issue definition process focused on the emerging technologies for crude-oil washing. When the working groups that were looking at the issues and preparing for the conference were no longer able to make any more progress on determining which of these technologies to advocate in the protocol (largely because they did not consist of the high-level diplomats or government officials who could make the necessary political decisions), it was time to bring in the diplomats who could make some of the necessary political choices. Another internal factor that contributed to this turning point in the MARPOL negotiations was a deadline – preparation time ran out as the predetermined date for the conference approached.

In the tropical timber negotiations, the turning point occurred as the result of an agreement on the objectives and general content of the new agreement. Once governments agreed on the objectives, they were able to move to the next phase and begin negotiating an agreement that would achieve these objectives. At the conclusion of the first ITTA preparatory meeting, the participants called for the preparation of position papers on appropriate measures and techniques to achieve the agreed upon objectives.

The turning point in the biodiversity negotiations was also the result of an agreement on goals – the purpose of a new convention. During the issue definition phase, the Ad Hoc Working Group determined that a new convention on biodiversity was needed to fill the gaps in cover of existing conventions. At the same time, increasing scientific evidence about species loss and growing technological advances in the relatively new field of biotechnology enabled the UNEP Governing Council to take the decision to convene additional sessions of the Ad Hoc Working Group and begin to negotiate a new convention.

The turning point in the Mediterranean negotiations was the result of an agreement to proceed with the negotiation of a legally binding instrument. The issue definition phase took place during the course of preparations for the first Intergovernmental Meeting on the Protection of the Mediterranean and it was at this meeting that delegates agreed that a legally binding instrument should be elaborated. At the Intergovernmental Meeting in Barcelona in February 1975, governments requested UNEP to convene a working group of governmental legal and technical experts to begin drafting this instrument.

Likewise, growing scientific evidence and an agreement on goals for harvesting krill triggered the decision to begin negotiations on a legally binding convention to conserve Antarctic marine living resources within the Antarctic Treaty system. As more scientific evidence became available, there was greater consensus on the need to promote and achieve the objectives of protection, scientific study, and rational use of Antarctic marine living resources.

Scientific evidence and an agreement on goals also played a role in triggering the turning point in the ozone negotiations. After the two informal workshops where delegates had the opportunity to examine the growing scientific evidence that CFCs are one of the causes of stratospheric ozone depletion and that ozone depletion is occurring and increasing rapidly, there was growing consensus that an international regime was required. Thus, the time was ripe for the delegates to come to the negotiating table.

The turning point in the long-range transboundary air pollution negotiations was motivated by the decision of a group of states to begin actual negotiations. When the Nordic Group submitted its draft convention on "Reduction of Emissions Causing Transboundary Air Pollution," this forced the other governments to move from a technical discussion of the issues to elaborating their positions and responses to the Nordic countries' proposal. This led the Special Group to invite governments to submit their comments or alternative proposals during the intersessional period.

External events without clear-cut agreement on goals motivated the turning point in the Basel Convention negotiations. The issue definition phase lasted for six years as a Working Group defined the issues, examined the facts, and agreed upon non-binding guidelines. But it was not until the media, the non-governmental community, and some governments started reporting and publicizing the presence of illegal waste dumps in several African countries that the UNEP Governing Council took the decision to convene a Working Group of Legal and Technical Experts to prepare a global convention on the control of transboundary movements of hazardous wastes.

In the climate change negotiations, scientific evidence prompted the turning point. Although many governments continued to call for more scientific research into the sources and effects of climate change, the release of the IPCC report was enough to convince the heads of UNEP and WMO and many governments to call for the establishment of a working group to negotiate a framework convention on climate change. It was the scientific evidence in the IPCC report that enabled the UN General Assembly to adopt the resolution establishing the Intergovernmental Negotiating Committee to elaborate this convention.

If governments decide not to negotiate an agreement, either the issue is dropped or the parties involved agree to further discuss the issue.

For example, in the Barcelona Convention for the Protection of the Mediterranean Sea against Pollution the parties agreed in 1976 to drop the issue of controlling pollution from the exploration and exploitation of the continental shelf and the seabed and its subsoil, and re-open discussions at a later date. A protocol on this issue was adopted in 1994. However, if governments decide there is a need to negotiate, the pre-negotiation process – consisting of the precipitants and issue definition phases – comes to a close and the first phase of actual negotiation – statement of initial positions – begins.

Turning point 3: Agreement to begin formula-building or drafting

At this point in the negotiating process, delegates must take a decision to move away from stating and restating their governments' positions and proposals towards drafting, formula-building, and the compromises that are necessary to bring the parties to an agreement. In most cases, this turning point takes the form of a decision to shift the work to informal drafting groups or to request the chair or the secretariat to prepare a draft text. Occasionally a state or group of states takes the initiative and signals its desire to begin actual negotiations and allow the process to move forward. The initiative may be triggered by an event outside of the negotiating process. This decision or turning point can also be motivated by events external to the negotiating process or by a predetermined deadline by which the negotiations should be complete. Whatever form this decision takes and whatever motivates it, the key to this turning point is timing. Delegates have to be ready to shift their focus from the development of their own positions to the recognition and evaluation of the positions of others so that they can start the process of drafting or formula-building.

In some cases, delegates take the decision to establish a drafting group or committee that attempts to incorporate the various drafts submitted by delegations into a consolidated draft text. This decision enables delegates to focus on elements that could form the basis of a consolidated draft. This was the case in the London Convention and the Montreal Protocol negotiations. In the London Convention negotiations, several governments (Spain, Sweden, and the United States) tabled draft texts during the statement of initial positions phase. With so many different texts, it was difficult to focus and advance negotiations. Thus, it was necessary to establish a drafting group to put together a single text to serve as the basis for further negotiations. In the Montreal Protocol negotiations, the first session (Geneva, December 1986) began chaotically with a general debate. Different delegations (Canada, the Soviet Union, and the United States) proposed texts for the protocol and there was no focus to the discussion. At the beginning of the second session (Vienna, February 1987), the United States and the chair, Winfried Lang (Austria), proposed organizing the work of the Vienna Group (as the negotiating body was known) by establishing separate working groups to address the unresolved major issues. This proposal was endorsed by the participants and allowed the Group to move forward and begin actual negotiations of the protocol without supporting any one of the three proposed drafts that were so incompatible with each other as to make a consolidated draft difficult to formulate.

Similarly, in the Mediterranean negotiations, once the delegates took the decision to negotiate a framework convention and protocols on oil pollution and tanker traffic, UNEP established a working group to draft the Barcelona Convention and the first two protocols.

In other cases, a decision to ask the chair or the secretariat to prepare a draft text marks the turning point. This decision usually occurs when delegates cannot move forward because no draft text has emerged during the statement of initial positions phase or when so many drafts have emerged that there is no focus to the negotiations. When no state-sponsored text emerges, delegates often request that the chair or the secretariat draft a text that will give delegates a starting point for the drafting/formula-building phase. In other cases, multiple texts are tabled and the chair or the secretariat takes the responsibility for formulating a single draft text to serve as the basis for the next round of negotiations.

In the case in the Antarctic negotiations, nine draft conventions were tabled and discussed during the first Special Meeting of Antarctic Treaty parties in March 1978. It proved difficult to focus discussions with so many draft texts, so the chair (John Rowland of Australia) prepared a draft text for the convention. The first draft was based on statements and drafts presented by delegations and was discussed and revised following intensive comment and debate. This served to focus the negotiations and allow the delegates to identify key issues where there was already consensus and those issues where further negotiation was still needed.

Similarly, in the climate change negotiations, delegates requested the co-chairs of the two Working Groups to prepare a negotiating text based on the statements and written proposals submitted by governments. These draft provisions served to streamline the work of the two Working Groups and allow delegates to identify areas of convergence and divergence.

In the case of the biodiversity negotiations, no draft texts were tabled at the first session of the Ad Hoc Working Group of Legal and Technical Experts in November 1990. This meeting had been convened to consider the work of the three sessions of UNEP's Ad Hoc Working Group of Experts on Biological Diversity and its Sub-Working Group on Biotechnology and to prepare for the negotiation of the convention. At the conclusion of that meeting, the Working Group requested that the UNEP secretariat prepare a draft convention. At this point, delegates had noted several areas where there was agreement and other areas that still needed further consideration. The discussion of these issues, as well as the preparatory work by the Working Groups on biodiversity and biotechnology, provided the secretariat with the necessary guidance to draft the convention.

By the conclusion of the first session of the Basel Convention negotiations (Budapest, 1987), delegates agreed that there should be a convention on hazardous wastes, although there was disagreement about how general or specific the treaty should be. The secretariat (UNEP) was asked to prepare a first draft of the convention based on the statements given at the first meeting as well as on the experiences of the OECD and the European Community. This way, governments could immediately focus on the draft text at the second session in February 1988.

Sometimes one or more states propel the negotiations to the next phase by expressing their desire to consider some of the proposals made by other states. This serves not only as a message of cooperation and good will, but also as a means to propel the negotiations towards the drafting phase. This happened in the air pollution negotiations when, at the end of the third session, France and West Germany declared their willingness to discuss the Nordic Proposal.

In the MARPOL negotiations, the initiatives of the United States, the United Kingdom, and the Nordic states shifted the focus from statements of initial positions to formula-building. Once these governments tabled their proposals for tanker standards, other governments had little choice but to respond and suggest different ways to address this issue that was at the core of the negotiations. The turning point in the CITES negotiations was the decision of one government, the United States, to announce that it would convene a ministerial conference with a target date of February 1973. The establishment of this date set a concrete goal for the ad hoc dialogue that had been going on for nearly a decade.

Finally, this turning point can be the result of an agreement on the basic elements to be included in the convention. In the ITTA negotiations, agreement on four elements that would form the basis for an international arrangement on tropical timber – reforestation and timber management; increased and further processing in the producing countries; research and development; and market fluctuation – created the necessary framework to begin the drafting/formula-building phase.

There is always the possibility that governments will not take the decision to move on to the drafting/formula-building phase of the negotiations and, instead, an impasse or lack of good will could move the negotiations backward instead of forward. This impasse or crisis can be either internally or externally motivated. For example, during the UN Conference on Environment and Development negotiations, the working group responsible for elaborating the Earth Charter (later renamed the Rio Declaration on Environment and Development) was not ready to take a decision that would enable the transition from the statement of initial positions phase to the drafting/formula-building phase at the conclusion of the third session of the Preparatory Committee. The chair thought otherwise and during the intersessional period put together a chair's draft of the Earth Charter to serve as the basis for negotiation at the fourth session. The delegates at the fourth session, however, were not prepared to accept the chair's draft and, instead of moving the process forward, the chair's draft was discarded and the participants resumed stating their positions and tabling their own drafts.

Turning point 4: Agreement on a formula or general framework

The turning point between the drafting/formula-building phase and the final bargaining/details phase occurs when negotiation has progressed to a point where there is agreement on either the majority of the text (if the inductive approach is used) or on a formula (if the deductive approach is used) and only the most contentious details remain to be resolved. This turning point does not necessarily happen only once in the negotiating process. Sometimes negotiators reach consensus on most of the agreement and think that they can move on to the final bargaining/details phase, only to find that one country or group of countries cannot accept a major part of the agreement; rather than moving ahead, they are forced to backtrack and revisit the drafting/formula-building phase. In other cases, delegates may not be able to turn their formula into an agreement on details and they must go back to the previous phase to reformulate a framework that works (Zartman and Berman 1982, 147). Nor does this turning point necessarily happen at the beginning or end of a negotiating session. Four different categories of events make this turning point possible: agreement on a single draft text (inductive approach); consensus on a formula or basic elements to be included in the agreement (deductive approach); a deadline; or stalemate in the drafting/formula-building phase that requires the intervention of high-level political officials.

When the inductive approach is used and the agreement is put together piecemeal, this turning point is often made possible by agreement on a single draft text, although some crucial provisions may still need further negotiation in the final bargaining/details phase. This was the case in the London Convention negotiations. The delegates were able to reach agreement on the regulatory structure of the convention by basing it on the Oslo Convention for the Prevention of Marine Pollution by Dumping from Ships and Aircraft (15 February 1972) and the US Marine Protection, Research and Sanctuaries Act of 1972. Once the draft text was complete, the delegates were able to begin the conference by focusing on the remaining unresolved issues, including the central question of jurisdiction, rather than reopening discussion on the framework for the agreement as a whole. Similarly, this turning point occurred in the Mediterranean negotiations at the last UNEP-sponsored preparatory meeting in January 1976 once there was agreement on the framework and on most of the elements in the draft convention. By the conclusion of the second session of the CCAMLR negotiations in Buenos Aires (July 1978), substantial consensus existed on the draft articles that addressed the core issues of the objectives of the convention, conservation measures, and the principles for a system of inspection and observation.

In the CITES negotiations, this turning point was reached only once the sponsors of the three draft conventions – the United States, Kenya, and the IUCN – were able to agree on a Unified Working Paper. Although the sponsors did not expect this paper to receive unconditional acceptance by the other countries, it did provide delegates with a starting point at the final conference. After an initial review of the Working Paper, delegates were then able to focus on the provisions that lacked consensus.

When the deductive approach is used, this turning point may be made possible by agreement on a formula or the basic elements to be included in the treaty. With agreement on the formula, the delegates can then turn their attention to the details that will operationalize this formula. The turning point in the MARPOL negotiations was the agreement on the concept of tanker standards – the key issue that underlies the entire Protocol – and related trade-offs. Only once delegates had achieved consensus on this point could the negotiations on the remaining details of the Protocol move forward.

The turning point in the long-range transboundary air pollution negotiations occurred when the Nordic countries expressed their willingness to compromise on one of the core issues of the agreement – the timetable to control air pollution caused by sulfur compounds. The Nordic countries had wanted a stricter timetable than many of the European Community nations and had refused to compromise on this position. At this point, however, they did agree to compromise on a strict timetable in return for a commitment to address the issue in future negotiations. Without agreement on this point, no further progress could be made. This trade-off is an example of how the good will of one party or group can propel the negotiations along from one phase to the next. In the ITTA negotiations, this turning point was made possible by agreement on a broad-based formula for cooperation between producing and consuming states in the four basic elements in the agreement. With agreement on this formula, delegates were then able to focus on the exact phrasing and details that would comprise the final agreement.

Sometimes this turning point is made possible only by a change in the composition of the delegations or a change in venue to the more public forum of a Conference of Plenipotentiaries. This was the case in the Montreal Protocol and the Basel Convention negotiations. In both of these negotiations there was a single draft text early on in the drafting/ formula-building phase, but there was no agreement on a formula or even on the basic provisions of the draft agreement. As a result, this phase was more of a re-drafting exercise than either initial drafting or formula-building. Even after many sessions, delegates were not able to reach agreement on a number of key issues, articles, or provisions without which the convention or protocol would be worthless. These issues tend to be politically or economically sensitive and may require the presence of high-level political officials who are able to make the difficult concessions that are necessary to achieve consensus on the final text. Faced with the possibility of extended stalemate or even failure, governments often send higher-level political officials who will focus primarily on these sensitive, unresolved issues.

Although the change in venue or the change in the level of the delegation makes the turning point possible, time pressure often plays a major role. In some cases, the date for the final Conference of Plenipotentiaries has been set either before the negotiations begin or at some point earlier in the process. As this date approaches there is usually a change in the atmosphere as the parties are under greater pressure. However, deadlines can have the opposite effect because the parties may harden their positions in preparation for a last-minute proposal that will present the others with an offer that will be barely acceptable but too late to improve on (Zartman and Berman 1982, 195).

During the Montreal Protocol negotiations, a number of provisions still remained "bracketed" or subject to further negotiation on the eve of the final Conference of Plenipotentiaries. Although progress was made on many of the procedural articles in the Protocol, there was still no agreement on the core issues: what chemicals should be included, what the amount of the reduction of these chemicals should be, and how long the phase-out should take. Likewise in the Basel Convention negotiations, although the first draft had been tabled by UNEP in February 1988, five sessions later the list of outstanding issues included: developing countries' desire for a complete ban on hazardous waste exports; liability and compensation rules; responsibility for "illegal" shipments; monitoring and enforcement; and provisions for technology exchange.

Neither the climate change nor the biodiversity negotiations concluded with a final Conference of Plenipotentiaries. Instead, delegates were scheduled to complete the negotiation of the convention prior to the UN Conference on Environment and Development (UNCED) where the conventions were to be opened for signature. However, in the bio-diversity negotiations, after six sessions there was still no agreement on a number of core issues: the relationship between *ex situ* and *in situ* con-servation; the establishment of global lists of threatened and/or otherwise important species and ecosystems; rights of the country of origin; and financial support for the convention. Similarly, after five negotiating ses-sions, the climate change convention still had the following key provi-sions in brackets: targets and timetables for stabilizing carbon dioxide emissions; financing the convention; and specific commitments to be made by the industrialized countries. The turning point in these negotiations was influenced by time pressure, growing media and NGO attention, and pressure from the UNCED secretariat and Preparatory Committee. Fail-ure to complete these conventions prior to the Rio Conference could also have affected the success of this major global conference. Owing to this pressure on the climate change negotiations, the chair stepped in and prepared a compromise text bridging the different views expressed by delegations at earlier sessions.

Sometimes when the negotiations reach this point there is an impasse and the negotiations are not able to proceed to the next phase. In this event, governments have to ask themselves whether the negotiations should continue. This usually means weighing the cost of failure against the cost of compromise. In most cases of environmental negotiation, the negotiators determine that the cost of failure is too high and they return to the negotiating table. One example of this was during the UN Confer-ence on the Law of the Sea. During the summer of 1981, the United States threatened to stop participating in the negotiations over the ques-tion of who would control mining minerals from the seabed. At this point only one more negotiating session was scheduled before the signing of the Law of the Sea Convention and there was concern that the negotia-tions would end in failure. Although the negotiations did resume the fol-lowing spring and the Law of the Sea Convention was adopted on 30 April 1982, the United States voted against the agreement and it was not until November 1993 that the Convention entered into force.

Turning point 5: Conclusion of the negotiations

The final turning point in the multilateral environmental negotiating process occurs when the negotiations come to a close and the agreement is adopted. Of all the turning points, this one is the most concrete as it is marked by adoption of the agreement.

The event that usually influences this turning point is a deadline. Most environmental agreements are finalized and adopted at a Conference of Plenipotentiaries that has fixed dates. It is very rare that the negotiators are unable to reach consensus and adopt the agreement by the close of the conference. At this point there is usually a great deal of external pressure on the negotiators to conclude an agreement. Not only does the final conference attract high-level government officials, but there is usually an increase in NGO participation, media attention, and public awareness. So, even if the negotiators have to work all night during the last night of the conference, agreement is usually reached.

A number of tactics can be used to bring governments towards this turning point, including public or peer pressure on a blocking coalition, the use of a mediator, the creation of a small informal "Friends of the Chair" group that negotiates behind the scenes, small meetings of "interested" parties, a vote, or postponing further consideration of a difficult issue. It is often a combination of two or more of these tactics that makes this turning point possible.

In the MARPOL Protocol negotiations, the final agreement was reached not by consensus but by a vote. In cases where it does not appear as though all of the delegates will agree on all parts of the convention or protocol and time is running out, the negotiators can either admit failure, schedule another session, postpone consideration of some of the more controversial articles, or put the entire agreement forward for a vote. This action can be taken only if the supporters of the agreement believe they have enough votes to adopt the convention in spite of the presence of a potential blocking coalition.

In the Montreal Protocol negotiations, a number of factors have been credited with forging the final compromise that made this turning point and the agreement possible. UNEP Executive Director Mostafa Tolba played a key role as mediator through the final two phases of the negotiations. Relentless diplomatic pressure by the United States, the role of NGOs in bringing the final negotiating session to the attention of the public and the media, and a certain reluctance of delegations to be blamed for the failure of the conference all contributed to this turning point. The final compromise, which included a pledge by industrialized countries to reduce CFC pollution by 50 percent of 1986 levels by 1999, was reached only after hours of behind-the-scenes negotiations between the United States and the European Community. In the final days of the CITES negotiations, delegates met throughout the night in an effort to reach agreement on the final details so that the Convention could be adopted on the last day of the conference. Intense efforts by the United States (as the host country) and other concerned delegations in the face of a deadline enabled the CITES agreement to be completed and adopted on schedule.

The adoption of the Biological Diversity Convention was facilitated by events in a parallel negotiating process. Until the last moment it was uncertain whether there would actually be a convention to be signed in Rio owing to North–South polarization over whether the Global Environment Facility (GEF) would become the financial mechanism for the Convention. Progress was finally made once the parallel negotiations on climate change had agreed to use the GEF as an interim arrangement and the biodiversity negotiators agreed to follow suit. As more negotiations are taking place simultaneously in the post-UNCED era, this type of turning point and the linkages between processes may be more frequent in the future.

Sometimes final obstacles are overcome by postponing further consideration of a difficult issue. This was the case in the London Conference, where delegates shelved the controversial issue of jurisdiction of states over water adjacent to their coasts until the UN Conference on the Law of the Sea. The Mediterranean Convention negotiators decided to eliminate reference to the creation of an "Interstate Guarantee Fund" to compensate states for the costs of cleaning up in case of emergencies. The Convention on Long-Range Transboundary Air Pollution did not set a strict timetable to control air pollution caused by sulfur compounds and this issue was not addressed until the time was ripe for negotiation and more scientific evidence supported the Nordic claims about acid rain. The 1985 Protocol on the Reduction of Sulphur Emissions or Their Transboundary Fluxes by at Least 30 percent addressed this issue. The Conference on the Conservation of Antarctic Marine Living Resources sidestepped the sovereignty issue as well as the monitoring of harvesting levels during the interim period between signature and entry into force. The Conference on Tropical Timber postponed the decision on the location of the International Tropical Timber Organization headquarters in order to facilitate conclusion of the negotiations. The Basel Convention does not include liability provisions, as this issue was postponed until negotiations began on a protocol. The Climate Change Convention did not include any specific targets or timetables for the reduction of carbon dioxide emissions. A decision on the financial mechanism for the Convention was postponed until the first meeting of the Conference of the Parties, although delegates agreed to use the Global Environment Facility as an interim mechanism.

In some cases, just when the participants think that the treaty is ready for signature, a last-minute problem develops and a state or group of states can no longer accept a provision or article that it had previously or conditionally accepted. In these cases, instead of moving forward to the ratification/implementation phase, the negotiations backtrack to the final bargaining/details phase, or, on rare occasions, to the drafting/formula-building phase, where negotiations are re-opened. During the long-range transboundary air pollution negotiations a last-minute problem emerged when the Eastern bloc countries resisted the European Community's claim to represent its member states in negotiating the agreement and to be a signatory to the agreement. The European Community and its member states, which had no heavy investment in concluding the convention, were adamant that, if the Community itself was not a signatory to such an agreement, none of the member states would sign it. The meeting was adjourned and all further work on the convention was suspended. After informal consultations, the obstacle was removed when the Eastern bloc agreed to amend the convention, entitling regional economic integration organizations to sign the convention if, and only if, they had been granted authority to act internationally on behalf of their constituent states.

Summary

Turning points are events or actions that are necessary to move the negotiations from one phase to the next. In multilateral environmental negotiations, the turning points can be triggered either by events from within the negotiating process (change in a country's or group's position, internal time pressure, or the establishment of a working group) or by external events that influence the negotiating process (public pressure, scientific discoveries, or media attention). Figure 5.2 provides a summary of the different types of turning points that tend to influence the transition between different phases of the process.

Conclusions

The model developed in this chapter represents a convergence of the theoretical – the use of phased process analysis – and the empirical – an examination of the historical record as presented in 11 cases of multilateral environmental negotiation. The resulting model contains six phases: precipitants, issue definition, statement of initial positions; drafting/formula-

TURNING POINTS	TYPE			
1. FROM PRECIPITANTS TO ISSUE DEFINITION	INTERNATIONAL COMMUNITY AGREES TO ADDRESS THE PROBLEM			
	Initiative of a state or group of states	Initiative of a non-governmental organization	Decision of an intergovernmental body	
2. FROM ISSUE DEFINITION TO INITIAL POSITIONS	AGREEMENT TO BEGIN NEGOTIATIONS			
	Stalemate in the issue definition phase	Call for comments and/or proposals	Agreement on goals	Impact of external actors or events
3. FROM INITIAL POSITIONS TO DRAFTING	AGREEMENT TO BEGIN FORMULA-BUILDING OR DRAFTING			
	Decision to establish a drafting or working group	Request for the chair or secretariat to draft the text	Initiative of one or more countries	Agreement on basic elements to be included in the text
4. FROM DRAFTING TO FINAL BARGAINING	AGREEMENT ON A FORMULA OR GENERAL FRAMEWORK			
	Agreement on a single draft text	Consensus on formula or basic elements	Introduction of high-level officials	Time pressure/ media attention
5. FROM FINAL BARGAINING TO ADOPTION	CONCLUSION OF THE NEGOTIATIONS			
	Internal efforts towards compromise	Postponing consideration of difficult issue	Influence of external events	

Fig. 5.2 Turning points in multilateral environmental negotiation (Note: These are representative of the different types of turning points that may occur during the negotiations. They are not exclusive and more than one type may occur during the negotiating process)

building, final bargaining/details, and ratification/implementation. The first two phases represent the prenegotiation period, the next three phases comprise the actual negotiations, and the final phase is the post-agreement negotiating process. These phases are not rigid, may not always be chronological, and can overlap with each other (see figure 5.3).

The turning points that enable passage from one phase to the next are often the key points in the process where a decision is taken, a compromise is agreed upon, a concession is made, or an external event has an impact that allows the negotiations to proceed. Alternatively, the absence of one key turning point could lead to the failure of the negotiations as negotiators are unable to make the necessary concessions or com-

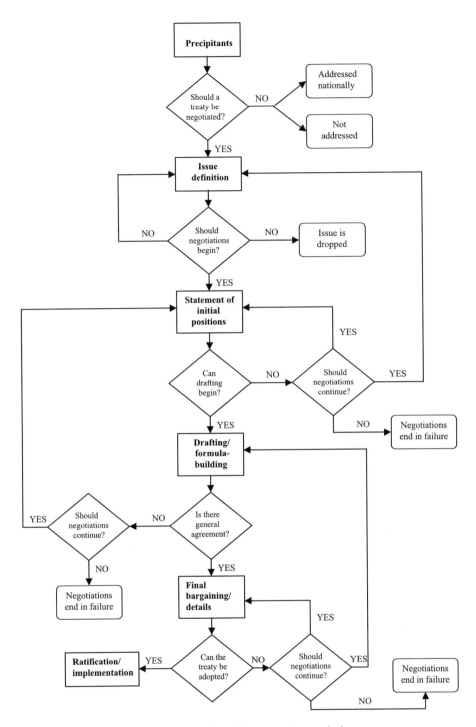

Fig. 5.3 The multilateral environmental negotiation process

promises that will allow them to move forward. These turning points can be motivated or characterized by a number of different events, activities, or decisions. The first turning point is usually externally motivated because the negotiating process has not yet begun. The second turning point can be influenced either by external events, as in the first turning point, or by internal events, such as agreement on goals, a call for comments or proposals, or a stalemate. The third and fourth turning points tend to be motivated from within the process. A state or group of states, the secretariat, or the chair often takes the necessary initiatives to coax the process along. Time pressure and the media or NGOs may also play a supporting role. The final turning point is almost always influenced by a deadline. At this point, it is likely that the public or media pressure will also play a role in bringing about the final turning point that results in adoption of the agreement.

What this model demonstrates is that, by analyzing the negotiations in terms of phases and turning points, both participants and observers are able to better understand the nature of both the negotiating process and the events or actions that motivate it. Using this model, anyone can walk into a negotiating chamber and by listening to the delegates determine which phase they are in and what needs to happen to enable the negotiations to move forward. Although this model does not address the nature of a specific compromise that produces a turning point – or tell negotiators how to put together their positions or strategies – its generality enables it to be applied to large-scale multilateral negotiations as well as to more regional ones, to negotiations on different environmental issues, and to negotiations both within and outside the UN system.

I have shown that different internally and externally motivated events (change in a country's or group's position, time pressure, the establishment of a working group, public pressure, or scientific discoveries) have different effects on the negotiating process. But what is the nature of these effects and does the presence or absence of any of these events affect the outcome of the negotiations? Unlike many bilateral negotiations and multilateral negotiations on non-environmental subjects, environmental negotiations rarely break down and end in failure. As was explained in Chapter 4, this is due to the subject matter of the negotiations, the large number of participating countries, and the use of consensus decision-making. Therefore, the success of the outcome is usually judged by the contents of the resulting agreement and by improved management of natural resources or control of environmental pollution.

Now that the phases and turning points have been identified, the next step is to determine if there are statistically significant relationships among these phases and turning points and the outcome.

Notes

1. All descriptions of the cases in this chapter are based on the information contained and cited in Chapter 4.
2. At the insistence of the Nordic countries, one token sentence was included on the military in Chapter 20 of Agenda 21 (the program of action adopted in Rio), which reads: "Governments should ascertain that their military establishments conform to their nationally applicable environmental norms in the treatment and disposal of hazardous wastes."

6

Comparing cases, process, and outcome

In the previous chapter a model was developed to help explain multilateral environmental negotiations by breaking down the complex process into a series of phases and turning points. But what about the outcome? An analysis of the negotiating process is not complete without an evaluation of the results or outcome of the process. According to Arild Underdal (1991, 100), "[t]he ultimate aim of negotiation analysis is to predict, explain or find ways of influencing the outcome." Outcomes may be defined in several different ways, all of which may be important for an evaluation of the impact that the process has on the results.

First, the mere act of reaching agreement itself constitutes an outcome (Hopmann 1996, 28). However, the nature of the agreement has its own implications. An agreement may be partial in at least three respects: it may be vague and shallow, it may cover only some of the agenda items (perhaps only the least important ones), and it may be signed by only some of the parties involved (Underdal 1991, 102). As a result, the fact of reaching agreement alone should not be used as a main indicator of a successful outcome.

Another means of evaluating the outcome is in terms of efficiency. "An agreement will be considered to be optimally efficient if it is the best agreement that the parties could achieve jointly under the circumstances" (Hopmann 1996, 29). In other words, if the parties could have found alternative agreements where they would all be better off than under the present agreement, the present agreement could be considered to be inefficient or suboptimal. However, when the parties have negotiated an agreement where there are no more mutually beneficial changes available in their positions, they may be considered to have done the best possible within the constraints of the process.

Outcomes can also be evaluated by their stability. If no actor has any incentive to defect unilaterally or to form a sub-coalition of defectors, the outcome is considered to be stable (Underdal 1991, 108). Defections could include renunciation of the agreement, cheating on the agreement, or willfully failing to implement the agreement effectively (Hopmann 1996, 29). Underdal (1991, 110) outlines four basic states of stability: (1) stable, which does not provide incentives to expand cooperation or to defect; (2) unstable, which does not provide incentives to expand cooperation but does provide incentives to defect; (3) stable and dynamic, which provides incentives to expand cooperation but not to defect; and (4) empty, which provides incentives to expand cooperation and incentives to defect.

Finally, outcomes can be evaluated in terms of the distributions of the benefits. In other words, are the gains from the agreement spread equally or unequally across the parties to the negotiation? This could be determined by measuring the change from the opening positions and comparing the magnitude and frequency of concessions by the parties. The distribution of the benefits can also be measured by comparing the absolute gains by the parties, or by examining the relative gains in comparison with their next-best alternative had the negotiations failed (Hopmann 1996, 30).

Given these thoughts on outcomes, can a model such as the one developed here help understand the logic of the mechanisms that shape the outcome and the instruments whereby it can be successfully influenced or engineered? Can it help policy analysts or practitioners determine what actions should be taken during any of the phases in the process to influence the outcome? One method might be to use the model to identify key characteristics of the process, the phases, and the turning points, as well as the outcome to test the following two guiding statements or hypotheses:

(1) The characteristics of the phases and turning points late in the process are influenced by which type of actor plays the lead role in the early phases.

(2) The outcome, as measured by the strength of the resulting agreement and ratification time, is shaped more by the nature of the final phases and turning points than by the earlier ones.

If there is indeed a statistical relationship between the nature of the phases and turning points, the presence of certain characteristics in the process itself, and the nature of the outcome, the results would enable us to move one step further toward improving our understanding of the conditions and strategies for achieving the best possible outcomes. To accomplish this, it is necessary first to identify the predominant characteristics of each of the phases and turning points and determine which cases have which characteristics. Second, it is necessary to develop an index to measure the comparative strength of each agreement. Once the information is assembled in this manner, the third step will be to examine the data and determine if, indeed, there is any correlation between the phases and the turning points at different stages in the process, as well as between the phases, the turning points, and the outcome of the negotiations. Finally, the implications of these correlations for the negotiation process will be examined to determine just how the process influences the outcome and how negotiators could respond in practice.

Characteristics of the phases and the turning points

Upon close examination of the negotiating process, it becomes apparent that there are several predominant characteristics in each phase or turning point. To compare each of the cases, each of these characteristics was assigned a numerical value. Wherever possible the numerical values were assigned to the different characteristics of each phase in a gradated scale so that similar characteristics are at one end of the scale (see table 6.1). For example, in the Precipitants phase, the characteristics range from those that are external to the international community (incidents of human-induced pollution and growing scientific evidence) to those that involve government concern (concern about overexploiting biological resources and economic concerns). Similarly, in Turning Point 1, the characteristics are scaled from institutionalized (decision of an intergovernmental body) to ad hoc (initiative of a non-governmental organization).[1]

In some of the cases, more than one of the options characterized a particular phase or turning point. For example, the CITES negotiations were precipitated by some countries' concerns about overexploiting biological resources and other countries' economic concerns. In cases such as this one, the average of the two responses was used.

Strength Index

The next question was how the outcomes should be measured. Evaluating the outcomes of multilateral environmental negotiations poses some difficult questions, largely because of the nature of the issues involved. For example, mitigating a global danger, such as ozone depletion or

Table 6.1 Characteristics of the phases and turning points

Phase/turning point	Scale	Predominant characteristics[a]
Precipitants	1	Incidents of human-induced pollution (MAR, MED, BAS)
	2	Growing scientific evidence (LDC, TAP, OZO, FCCC)
	3	Concern about overexploiting biological resources (CIT, CCA, CBD)
	4	Economic concerns (CIT, ITTA)
Turning point 1	1	Decision of an intergovernmental body (MED, CCA, ITTA, OZO, BAS, FCCC, CBD)
	2	Initiative of a state or group of states (LDC, MAR, TAP)
	3	Initiative of a non-governmental organization (CIT)
Issue definition	1	Through discussion of a draft agreement (LDC, MAR, CIT, TAP)
	2	Within the framework of a UN agency (MED, ITTA, OZO, BAS, CBD)
	3	During scientific studies or meetings (CCA, FCCC)
Turning point 2	1	Agreement on goals (MED, CCA, ITTA, OZO, CBD)
	2	Call for comments and/or proposals (TAP)
	3	Stalemate in the Issue Definition phase (MAR)
	4	Impact of external actors or events (BAS, FCCC)
	0	None of the above (LDC, CIT)
Statement of initial positions	1	UN agency working group meetings (MED)
	2	Meetings of a special negotiating group (TAP, CCA, ITTA, OZO, BAS, FCCC, CBD)
	3	Opening of a conference (MAR)
	0	None of the above (LDC, CIT)
Turning point 3	1	Request for the chair or secretariat to draft the text (CCA, BAS, FCCC, CBD)
	2	Decision to establish a drafting or working group (LDC, MED, OZO)
	3	Agreement on basic elements to be included (ITTA)
	4	Initiative of one or more countries (MAR, CIT, TAP)
Drafting/formula-building	1	Negotiations based on prepared text (CCA, BAS, FCCC, CBD)
	2	Competing drafts form basis for negotiation (LDC, TAP)
	3	Initial drafting begins (MAR, MED, ITTA, OZO)
	4	Drafting on an ad hoc basis (CIT)

Table 6.1 (cont.)

Phase/turning point	Scale	Predominant characteristics[a]
Turning point 4	1	Consensus on formula or basic elements (MAR, TAP, ITTA)
	2	Agreement on a single draft text (LDC, CIT, MED, CCA)
	3	Introduction of high-level officials (OZO, BAS)
	4	Time pressure/media or NGO attention (FCCC, CBD)
Final bargaining/ details	1	Focus is on the majority of the agreement (MAR, ITTA)
	2	Focus is on outstanding core details of the agreement (OZO, BAS, FCCC, CBD)
	3	Focus is on outstanding peripheral details (LDC, CIT, MED, TAP, CCA)
Turning point 5	1	Postponing consideration of difficult issue (LDC, MED, TAP, CCA, ITTA, BAS, FCCC)
	2	Vote (MAR)
	3	Internally motivated efforts toward compromise (CIT, OZO)
	4	Externally motivated efforts toward compromise (CBD)
Ratification/ implementation	1	No action until agreement enters into force (LDC, CIT, MED, TAP, CCA, ITTA, BAS)
	2	Interim mechanisms for meetings (OZO, FCCC, CBD)
	3	Interim mechanisms for the negotiation of amendments (MAR)

a. Key to abbreviations of agreements:
   LDC   Convention on the Prevention of Marine Pollution by Dumping of Wastes and Other Matters (London Convention)
   MAR   1978 Protocol to the 1973 International Convention for the Prevention of Pollution from Ships
   CIT   Convention on International Trade in Endangered Species
   MED   Convention for the Protection of the Mediterranean Sea against Pollution
   TAP   Geneva Convention on Long-Range Transboundary Air Pollution
   CCA   Convention on the Conservation of Antarctic Marine Living Resources
   ITTA International Tropical Timber Agreement
   OZO   Montreal Protocol on Substances That Deplete the Ozone Layer
   BAS   Basel Convention on the Control of Transboundary Movements of Hazardous Wastes and Their Disposal
   FCCC Framework Convention on Climate Change
   CBD   Convention on Biological Diversity

climate change, requires virtually universal participation to be truly effective. Therefore, at some point negotiators must determine whether to go ahead with a less than optimal number of signatories or to delay the process and obtain wider agreement. They must also assess the benefits of a formal agreement involving fewer nations against the potential of non-parties undermining the treaty's impact as free-riders (Benedick 1993, 240). Given these variables, although there are a number of ways of evaluating outcomes (as outlined in the beginning of this chapter), I used a combination of the nature of the agreement, its efficiency, and its stability through the development of a "Strength Index."

For the purposes of this analysis, the strength of an international environmental agreement is based on the strength of its components. Each of the agreements was compared on the basis of its textual provisions, not its implementation record or evaluations of its effectiveness. This was done for two reasons. First, the textual provisions of the treaty contain the language that was agreed upon by the negotiators – the true product of the compromises and concessions made during the negotiations. Second, accurate data about the implementation of a convention are not always readily available or complete since reporting requirements are not always fulfilled by all of the parties. Therefore, the characteristics that were measured are: provisions for a secretariat; provisions for reporting by parties; provisions for reservations; power given to the secretariat to monitor compliance; mechanisms for dealing with non-compliance; provisions for observations or inspections as a monitoring tool; dispute settlement mechanisms; provisions for amending the agreement; the presence of explicit measurable performance standards; liability provisions; and financial arrangements.[2] One other variable was taken into consideration along with the provisions written in the agreements themselves. This variable relates to the "life" of the agreement: have the parties adopted protocols or amendments? The scientific uncertainties and the increasingly preventive objectives of environmental negotiations dictate a pragmatic and flexible approach. An agreement that continues to adapt to changing circumstances and is improved over time is stronger than an agreement that remains static.

The responses to the questions in the Strength Index were weighted according to their relative importance to the overall strength of the agreement. Provisions relating to environmental improvement, rather than administrative issues, were given more points or weight. Although the administrative provisions may help to facilitate implementation, they can be effective only if there are concrete objectives or standards to implement. Therefore, the presence of provisions that give the secretariat the power to monitor states' compliance with the agreement and the presence of measurable performance standards were given more weight

Table 6.2 Ranking of agreements on the Strength Index

Agreement	Score on Strength Index
Montreal Protocol on Substances that Deplete the Ozone Layer (OZO)	32.0
Convention on the Conservation of Antarctic Marine Living Resources (CCA)	32.0
1978 Protocol to the International Convention for the Prevention of Pollution from Ships (MAR)	29.0
Convention on International Trade in Endangered Species (CIT)	27.5
Framework Convention on Climate Change (FCCC)	26.0
Basel Convention on the Control of Transboundary Movements of Hazardous Wastes and Their Disposal (BAS)	25.0
Convention for the Protection of the Mediterranean Sea against Pollution (MED)	21.0
London Convention (LDC)	20.0
Convention on Biological Diversity (CBD)	20.0
International Tropical Timber Agreement (ITTA)	19.0
Convention on Long-Range Transboundary Air Pollution (TAP)	13.0

than the presence of provisions for reservations to parts of the agreement. The information on the provisions of the agreements was found within the text of the agreements themselves. The amendment and protocol information was provided by the United Nations Treaty Section. After the agreements were reviewed, the points for each agreement were added up to create the Strength Index. For more details about the Strength Index, see Appendix I.

According to the Strength Index, the strongest of the 11 agreements were the Montreal Protocol on Substances That Deplete the Ozone Layer and the Convention on the Conservation of Antarctic Marine Living Resources. The weakest agreement was the Long-Range Transboundary Air Pollution Convention (not including any of the protocols that considerably strengthened this framework convention). The highest possible score an agreement could receive is 45 and the lowest is 0. The average score in this sample was 24. The agreements are listed in order from strongest to weakest in table 6.2.

The cases can be divided into four groups based on their relative scores on the Strength Index, in a manner similar to the characteristics of the phases and turning points:
(1) Less than 18 (TAP)
(2) 18–22 (LDC, MED, ITTA, CBD)

(3) 23–27 (BAS, FCCC)
(4) 27.5–32 (MAR, CIT, CCA, OZO)
The division of the conventions into these four groups enabled the strength of the convention to be coded along with the other independent variables in the data matrix for the correlation analysis that follows.

Identifying the relationships between phases, turning points, and outcome

Now that the characteristics of the phases and the turning points have been identified and one method for measuring the strength of the outcome has been devised, the next step is to evaluate the relationships between the phases, turning points, and outcome. After the data were collected, the correlations among the phases, turning points, and outcomes were calculated. No attempt was made to establish causal relationships; correlations were computed among the characteristics across the 11 cases. The type of correlation computed is the gamma coefficient. This is a measure of non-parametric correlation that can be used with variables that cannot be stated precisely enough to be capable of quantification (Connolly and Sluckin 1971, 178). Although not strictly measurable, the characteristics of a negotiating process may manifestly correlate with one another to a greater or lesser extent and the gamma coefficient is one way to examine these relationships. For more information about the gamma coefficient and the statistical methodology used to determine these correlations, see Appendix II.

Relationship between early and late phases and turning points

The first guiding statement or hypothesis states that the characteristics of the phases and turning points late in the process are influenced by which type of actor plays the lead role in the early phases. The first step in testing this hypothesis is to determine if there is any relationship between the characteristics of the phases and turning points early in the process and those that follow. The early phases and turning points are defined as those that shape the prenegotiation activities: the Precipitants phase, Turning Point 1, the Issue Definition phase, Turning Point 2, and the Statement of Initial Positions phase. The following is a summary of the stronger correlations calculated between the early and late phases and turning points. The matrix of gamma coefficients can be found in Appendix II.
- **Turning Point 1 and Turning Point 3 (0.93 correlation).** There is a strong correlation between the first turning point – the decision to ad-

dress the problem – and the third turning point – between the Statement of Initial Positions phase and the Drafting/Formula-Building phase. In the majority of the cases where the negotiations began as the result of a decision of an intergovernmental body, delegates requested the chair or the secretariat to prepare the first draft text or a formal drafting or working group was established. In cases where the negotiations began as the result of an initiative by a state, group of states, or NGO, the third turning point was often the result of an initiative of one or more states.

- **Turning Point 1 and Turning Point 4 (−0.67 correlation).** There is a moderate correlation between the first turning point – the decision to address the problem – and the fourth turning point – between the Drafting/Formula-Building phase and the Final Bargaining/Details phase. In negotiations that resulted from the initiative of a state, group of states, or NGO, the fourth turning point was the result of consensus on a formula or basic elements or of agreement on a single draft text. In negotiations that resulted from the decision of an intergovernmental body, the fourth turning point in the majority of cases was the result of the introduction of high-level officials, time pressure, or media/NGO attention.
- **Issue Definition and Turning Point 3 (−0.94 correlation).** This strong negative correlation indicates that the nature of the Issue Definition phase influences the third turning point – between the Statement of Initial Positions and the Drafting/Formula-Building phases. When the Issue Definition phase took place within the context of a discussion of a draft agreement, the third turning point was usually marked by the initiative of one or more states. On the other hand, when the Issue Definition phase took place within the framework of a UN agency or during scientific studies or meetings, the third turning point was often marked by a request for the chair or secretariat to draft the text or by the establishment of a drafting group.
- **Issue Definition and Turning Point 4 (0.67 correlation).** This moderate correlation indicates that the nature of the Issue Definition phase also influenced the fourth turning point – between the Drafting/Formula-Building phase and the Final Bargaining/Details phase. When the Issue Definition phase took place within the context of a discussion of a draft agreement, the fourth turning point was marked by consensus on a formula or basic elements or by agreement on a single draft text. When the Issue Definition phase took place within the framework of a UN agency or during scientific studies or meetings, the fourth turning point was more likely to be characterized by the introduction of high-level officials, time pressure, or NGO/media attention.
- **Statement of Initial Positions and Final Bargaining (−1.00 correlation).** This perfectly negative correlation indicates that the nature

of the Statement of Initial Positions phase was related to the Final Bargaining/Details phase. Where the Statement of Initial Positions phase took place within the context of a special negotiating group, it is likely that the Final Bargaining/Details phase was characterized by a focus on outstanding core details of the agreement. When the Statement of Initial Positions phase overlapped with the Issue Definition phase, the Final Bargaining phase usually focused on outstanding peripheral details.

Two instances of high correlations between different phases and turning points in the early part of the negotiating process are worth noting. The first instance is a perfectly negative correlation (−1.00) between Turning Point 1 and the Issue Definition phase. In cases where the first turning point – the decision to address the problem – was the result of a decision of an intergovernmental body, the Issue Definition phase usually took place within the framework of a UN agency or during scientific studies or meetings. In cases where the first turning point resulted from the initiative of a state, group of states, or NGO, the Issue Definition phase usually took place within the context of a discussion of the draft agreement. The second instance is a high correlation (0.86) between Turning Point 2 and the Statement of Initial Positions phase. When the second turning point was marked by an agreement on goals, the Statement of Initial Positions phase usually took place within the context of meetings of a special negotiating group.

Relationship between phases, turning points, and outcome

The second guiding statement or hypothesis states that the outcome, as measured by the strength of the resulting agreement and ratification time, is shaped more by the nature of the final phases and turning points than by the earlier ones. To test this, the first step is to determine if there is any relationship between the process and the outcome. The outcome is measured by the Ratification/Implementation phase and the Strength Index. The outcome is considered stronger when the Ratification/Implementation phase was characterized by interim mechanisms for meeting or negotiation since this keeps the international dialogue alive during the period before an agreement enters into force and the Conference of the Parties holds its first meeting. The following is a summary of the stronger correlations calculated between the phases and turning points and the outcome.

- **Statement of Initial Positions and Ratification (1.00 correlation).** When the Statement of Initial Positions phase took place within the context of a UN agency working group meeting (or overlapped with the Issue Definition phase), the Ratification/Implementation phase was characterized by no action until the agreement entered into force. If the Statement of Initial Positions phase took place within the meetings of a special negotiating group, the Ratification/Implementation phase was characterized either by no action until the agreement entered into force or by an interim mechanism for meetings. The difference is that the most recent negotiations contained an interim mechanism for meetings.

- **Final Bargaining and Ratification (−0.78 correlation).** When the Final Bargaining/Details phase was characterized by a focus on outstanding peripheral details in the agreement, the Ratification/Implementation phase in this sample was characterized by no action until the agreement entered into force. When the Final Bargaining/Details phase focused on outstanding core details of the agreement, in three out of four cases the Ratification/Implementation phase included mechanisms for interim meetings.
- **Turning Point 5 and Ratification (0.68 correlation).** When Turning Point 5 was characterized by the postponement of consideration of a difficult issue, in six of seven cases the Ratification/Implementation phase was characterized by no action until the agreement entered into force. When Turning Point 5 was characterized by either internally or externally motivated efforts towards compromise, two of the three cases had mechanisms for interim meetings pending the entry into force of the agreement.
- **Turning Point 5 and Strength (0.62 correlation).** Postponing consideration of a difficult issue toward the end of the process (Turning Point 5) often means that the resulting agreement will be weaker than in cases where Turning Point 5 was characterized by a vote or internally or externally motivated efforts toward compromise.

Evaluating the relationship between phases, turning points, and outcome

This analysis set out to examine the relationship between the phases and turning points early in the negotiating process and those that occur later in the process as well as the relationship between process and outcome in terms of the following two hypotheses or guiding statements:

(1) The characteristics of the phases and turning points late in the process are influenced by which type of actor plays the lead role in the early phases.

(2) The outcome, as measured by the strength of the resulting agreement and ratification time, is shaped more by the nature of the final phases and turning points than by the earlier ones.

With regard to the first statement, this analysis has shown that, among the early phases and turning points, Turning Point 1, the Issue Definition phase, and the Statement of Initial Positions phase tend to have stronger relationships with different phases and turning points later in the process. The nature of the Precipitants phase and Turning Point 2 does not appear to have any significant relationship with what occurs subsequently in the process.

Turning Point 1 and the Issue Definition phase have a strong relationship with Turning Points 3 and 4. When Turning Point 1 – the decision to address the problem – was the result of a decision taken by an intergovernmental body, the Issue Definition phase usually took place within the framework of a UN agency or during scientific meetings, and Turning Point 3 – the decision to begin drafting an agreement – was usually characterized by delegates requesting the chair or the secretariat to prepare the first draft or establishing a formal drafting or working group. Following this pattern, Turning Point 4 – agreement on a formula or general framework – was usually the result of the introduction of high-level officials, time pressure, or NGO/media attention. On the other hand, when Turning Point 1 was the result of an initiative by a state, group of states, or NGO and the Issue Definition phase took place within the context of a discussion of a draft agreement, Turning Point 3 was often the result of an initiative of one or more states and Turning Point 4 was usually the result of consensus on a formula or basic elements or of agreement on a single draft text.

This four-way relationship (which is completed by strong correlations between Turning Point 1 and Issue Definition and between Turning Points 3 and 4) indicates that, where an intergovernmental body, such as one of the UN agencies or the UN General Assembly, took the decision to begin negotiations, the intergovernmental body tended to play a strong role throughout. The relevant UN agency may have provided the framework for the Issue Definition phase, and the secretariat (usually a UN agency) may have prepared the first draft of the agreement. Finally, this drafting and redrafting process often continued until pressure was put on the delegates in the form of a deadline such as a final conference to be attended by high-level officials, or NGO/media pressure. In the cases where the initial decision to address the problem in the international arena was the result of an initiative by a state, group of states, or NGO, the nature of the subsequent process was quite different. States, rather than an intergovernmental organization, tended to be the focal point. Usually a state or group of states (or in one case an NGO) would circulate a draft agreement to serve as the focus for both the Issue Definition phase and subsequent negotiations. States continued to take the initiative throughout the process and it was these initiatives that characterized Turning Points 3 and 4 during the actual negotiations.

There is also a strong relationship between the nature of the Statement of Initial Positions phase and the Final Bargaining/Details phase. In the cases where the Statement of Initial Positions phase took place within the context of a special negotiating group, it is likely that the Final Bargaining/Details phase focused on outstanding core details in the agreement. The findings for this sample of cases indicate that in the four recent cases of UNEP-sponsored negotiations (Montreal Protocol, Basel Convention, Climate Change Convention, and Biodiversity Convention) the special negotiating groups that were established used a more inductive than deductive approach and, thus, may have entered the Final Bargaining/Details phase without agreement on a formula or even the core objectives of the final agreement. There does thus seem to be a relationship between the actors that play the lead role in the early phases of the negotiations and the characteristics of the phases and turning points later in the process.

With regard to the relationship between process and outcome, the Final Bargaining/Details phase and Turning Point 5 are the only parts of the latter half of the process that have a significant relationship to the outcome, as measured in this analysis. This is not to say that if the outcome were measured in another way (such as speed of ratification, implementation record, or amendment record) the results would not be different. Thus, for these 11 cases and the measurement of outcome composed of the Strength Index and the nature of the Ratification/Implementation phase, Turning Points 3 and 4 and the Drafting/Formula-Building phase do not appear to have much of a relationship with the outcome.

In the four of the five cases where the Final Bargaining/Details phase focused on outstanding peripheral details in the final agreement (core issues and/or formula had already been agreed upon in the previous phase), Turning Point 5 was brought about by postponing consideration of a difficult issue. In all five of these cases, the Ratification/Implementation phase was characterized by inaction until the agreement entered into force. So, in cases where the process seemed to use a formula/detail approach (as described by Zartman and Berman 1982), the Ratification/Implementation phase tended to be weaker, since no further action was taken until the agreement entered into force. Yet, this is only one possible measurement of outcome and, since this sequence of events had no noticeable relationship to the Strength Index, it is possible that there would be different results if other measurements of outcome were used.

The only phase or turning point that has a significant relationship to the Strength Index is Turning Point 5, although even this correlation is not a particularly strong one. There were seven cases where Turning Point 5 was brought about by postponing consideration of a difficult issue and five of these cases (71 percent) had a Strength Index score of 22 or below. In fact, a total of five cases had a Strength Index score of 22 or below and they all postponed consideration of a difficult issue to arrive at Turning Point 5. In the one case where Turning Point 5 was the result of external pressure, the Strength Index score was also below 22. In the three cases where Turning Point 5 was brought about by a vote or by internally motivated efforts towards compromise, the resulting agreements were among the strongest, with Strength Index scores above 26. These findings suggest that postponing consideration of a difficult issue towards the end of the process means that the resulting agreement may be weaker than when time pressure is the major factor. There are two implications of this relationship. First, postponing consideration of a difficult issue may decrease the substantive value of the agreement and, thus, make it weaker. Second, as time pressure at the end of the negotiating process is manifested in terms of a vote (consensus is impossible) or consensus brought about by the desire of delegates to avoid failure, governments may be forced to make compromises that they would not have made given more time. So, in effect, time pressure may prevent the opportunity to weaken an agreement.

Conclusions

The correlation analysis highlighted several aspects of the negotiation process that the case-study method did not reveal. First, it appears that the characteristics of the phases and turning points late in the process were influenced by which type of actor played the lead role in the early phases: individual states or intergovernmental organizations. The early phases and turning points are defined as those that shape the prenegotiation period: the Precipitants phase, Turning Point 1, the Issue Definition phase, Turning Point 2, and the Statement of Initial Positions phase.

Several implications of the findings are echoed in research that has been done on opening and early moves in negotiations and games. Experimental studies have shown that the initial offer in a negotiation influences the perceptions of the bargaining set by the negotiators. A low initial demand expresses an attempt to reduce the other party's level of aspiration and increases the likelihood of an agreement. Negotiators attain higher outcomes if they start with extreme rather than moderate demands, although extreme positions may produce counter-effects (Dupont and Faure 1991, 46). This is not exactly the focus of the hypothesis tested in this chapter, but it does demonstrate that characteristics in the early phases of negotiation have a lasting impact throughout the process.[3]

These findings are important for practitioners, who frequently discount the early phases of negotiations as the posturing before the "real" negotiations begin. If they realized the important implications of these early phases for the negotiations down the road, it might increase coherence and consistency within delegations, which might serve to improve the negotiation process as a whole. Negotiation analysts should also take note because the answers to some of the process-oriented questions that arise when studying a negotiation process may be found in the early stages before the actual drafting and bargaining begin.

With regard to the second hypothesis, the findings allow a slight modification. In the majority of the cases examined, the Final Bargaining/Details phase and Turning Point 5 were the only two parts of the negotiating process to have any significant relationship to the outcome. However, this relationship was not as strong as expected.

Based on the correlation analysis, two different negotiating paths or processes have emerged. The first path can be called "UN-centered negotiations" (figure 6.1). Along this path, the United Nations or one of its specialized agencies tended to be the focal point throughout the negotiating process. Although the precipitants could vary, the first turning point was the result of the decision of an intergovernmental body, such as the United Nations, to address a specific environmental problem. Sometimes this decision actually established a special negotiating body; in other cases it authorized the relevant agency to study the problem and make further recommendations. The next phase, Issue Definition, also took place within the UN system or, occasionally, during a series of meetings of scientific experts.

In all the cases where the Issue Definition phase took place within the framework of a UN agency or during scientific studies or meetings, Turning Point 2 was the result either of an agreement on goals or of external events or pressure from the media or NGOs. Likewise, in 86 percent of the cases following this path, the Statement of Initial Positions phase took place within a special negotiating group established for the purpose of elaborating a treaty.

In most of the cases of UN-centered negotiations, Turning Point 3 was the result of a decision by the delegates to request the chair or secretariat to prepare a draft text for consideration. This text gave the delegates a focal point and enabled them to begin the process of drafting and consensus-building. The subsequent Drafting/Formula-Building phase was then based on this prepared text. Negotiations in this phase used an inductive approach and started to put the agreement together paragraph-by-paragraph, based on the language contained in the chair's or secretariat's draft and proposals made by delegates. This drafting and redrafting process continued until delegates reached the next turning point.

Turning Point 4 was usually influenced by time pressure. In many cases the final Conference of Plenipotentiaries was about to start and there was

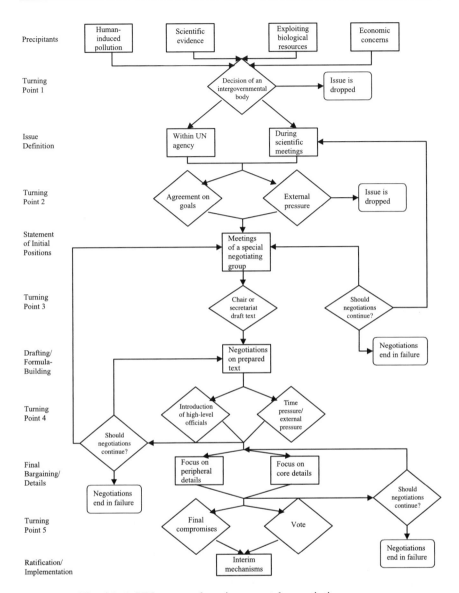

Fig. 6.1 A UN-centered environmental negotiation process

greater media or NGO attention and pressure on the negotiators. Occasionally the final conference was used as a stalling measure – delegates determined that they could make no further progress until their high-level officials or ministers arrived since these officials were able to make the tough political decisions that ordinary diplomats could not. The conference could also be used as a deadline, because delegates often did not want to leave too much text "bracketed." If their capitals did not think that an agreement was likely at the final conference, they might not send their ministers or heads of state, thus jeopardizing the status and possible conclusion of the final treaty.

The Final Bargaining/Details phase in UN-centered negotiations was characterized by numerous consultations on the remaining details in the agreement. The text of the agreement was usually complete with the exception of some provisions where there was a lack of consensus. Sometimes these provisions included details that were peripheral to the main thrust of the agreement. It was more likely in cases that followed this path, however, that there were still outstanding core details to be resolved. Without agreement on these provisions, the overall treaty would have been ineffective. The core details might still have been unresolved because delegates had postponed consideration of the difficult issues again and again. As a result, Turning Point 5 was usually characterized by a series of final compromises that allowed the treaty to be adopted or, when consensus was unlikely but there were not enough members of a blocking coalition to defeat the treaty, delegates might call for a vote. Once the treaty was adopted, the Ratification/Implementation phase tended to be characterized by the provision of interim mechanisms to allow governments to meet and continue the dialogue in the period before the agreement entered into force.

Finally, it is not clear if negotiations that followed this path resulted in treaties that are stronger because there were no significant correlations between most of the phases and turning points and the Strength Index. It is more likely that the resulting treaty will be stronger if the final turning point was characterized by final compromises or a vote than if the delegates decided to postpone consideration of a difficult issue in order to conclude the negotiations.

A second path that environmental negotiations tended to take can be called "state-centered negotiations" (figure 6.2). Even though "UN-centered negotiations" featured states as the primary actors, the United Nations played a major role as the initiator and host of the negotiating process. State-centered negotiations were those where a state or group of states initiated the negotiating process and guided it through until there was agreement on a final treaty. Although the precipitants varied, the first turning point was the result of an initiative by a state, group of states, or, possibly, an NGO to address a specific environmental problem. Usually the initiator circulated a draft text of an agreement to other states for their perusal. The next phase, Issue Definition, was then directed towards issues raised in the draft text.

When the Issue Definition phase and the Statement of Initial Positions

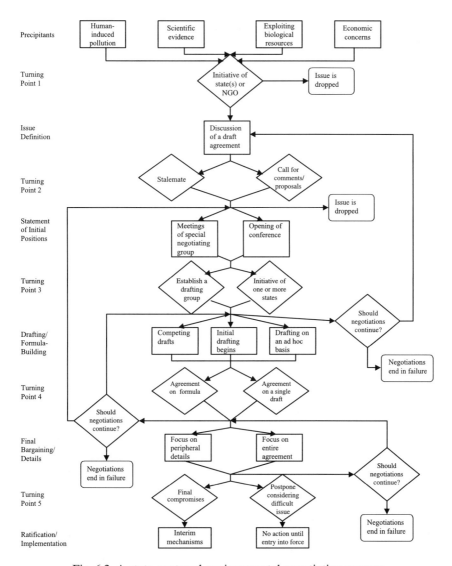

Fig. 6.2 A state-centered environmental negotiation process

phase did not overlap, Turning Point 2 was the result either of a stalemate in issue definition (technicians and scientists could go no further until the lawyers and diplomats entered the process and began drafting or formula-building) or of a call for comments on the draft or the submission of new proposals. The Statement of Initial Positions phase usually took place within a special negotiating group established for the purpose of elaborating a treaty or at the opening of a conference to address the issue and adopt the treaty.

In most of the state-centered negotiations, Turning Point 3 was the result of either the establishment of a drafting group (in 25 percent of the cases) or the initiative of one or more states (in 75 percent of the cases). The subsequent Drafting/Formula-Building phase could vary quite significantly. Unlike the UN-centered negotiations, which almost always used an inductive process for negotiating an agreement, these negotiations tended to take a more deductive approach in which delegates first agreed on a formula and then addressed the details. Sometimes competing drafts formed the basis for negotiation as delegates or a smaller drafting group tried to merge elements from the various drafts. In other cases, a drafting group or the Plenary began initial drafting or formula-building. Finally, the drafting or formula-building might also take place on an ad hoc basis, outside the framework of any negotiating body. This drafting or formula-building process continued until delegates reached the next turning point.

Turning Point 4 was usually influenced by agreement on a formula or on a single draft text. This turning point enabled the Final Bargaining/Details phase to focus on the details – specific provisions in the agreement that would implement the formula. When delegates had developed a formula in the previous phase, they used the Final Bargaining/Details phase to work out the details of the agreement. When a more inductive procedure was used, this phase was characterized by numerous consultations on the remaining peripheral details in the agreement. The text of the agreement was usually complete with the exception of some provisions where there was a lack of consensus. Rarely were core issues still the subject of negotiation in this phase.

Turning Point 5 was usually characterized by a series of final compromises that allowed the treaty to be adopted, or, when consensus appeared to be impossible, delegates might agree to postpone consideration of a difficult issue. Once the treaty was adopted, the Ratification/Implementation phase was likely to be characterized by a provision for governments to meet and continue the dialogue in the interim period before the agreement entered into force. If delegates had postponed consideration of a difficult issue, the Ratification/Implementation phase tended to be characterized by inaction until the agreement entered into force. As in the UN-centered negotiations, it is not clear if negotiations that followed this path resulted in treaties that are stronger since there were no significant correlations between most of the phases and turning points and the Strength Index. It is more likely that the resulting treaty will be stronger if the final turning point was characterized by final compromises than in cases where the delegates decided to postpone consideration of a difficult issue in order to conclude the negotiations.

There is no conclusive evidence that one of these paths is better or more effective than the other. The more recently negotiated environmental agreements, however, have taken the UN-centered negotiations path, rather than the state-centered one. In the 11 case studies, the more state-centered negotiations included the London Convention (1972), the MARPOL Protocol (1978), CITES (1973), and the Convention on Long-Range Transboundary Air Pollution (1979). This pattern echoes Kaufmann's (1996) observations on conference diplomacy in general. Kaufmann found that international conferences were originally called by one, or sometimes several, of the major powers. Over time, however, most conferences have been convened within the framework of the United Nations or its specialized agencies. Conferences convened by individual states have become the exception rather than the rule.

This shift from state-centered to UN-centered environmental negotiations may be related to a number of events within the UN system. First, the United Nations Environment Programme was established in 1972 and has been increasingly active in the development of environmental law. Former UNEP Executive Director Mostafa Tolba played a proactive role in organizing and mediating negotiations. Second, environmental issues began to receive greater attention in the UN General Assembly and other UN agencies, such as the FAO, WMO, WHO, and UNDP, have begun to expand their own mandates to include relevant environmental issues. Finally, given the North–South polarization over environmental and development issues within the international arena in general and the United Nations in particular, it is more prudent for the United Nations to host environmental negotiations so that the process and the outcome are not seen as biased toward either developed or developing countries.

These findings demonstrate that correlation analysis can be useful to the analysis of multilateral negotiations. The insights are valuable and, despite the methodological weaknesses, could prove useful in studying future environmental negotiations. Correlation analysis helped identify the two predominant paths – state-centered and UN-centered negotiations. These take different approaches to the negotiation of agreements, based primarily on the driving force behind the negotiations. Although one approach is not necessarily better than the other, the motivations behind the compromises and the final language in the agreement may differ greatly. In UN-centered negotiations, the secretariat tends to play a stronger, more proactive role than in state-centered negotiations, where the chair or certain negotiators play a stronger role than the secretariat in both the drafting and the consensus-building. UN-centered negotiations of this nature rarely use the deductive approach of establishing the formula first and then working out the implementing details. Instead, the chair or the secretariat put together a draft text of the agreement, based on government submissions, and negotiation takes the inductive approach of putting an agreement together through mutual compromise or exchanged concessions. Although state-centered negotiations do not necessarily use a deductive approach, the greater flexibility in this nego- tiation process may encourage the use of such a methodology. These and other characteristics of these two approaches described earlier in this chapter can help negotiators assess their strategies and determine how best to proceed at different stages of the negotiations. Along these lines, a series of recommendations for negotiators is outlined in Chapter 8. First, however, there have been changes in the UN system since 1992. The next chapter will outline these changes and determine if the phased process model is useful in explaining, analyzing, and determining strategies for current and future multilateral environmental negotiations.

Notes

1. To determine the primary characteristic of each phase and turning point, each of the 11 cases was examined in detail and coded appropriately. Information about each case was gathered from primary source material, such as UN documents, secondary source mater- ial, including articles and books written about the subject, and interviews conducted by me. Although it is desirable to have others with knowledge of each case perform the coding, in this analysis the coding was done solely by me. This analysis was conducted primarily to see if cases can be compared on the basis of the nature of different phases and turning points.
2. I developed the characteristics or provisions in the agreement that were measured in the Strength Index in consultation with academics and diplomats who had been involved in negotiating environmental agreements, in addition to reviewing relevant literature.
3. For more information on these studies, see Bartos (1974), Hamner (1974), Chertkoff and Conley (1967), and Hinton, Hamner, and Pohlen (1974).

7

Recent trends in multilateral environmental negotiation: The post-UNCED era

Models may be useful at explaining negotiations from the past, but a test of their true effectiveness is if they can be used to help explain current negotiations and, possibly, enable negotiators and secretariats prepare for future negotiations. The phased process model of multilateral environmental negotiations provides useful insights into the relationship among different characteristics and phases in the process and between process and outcome. Phased process analysis itself is a useful means of explaining negotiations as it allows the analyst to reduce the number of complexities inherent in multilateral environmental negotiation to a more manageable and understandable level. The question now is whether or not the phased process model can adapt to new developments and changing practices in multilateral environmental negotiations and explain and predict their evolution.

In recent years there have been a number of new developments within the UN system that have affected the means by which environmental agreements are negotiated. Many of these developments emerged as part of the 1992 UN Conference on Environment and Development (UNCED). During the UNCED preparatory process, governments and international organizations conducted evaluations of the effectiveness of existing agreements and instruments related to environment and development, reviewed the international treaty-making process, and made recommendations for future practice. The UNCED review stimulated non-governmental organizations, academics, and other practitioners to perform their own analyses of the weaknesses of the treaty-making process and make suggestions for its improvement. In addition, the nature of UNCED itself – specifically the multiplicity of issues and participants – stimulated change in the negotiation process itself.

This chapter will examine recent changes in the international environmental negotiating process, stimulated, in part, by the 1992 UN Conference on Environment and Development. Then the phased process model of multilateral environmental negotiations will be applied to two different cases of post-UNCED negotiations to determine (1) if the model is still applicable, despite changes in the nature of the process, and (2) if the model can be used to explain the evolution of the negotiations.

UNCED as a watershed

On 22 December 1989, the United Nations General Assembly adopted Resolution 44/228 calling for a global meeting on environment and development issues. The conference was to be convened to "elaborate strategies and measures to halt and reverse the effects of environmental degradation in the context of increased national and international efforts to promote sustainable and environmentally sound development in all countries." Thus, the UN Conference on Environment and Development was born.

During the course of four Preparatory Committee meetings between August 1990 and April 1992, delegates from more than 150 countries examined a wide range of environmental issues as well as the underlying patterns of development that cause stress to the environment – poverty in developing countries, levels of economic growth, unsustainable patterns of consumption, demographic pressures, and the impact of the international economy, particularly trade and investment. This was the first time that an intergovernmental conference addressed these crucial economic and social development issues in conjunction with the natural environment.

UNCED also marked the first time since the end of the Cold War that the international community addressed a new set of issues on environment and development that call into question the concepts upon which the United Nations was created and its future role as a center for harmonizing the actions of nations. Peter Thacher (1992) noted that, when the UN Charter was signed,

Governments were the dominant actors on the international stage, and keeping the peace among member states was the primary task for the international community. As the 50th anniversary [of the United Nations] approaches, the end of the Cold War brings new issues to the fore in an organization whose membership – in terms of states – has more than trebled and is still growing. But the comparative influence of states on the international scene has diminished as significant roles are acquired in an interdependent and more transparent world by non-state actors of all sorts, including science, multinational corporations and financial institutions, media, as well as a host of international organizations.

In addition to the presence of new actors on the negotiating scene, there are new and more complicated issues, growing UN membership (not to mention the inclusion of many non-member states and territories in multilateral negotiation, such as Switzerland, the Holy See, and numerous small island states or territories), and higher, more interdependent political and economic stakes. There is no doubt that these changes have had an impact on the way in which international environmental agreements are negotiated.

Non-governmental actors

Non-governmental organizations (NGOs) were allowed to participate to an unprecedented extent during the UNCED preparatory process and the conference itself. The preamble to Section 3 of Agenda 21 (United Nations 1992), the action program for sustainable development adopted by UNCED, states that "[c]ritical to the effective implementation of the objectives, policies and mechanisms agreed to by Governments in all programme areas of Agenda 21 will be the commitment and genuine involvement of all social groups." As a result of the recognition of the increased role of NGOs, the scientific community, and other major groups (including business and industry, women, indigenous people, youth, local authorities, and trade unions) in the formulation of environment and development programs and policies, Agenda 21 recommended the following in paragraph 27.9:

The United Nations system, including international finance and development agencies, and all intergovernmental organizations and forums should, in consultation with non-governmental organizations, take measures to:
    (a) Review and report on ways of enhancing existing procedures and mechanisms by which non-governmental organizations contribute to policy design, decision-making, implementation and evaluation at the individual agency level, in inter-agency discussions and in United Nations conferences ...

Since the early 1990s, coinciding with the UNCED preparatory process, non-governmental actors have played a more prominent role in multilateral negotiations. According to Thomas Princen (1994, 36), NGOs gain influence by "building assets based on legitimacy, transparency, and transnationalism." NGO legitimacy is based on their ability to command media attention, promote communication, and muster support, or opposition, for environmental policies, and to provide scientific and earth-centered knowledge from their own research, as well as their ties with the scientific and land-based communities (Princen 1994, 34). As an example of increased NGO legitimacy, during the first session of the Intergovernmental Negotiating Committee to elaborate an international convention to combat desertification in those countries experiencing serious drought and/or desertification, particularly in Africa (INCD), which was held in Nairobi in May 1993, NGOs, scientists, academicians, and other non-governmental technical experts participated in a week-long information-sharing segment. In fact, some governments included non-governmental experts on their official delegations and even gave them the opportunity to present reports on their experiences with land degradation and desertification.

Furthermore, governments, including some from developing countries, are now including non-governmental representatives on their official delegations to UN-sponsored negotiations. NGO representatives are often given more opportunities to make interventions during formal negotiating sessions and are even allowed to observe many informal sessions as well. This has greatly increased the leverage that NGOs can have in presenting technical information and suggestions, drafting text, and influencing government positions. For the most part, however, the crucial final bargaining/details phase continues to be closed to NGOs (even those on official government delegations). During this phase of the process, NGOs have had to resort to traditional ways of influencing the process in the form of press conferences, demonstrations, and lobbying delegates in the corridors.

The greatest effect that NGOs have had on the negotiating process thus far has been in forcing increased transparency on the process. Only the most sensitive negotiations are still taking place behind closed doors. As more people outside the UN system and diplomatic circles are informed about what is going on in the international treaty-making process, governments will be held more accountable for their actions. NGOs bring with them both the ability to provide information that could help the negotiations but also the threat of publicizing the positions and actions of governments within the negotiations.

Government actors

Despite the presence of more non-governmental actors, governments still are the predominant force in multilateral negotiation on environmental issues and there are more of them than ever before. Whereas negotiations in the 1970s and 1980s often involved fewer than 70 states, dominated by industrialized countries, negotiations in the post-UNCED era have included, on average, at least 100 states, dominated by developing countries. There are now 188 member states of the United Nations – 58 more than in 1972. Participation of developing countries in UN-sponsored negotiations has become increasingly important and almost every conference and negotiating process includes the establishment of a "voluntary fund" to which industrialized countries contribute in order to underwrite the participation of developing countries.

The increase in the number of participants has had several effects on the process as new methods for managing the size of the negotiating body have had to be developed. These methods include the reorganization of the group system and the institutionalization of greater numbers of small, informal negotiating sessions. The group system has almost always been used in UN-sponsored negotiations. UN member states are divided into five regional groups that have traditionally been responsible for nominating officers to a conference or committee bureau and electing their representatives to limited-member organizations, such as the Economic and Social Council (ECOSOC), the UN Commission on Sustainable Development, and the Governing Council of the United Nations Environment Programme (UNEP). These five regional groups – Asia, Eastern Europe, Africa, Latin America and the Caribbean, and Western Europe and Others – have rarely been used as a means for consolidating negotiating positions. There are several reasons for this. First, within the United Nations' consideration of economic, social, and environmental issues, the Group of 77 (G-77) has been the primary forum for the development of a common negotiating position for all of the developing countries, which comprise the vast majority of the Asian, African, and Latin American regional groups.[1] During the Cold War, two other major groups existed: the Communist Bloc (made up of the Eastern Europe Group) and the Western Europe and Others Group (WEOG) and Japan. Of course, as the case studies have demonstrated, these groups rarely share negotiating positions on environmental issues and, thus, have not been used extensively to formulate negotiating strategies. For example, the London Convention and MARPOL negotiations divided the WEOG countries by their maritime interests. The Montreal Protocol negotiations had the Toronto Group (the Nordic countries, Canada, and the United States) in opposition to the European Community, Japan, and the Soviet Union.

In the 1990s, several events contributed to a further breakdown of these traditional groups. The first was the end of the Cold War. With the break-up of the Soviet Union and the transition to market economies in the former Soviet bloc, a new dimension has been added to UN negotiations. In the environmental arena, these countries still make up a negotiating bloc as they work together to ensure that they receive preferential treatment when it comes to the allocation of financial resources and the transfer of environmentally sound technology. These transitional countries are often at odds with the G-77, which does not want to lose bargaining leverage or financial and technical assistance from the western industrialized countries. The break-up of the Soviet Union has also had an impact on the Asia and Eastern Europe regional groups. The Asia Group is the most diverse of the five regional groups as it includes countries from Jordan to Japan, and the presence of the former Soviet republics in Central Asia has added yet another disparate element to the group – countries with economies in transition. Similarly, the break-ups of the Soviet Union and the former Yugoslavia have had an impact on the Eastern Europe Group. This group has more than doubled in size and, since it is no longer dominated by the Soviet Union, is less unified than before. Furthermore, some countries are trying to join the European Union and/or NATO, which has affected their negotiating position in other forums such as the United Nations. Nevertheless, the political and economic changes in the region have left it nearly powerless as a negotiating bloc on environmental issues, except in the crucial areas of access to financial assistance and technology transfer.

Some of the post-UNCED environment and development negotiations have also demonstrated that the G-77 is no longer the unified voice of the developing world. In fact, the G-77 appears to be united only as far as to ensure that the industrialized countries' commitments in Agenda 21 in the areas of finance and technology transfer are not lost in the post-UNCED era. Disparities in economic growth between some Latin American countries and Asian countries and the least developed countries, primarily in Africa, have led to a rift within the G-77. This rift was apparent at the first session of the Intergovernmental Negotiating Committee to elaborate an international convention to combat desertification in those countries experiencing serious drought and/or desertification, particularly in Africa (INCD). Since the title of the INCD specifically mentions Africa, the INCD chair, Ambassador Bo Kjellén of Sweden, proposed that the committee negotiate both a framework convention and an instrument for action in Africa (either a protocol or an annex). He envisioned that this instrument would serve as the model for the development of additional instruments to address drought and desertification in other regions of the world (Kjellén 1992). Despite these intentions, the Latin Americans (particularly Brazil and Mexico) and some Asians argued that they suffer from desertification as much as Africa does and, thus, regional instruments for Latin America, Asia, and Africa should be negotiated simultaneously. The Africans resisted, stating that the mandate of the INCD places special emphasis on desertification in Africa. As this became the primary issue at the first negotiating session, the G-77 ceased to meet because regional interests predominated over North–South interests (Chasek et al. 1993).

Likewise, during the negotiations of the Kyoto Protocol to the Framework Convention on Climate Change, the developing countries were divided between states producing oil and other fossil fuels, which were advocating no reductions in carbon dioxide emissions that might affect their fossil fuel exports, small island developing states, which are concerned about sea-level rise related to climate change, and a group of other developing countries that wanted to ensure that they did not have to undertake any commitments to reduce greenhouse gas emissions under the protocol.

Both new and old divisions of the regional groups have emerged or have been strengthened in recent years as the number of participants in negotiations has increased. It is now common to see unified positions from the European Union, the North African states, the Alliance of Small Island States (AOSIS), the Central American states, the Caribbean Community (CARICOM), the Arab states, and JUSCANZ (Japan, the United States, Norway, Canada, Australia, and New Zealand). These smaller groups are better suited for the elaboration of common negotiating positions and drafting than are the large, unwieldy regional groups. The institutionalization of these smaller groups also means that each one has only one spokesperson, thus decreasing the potential number of interventions that are made on any given topic during the negotiations. If each government wants to state its position, and more than 180 governments are present, the so-called "general debate" – the statement of initial positions phase – would last for days, if not weeks, and little substantive negotiation would take place.

In addition to affecting the composition and role of regional and interest groups in the negotiating process, the increased participation of developing countries has altered the focus and the substance of multilateral environmental negotiations. The most visible effect is that environmental negotiations are no longer focused solely on the environment. Related development issues, such as poverty, patterns of consumption, and human settlements, are now being considered with the environmental issues in this new era of "sustainable development." Developing countries are ensuring that the debt crisis, trade barriers, commodity prices, and other economic issues that hinder their development are also put on the negotiating table. Their argument is that, unless there is a favorable international economic climate for their own economic and social development, they can ill afford to implement international environmental agreements and other forms of environmental protection. Thus, the developing countries have increased their bargaining leverage by threatening to walk out of the negotiations, or at least not to sign, ratify, or implement environ-mental agreements, unless there are provisions for "new and additional" financial resources, new and improved mechanisms for the transfer of these resources, and favorable transfer of environmentally sound tech-nology. Because of the large number of developing countries that are now participating in these negotiations, these demands carry a lot of weight. In addition, the industrialized countries realize that, without the participation of developing countries in the implementation of envir-onmental agreements, the effect and impact of the agreement would be minimal. As a result, special provisions are now incorporated into agree-ments to ensure the participation of developing countries.

Emerging issues

Agenda 21 identified a number of environment and development issues that should be the subject of future negotiations. These include more ef-ficient commodity agreements (Chapter 2), new regional agreements for limiting transboundary air pollution (Chapter 9), an international con-vention on forests (Chapter 11), an international convention to combat desertification (Chapter 12), an international agreement on biotech-nology safety procedures (Chapter 16), agreements on protection of the marine environment from land-based sources of pollution (Chapter 17), an international agreement for the effective management and conserva-tion of fish stocks (Chapter 17), legal instruments to protect the quality of fresh water resources (Chapter 18), the establishment of prior informed consent procedures to manage trade in hazardous chemicals (Chapter 19), a protocol on liability under the Basel Convention (Chapter 20), and a legally binding instrument on the transboundary movement of radio-active waste (Chapter 22). Most of these negotiations have either con-cluded or are underway.

Likewise, other environmental issues that have already been the sub-ject of international negotiations are being revisited in response to chang-ing circumstances and demands for strengthening the enforcement of regimes already in existence.

By UNCED's first anniversary, new rounds of negotiations had already begun on combating desertification and drought, sustainable develop-ment of small island states, high seas fisheries, and land-based sources of marine pollution. At the same time, negotiations continued on climate change, ozone depletion, amending the London Convention, the renego-tiation of the International Tropical Timber Agreement, and a liability protocol for the Basel Convention. By the year 2000, much had been ac-complished. The revised ITTA was adopted in January 1994; the Convention to Combat Desertification was adopted in June 1994; the Agreement on the Conservation and Management of Straddling Fish Stocks and Highly Migratory Fish Stocks was adopted in August 1995; the Kyoto Protocol to the Framework Convention on Climate Change was adopted in December 1997; the Rotterdam Convention on the Prior Informed Consent (PIC) Procedure for Certain Hazardous Chemicals and Pesticides in International Trade was adopted in September 1998; the Liability Protocol to the Basel Convention was adopted in December 1999; the Cartagena Protocol on Biosafety to the Convention on Biological Diversity was adopted in January 2000. Negotiations on a convention to control persistent organic pollutants began in March 1998 and are expected to be completed in 2001. Several new protocols have been adopted under the Convention on Long-Range Transboundary Air Pollution, and a number of conventions, including the Montreal Protocol and MARPOL, have been amended.

The proliferation of negotiations has had a strong effect on the negotiating process. Many developing countries do not have the personnel or financial resources to attend such a large number of negotiating sessions. As a result, there are more and more instances where a developing country or group of "like-minded" countries is forced to rely on another country to represent their interests. It is becoming increasingly common to see only one Central American country present in the conference room. The East African, West African, Caribbean, and South Pacific nations are also relying more and more on this type of surrogate representation. Although this may serve to improve the management of the large number of parties to negotiations, it also has the potential to cause more last-minute problems during the final bargaining/details phase. Sometimes the countries that have relied on surrogate representation throughout the process suddenly appear at the last session because there is some article or phrase that they see as inimical to their interests. Although this particular phrase may have been agreed to months before, it is suddenly reopened because a new country has entered the conference room.

Some of these issues are complicated in nature and may stimulate other changes in the negotiating process. Most environmental issues that are being discussed in the international arena today are highly technical in nature and many of the negotiators are career diplomats or government officials with little technical expertise. As a result, the issue definition phase of the process takes on greater importance. In the past, this phase took place outside of the negotiating chambers. Meetings of scientific and technical experts often did not include the diplomats who would eventually negotiate the agreement. Yet, unless diplomats have a basic understanding of the scientific and technical aspects of the problem, the nego-tiations will be dominated by politics and the resulting agreement will do little to address the actual problem. During the negotiation of the resolution establishing the INCD, delegates realized this problem and recommended that the first session of the INCD include a week-long technical information-sharing segment. During this week, scientists, rep-resentatives from some of the UN technical agencies, and government experts on desertification, dryland management, and drought shared ex-periences and knowledge about the issue under negotiation. This seg-ment proved to be highly successful. By the end of the week, it was clear from the presentations, the overhead projections, and the color slides that desertification and drought are problems faced in many parts of the world, in both developed and developing countries (Chasek et al. 1993). It is likely that this new model for the issue definition phase will be used in other UN-sponsored negotiations.

The negotiation of these increasingly complicated environmental issues will likely change the face of many government delegations. Tradition-ally, governments have relied on their UN representatives in Geneva, New York, or Nairobi to negotiate environmental and other multilateral agreements. However, as environmental negotiations become more spe-cialized, governments will have to supplement their delegations with sci-entists, technical experts, industry representatives, and representatives from a wide range of government ministries. For example, environmental issues such as pesticide control, toxic chemicals, radioactive waste dispo-sal, and climate change touch on issues relevant to industry, trade, eco-nomics, health, medicine, law, environment, and agriculture. To discuss these issues effectively and negotiate an adequate agreement, govern-ments must get input from these sectors. This complicates the formula-tion of initial positions and the formation of groups and alliances because industrial interests will invariably disagree with environmental inter-ests, which will disagree with trade interests, and so on. Unfortunately, many developing countries do not have the level of capacity or expertise necessary to supplement their delegations or increase their delegations' expertise.

Higher political and economic stakes

More states are now attaching greater political and economic importance to natural resources and the environment. As the effects of environmen-tal degradation on present and future generations become clear, the costs of global environmental and resources conservation are also rising for all states. Meanwhile, the linkages among global environmental, economic, trade, and security issues are becoming increasingly apparent, as was demonstrated during the 1999 World Trade Organization (WTO) meeting in Seattle as well as the recent negotiation of the Kyoto Protocol to the Framework Convention on Climate Change and the Cartagena Protocol on Biosafety.

The most notable effect of this on environmental negotiations will be to prolong them. As is demonstrated by the length and divisiveness of negotiations on issues such as trade and arms control, the stronger the economic and political effects and repercussions of the agreement, the more difficult it is to negotiate. If UNCED succeeded in accomplishing anything, it was to demonstrate that environment and development are closely linked and that environmental policy is inextricably tied to policies on a wide range of issues, including foreign policy, trade, debt, and economic development. As a result, a larger number of policy makers now have an interest in environmental negotiations to ensure that the outcome and proposed policy measures do not have a negative effect on their short- and long-term interests. This will have the greatest impact on the two negotiating phases: drafting/formula-building and final bargaining/details. The earlier prenegotiation phases and the transition phase (the statement of initial positions) will still largely be the domain of diplomats and environment ministries.

The impact of a large number of policy makers and interests was evident in the US government's approach to the UNCED negotiations. In the middle of the fourth and final session of the Preparatory Committee, the Bush administration sent a group of high-level officials from different departments to review the text of Agenda 21, which had been painstakingly negotiated over the previous year. These high-level officials represented the administration's interests in industry, trade, and foreign aid, to name a few. As a result of their review, portions of text that had earlier been agreed to in principle by the US delegation were no longer considered acceptable. During the final sessions of each of the working groups and the Plenary, the US delegation proposed numerous changes, which served to open debate anew. This not only prolonged the negotiations, but contributed to a general sense of frustration among government delegates, NGOs, and the secretariat during the final days of the Preparatory Committee meeting. Had the various interests of the administration been present earlier in the process and had there been more cooperation and coordination among the agencies and departments, these last-minute changes would not have been necessary. In many cases, it is not until the eleventh hour that governments realize the high political and/or economic stakes of the agreement under negotiation and decide that the negotiations should not be left solely to the diplomats.

Applying the model to future negotiations and negotiations in progress

As times and political realities change, there is a ripple effect into various international forums, including the negotiation of environmental agreements. The post-Rio era (1992 to the present) has been characterized by increased participation of non-governmental actors, increased numbers of governmental actors, new and more technically challenging environmental issues, and increased political and economic stakes. Can the phased process model of multilateral environmental negotiations adapt to changing circumstances and continue to be useful in ongoing and future environmental negotiations? Can this model help to explain the process and the relationship between process and outcome, and assist practitioners in avoiding unnecessary pitfalls?

To test its adaptability, the model will be applied to two examples of post-Rio environmental negotiations: the negotiations towards a protocol to strengthen the Framework Convention on Climate Change, and the negotiations on a biosafety protocol under the Convention on Biological Diversity.[2] Both of these cases involve a large number of governmental actors (more than 100 states), intergovernmental organizations, and non-governmental actors. Both issues were relatively new to the international environmental negotiating arena, considering that the negotiation of the FCCC had concluded no more than five years before and no international agreement existed on biosafety. In addition, both cases are seen to have major economic implications. The reduction of greenhouse gas emissions, primarily through energy conservation and conversion, would have a major effect on countries exporting fossil fuels, as well as on the industries that rely heavily on fossil fuels – the automobile industry, electricity utilities, and large manufacturers. The biosafety negotiations were of major concern to the biotechnology companies as well as to some of the major agricultural exporting countries and their various agricultural industries, which were concerned about increased bureaucratic red tape which would affect agricultural trade, as well as about a backlash against genetically modified crops.

Precipitants

Biosafety

The precipitants phase of the biosafety negotiations encompassed a combination of the overexploitation of biological resources, specifically concern about the effect of living modified organisms (LMOs) on biological diversity, and economic concerns about the sharing of benefits from LMOs.

Climate change

In the case of the climate change negotiations, the precipitant was increased scientific evidence about the relationship between certain greenhouse gases, particularly carbon dioxide, and climate change.

Turning point 1

In both cases, the negotiating process resulted from a decision of an intergovernmental body.

Biosafety

The second meeting of the Conference of the Parties (COP-2) to the Convention on Biological Diversity (CBD), which met in Jakarta, Indonesia, in November 1995, adopted Decision II/5, Consideration of the need for and modalities of a protocol for the safe transfer, handling and use of living modified organisms. This decision established an Open-ended Ad Hoc Working Group on Biosafety (BSWG) to elaborate a protocol on biosafety, specifically focusing on the transboundary movement of any LMO that might have an adverse effect on biodiversity.

Climate change

COP-1 to the UN Framework Convention on Climate Change (FCCC), which met in Berlin, Germany, in March–April 1995, adopted Decision 1/CP.1, also referred to as the "Berlin Mandate." The COP agreed to begin a process to enable it to take appropriate action for the period beyond 2000, including the strengthening of commitments of Annex I (developed country) parties in Article 4.2(a) and (b) of the Convention, through the adoption of a protocol or another legal instrument. The COP also established the Ad Hoc Group on the Berlin Mandate (AGBM) to undertake this action.

Issue definition

In both protocol negotiations, issue definition took place both within the context of a scientific meeting and within a UN agency or body, which fed into the work of the negotiating bodies established by the two conventions.

Biosafety

The first meeting of the BSWG took place in July 1996. The initial discussions were framed by the reports of two related meetings: the July 1995 Madrid meeting of the Open-ended Ad Hoc Group of Experts on Biosafety and the December 1995 Cairo meeting of the UNEP Panel of

Experts on International Technical Guidelines for Biosafety. Using these reports, delegates tried to define a number of key concepts and terms, the form and scope of advance informed agreement (AIA) procedures, and relevant categories of LMOs to be covered under the protocol. There was also discussion on some issues on which the Madrid meeting was unable to reach consensus: socio-economic considerations, liability, and compensation and financial issues.

Climate change

The AGBM focused on issue definition during its first two sessions in August and October–November 1995. These discussions were framed by the Second Assessment Report of the Intergovernmental Panel on Climate Change, adopted in December 1995, which stated for the first time that climate change is the result of human activities. The Berlin Mandate stated that the parties would focus on analysis and assessment in the early stages of the process, to identify possible policies and measures for Annex I parties. At the second session of the AGBM, the secretariat introduced a document describing policies and measures identified in national communications from Annex I parties. Over 1,000 policies and measures were included in the 27 national communications submitted. Delegates also started defining options for quantified emission limitation and reduction objectives within specified time-frames.

Turning point 2

In both of these cases, the turning point that allowed passage from the issue definition phase to the statement of initial positions phase was a call by the chair for comments and/or proposals. This shifted delegates' focus away from issue definition and towards elaboration of the protocol.

Biosafety

In the biosafety negotiations, this turning point took place at the middle of the first meeting when the chair called on delegates to make their initial statements on the structure of a future protocol and to submit all written comments and proposals to the secretariat by 31 December 1996.

Climate change

In the Kyoto Protocol negotiations, this turning point took place during the second meeting, when the chair called on delegates to provide an initial exchange of views on possible features of the protocol.

Statement of initial positions

As in the pre-UNCED cases, the length of the statement of initial positions phase tends to vary, but its nature has not changed. Governments still use this phase to make their initial statements, form coalitions, and prepare suggestions for elements to be included in the agreement.

Biosafety

This phase began during the second half of the week of the first session of the BSWG. During the course of the debate, governments, intergovernmental agencies, and NGOs stated their positions and tabled formal proposals about the structure of the protocol. This phase continued at the second session (Montreal, May 1997), where the secretariat tabled a document entitled "Compilation of Views of Governments on the Contents of a Future Protocol." In their opening statements, delegates emphasized a number of priority issues for consideration. These included: the inclusion of socio-economic considerations (Malaysia and the Philippines); establishing procedures in case of international transboundary movement of LMOs (European Union); ensuring consistency with the objectives of the CBD and not exceeding its scope (Japan, Norway, Republic of Korea); focusing on AIA, information-sharing, and capacity-building (United States and Australia); and consistency with WTO rules (Republic of Korea, Argentina, Australia, Japan, and South Africa).

Delegates also stated their initial positions on AIA. They raised more questions than they answered, such as: whether AIA would be required for all LMO imports or only under certain conditions; whether importing or exporting countries would be responsible for assessing and managing risks from LMOs; which party would be responsible for notifying and taking action in case of unintended movements; whether there would be any legal requirement for compensation or liability placed on producers or exporters of LMOs; and whether LMO-containing commodities would be treated under the protocol at all. Initial views were also exchanged on information-sharing, capacity-building, risk assessment, unintentional transboundary movements, and monitoring and compliance.

By the end of the session, there was little agreement on most of the substance, much less on a formula. At this point in the negotiations, the only two coalitions that had emerged were developing versus developed countries. The developing countries rallied around a common desire for the protocol to address the impact of the movement of LMOs on socio-economic conditions. Many developed countries, which were initially opposed to the negotiation of a protocol, appeared to be cooperative but cautious.

Climate change

The statement of initial positions phase of the climate change negotiations took place during the latter part of the second session in October–November 1995 and continued into the third session in March 1996 and the fourth session, which coincided with COP-2, in July 1996. During this period, delegates also considered two draft protocols that had been put forward by the Alliance of Small Island States and the European Union. Although delegates moved closer to making the determination that they should negotiate an actual protocol, no decision was made until the end of the fourth session.

There was also divergence of opinion on the pros and cons of mandatory approaches and their market-based alternatives to reducing emissions. Different positions began to emerge and some coalitions began to form, primarily along the same lines as those coalitions that negotiated the FCCC. The United States argued that no single set of policies and measures could apply to all countries, given their divergent circumstances. The European Union, calling for the widest possible measures and significant emissions reductions, proposed three categories of policies and measures, ranging from required elements to a broad list from which parties might choose. A number of developing countries were concerned about existing Annex I party implementation and continued to insist that they would undertake no new commitments under the protocol. The oil-producing countries wanted to focus on socio-economic assessment of various policies and measures to reduce emissions, before discussing the framework for a protocol or other draft instrument. The countries with economies in transition stressed the need for flexibility in the types of steps a country might take to reduce greenhouse gas emissions.

Turning point 3

The turning point in both cases was triggered when the negotiators requested the chair or the secretariat to prepare a draft negotiating text to move the process to the drafting/formula-building phase. This has become almost the de facto nature of this turning point in UN-sponsored negotiations.

Biosafety

At the conclusion of the second session of the BSWG, governments were invited to submit legal texts on the following issues by 1 August 1997: AIA; notification procedures; risk assessment and management; unintentional transboundary movements; handling, transportation, packaging, and transit requirements; competent authorities/focal points; an information-sharing/clearinghouse mechanism; capacity-building; and public awareness/ participation. The secretariat was requested to develop draft articles on: financial issues; the institutional framework; the scope of jurisdiction; the relationship with other international agreements; and the settlement of disputes. The preparation of a draft text served to shift the focus of the governments from statements of general principles and elements to be included in a convention to concrete language and provisions to be reviewed, discussed, and negotiated.

Climate change

At the conclusion of the fourth session of the AGBM, governments were invited to submit proposals by 15 October 1996. The chair was going to summarize these proposals and present them to AGBM-5 in December. The chair expressed the hope that this summary would provide a framework tool for discussion and would be a major step forward in developing a negotiating text.

Drafting/formula-building

When examining pre-UNCED cases, the phased process model indicated that, if turning point 3 was characterized by a request for the chair or the secretariat to draft the negotiating text, the subsequent drafting/formula-building phase would be characterized by negotiations on a draft text, rather than a more deductive approach where the general principles or a formula are agreed on first and then the details are negotiated. In these cases, even if there is no agreement on a formula, the chair or secretariat is still requested to draft a negotiating text to focus the negotiations at the next session. In an inductive type of drafting/formula-building phase, delegates examine the draft paragraph-by-paragraph and propose new language, begin to work out compromises among themselves, and generally ensure that their concerns are met in the draft as it evolves. This is usually a lengthy process and some of the more controversial issues can get quite contentious. This was the process followed by both of these negotiations.

Biosafety

At the third, fourth, and fifth negotiating sessions, held in Montreal in October 1997 and February and August 1998, delegates focused their attention on the draft negotiating text of the convention that was prepared by the secretariat. Two sub-working groups were established, along with two open-ended contact groups. The sub-working groups addressed the draft articles of the protocol, while the contact groups addressed definitions, institutional matters, and final clauses. The objective of each group was to develop a "consolidated draft negotiating legal text." The two working groups examined the draft article-by-article, paragraph-by-paragraph, proposing alternatives, bracketing text or even entire articles that were not acceptable to one or more states, and reaching consensus language on other parts. At the end of each reading of the text, the secretariat prepared a revised draft and the delegates would examine and discuss the text once again.

Delegates at the third session had difficulty making the transition from statements of initial positions to drafting and negotiating. They were more interested in ensuring that their government's preferred options continued to be represented in the text rather than making compromises. At the fourth session, delegates moved forward in consolidating options contained in the draft text, while beginning the process of negotiation to clearly define divergent positions and to identify common ground for moving forward.

As the drafting progressed, new coalitions emerged and by the fifth session the dynamics of the negotiations had become more political and fractured. The developing countries started to negotiate as regional blocs rather than as part of the Group of 77. The division was based vaguely on differing levels of economic development and biotechnological capacity, but even the Latin America and Caribbean Group was unable to remain united for long as the agricultural exporting countries began to split apart from the rest of the region. The developed countries were also divided between the major agricultural exporting countries (the United States, Canada, and Australia, among them) and the European Union.

At the outset of the fifth session, BSWG chair Veit Koster said his objective was to reduce each draft article to a single option. By the end of the meeting, the text was 50 percent shorter and appeared to contain one option for each article (although closer evaluation revealed that options still remained in the form of brackets). Greater progress was made during the drafting phase on the protocol's procedures rather than on the core issues of scope, liability, socio-economic considerations, and trade issues. Delegates still differed widely in terms of "what" they were actually negotiating about: what exactly was the scope of the protocol? Trade also began to emerge as a central issue and questions developed about the protocol's relationship to the WTO. Liability was still one of the most hotly debated issues that continued to be divided along North–South lines. One of the few things that was clear after delegates concluded this round of negotiations was that, with the range of actors and issues, the trade-offs were not as apparent as in other negotiations, such as the climate change negotiations, where the bargaining chips were more easily defined.

Climate change

The drafting/formula-building phase of the Kyoto Protocol negotiations took place at the fifth, sixth, seventh, and eighth sessions, convened in December 1996 and March, August, and October 1997. At AGBM-5 in December 1996, delegates discussed the options presented in the chair's synthesis document of proposals by parties on the strengthening of Annex

I party commitments, possible elements of a protocol or another legal instrument, and additional proposals submitted by 14 parties or groups of parties. At the end of this meeting, delegates requested the chair and the secretariat to prepare a framework compilation, incorporating textual proposals from parties as well as other proposals for elements of a protocol or another legal instrument, and identifying the sources. Proposals received by 15 January 1997 would be taken into account in the preparation of the framework compilation text.

At the sixth session in March 1997, delegates to the AGBM focused their deliberations on the framework compilation text. Delegates streamlined the text by merging or eliminating some overlapping provisions within the myriad of proposals contained in the text. Much discussion centered on a proposal from the European Union for a 15 percent cut in a "basket" of greenhouse gases by the year 2010 compared with 1990 levels. The European Union, Switzerland, and Norway were the only Annex I countries proposing specific targets. The United States, on the other hand, proposed flexible measures such as emissions trading, multiyear emissions budgets, borrowing of emissions from future budgets, and joint implementation with developing countries for credit. Australia and New Zealand also supported flexible measures. Other countries supported flexibility with regard to different levels of commitment. The oil-producing countries called for compensation for adverse impacts on developing countries arising from the implementation of response measures. AOSIS delegations responded that compensation should not concern lost revenues, but should address damage arising from temperature and sea-level rise.

Delegates continued to work on the main negotiating text compiled at AGBM-6 when they convened for their seventh session in August 1997. However, countries were still making new proposals, except for the eagerly awaited proposals for emissions reduction targets by the United States and Japan. There was a widespread sense that most of the progress achieved at this session was limited to a reduction in the number of proposals in the chair's negotiating text. The European Union's bid for a leadership role on strong targets, along with policies and measures, was frustrated by the near absence of support from the other developed countries and the G-77. A US Senate resolution demanding that the US negotiators dig in their heels to avoid any unilateral commitments by industrialized countries helped to put the brakes on the process. The G-77 and China responded to the Senate resolution by hardening their position and declaring that non-Annex I parties would accept no new commitments.

Drafting continued at AGBM-8 in October 1997. The G-77 and China, Japan, and the United States finally announced their proposals for targets, timetables, and options for reducing greenhouse gas emissions. The US proposal included a call for "meaningful participation" by developing countries, which did not help the negotiating climate. The G-77 and China used every opportunity to distance themselves from any attempts to draw developing countries into agreeing to anything that could be interpreted as new commitments.

Chair Raúl Estrada introduced a consolidated negotiating text that he hoped would facilitate completion of the protocol. By the end of the meeting, however, delegates could still not reach agreement on any of the alternatives presented in the chair's draft. Three alternatives remained on commitments for Annex I parties, two alternatives remained on the process for the establishment of Annex I party commitments, and all of the flexibility mechanisms, such as emissions trading, joint implementation, and so on, also continued to be disputed. As the end of the session approached with little hope of completing negotiations, Estrada suspended AGBM-8 and announced that it would reconvene for a day in Kyoto just prior to COP-3, where the protocol was supposed to be adopted.

Turning point 4

Turning point 4 was triggered by time pressure in both cases. Both the biosafety and the climate change negotiations were bound by COP decisions that established deadlines for the adoption of the agreements.

Biosafety

COP-4 of the CBD called for the final meeting of the BSWG to take place in early 1999, followed by an extraordinary meeting of the COP (ExCOP) to adopt the protocol. At the beginning of BSWG-5, Colombia offered to host the final meeting of the BSWG and the ExCOP in Cartagena in February 1999. Thus, in a sense, turning point 4 was triggered by the existence of an externally imposed deadline. Yet, other factors in both processes also played a role. Turning point 4 occurred at the end of the fifth session when delegates shifted their focus to achieving consensus. This change in focus was due in part to the fact that there was only one more negotiating session in Cartagena. In addition, this turning point was facilitated by the agreement on a single draft text, although many key issues were still to be resolved.

Climate change

In the climate change negotiations, turning point 4 had not yet taken place by the end of the final session of the AGBM. The chair announced that AGBM-8 would be reconvened on 30 November to continue discussions. He also said he would produce the text in the form of a protocol on that date. Therefore, with only one day left before COP-3 was set to convene on 1 December 1997, turning point 4 was triggered by time pressure.

Final bargaining/details

In cases where the inductive method is used, this phase tends to focus on the negotiation of outstanding core details of the agreement. If a deductive method is used in the earlier phases, there is agreement on a formula by this stage of the process and delegates focus more on the peripheral details. In both of these negotiations, an inductive process was used. Since delegates had not agreed on a basic framework or formula earlier on in the negotiating process, it was more likely that there would still be disagreement on core issues into the final bargaining/details phase.

The final bargaining/details phase of both of these negotiations took place at the final session of the negotiating committee and at the conference scheduled to adopt the protocol – the extraordinary meeting of the Conference of the Parties to the Convention on Biological Diversity and the third session of the Conference of the Parties to the Framework Convention on Climate Change.

Biosafety

The final bargaining/details phase started at the sixth session, which was held in Cartagena, Colombia, from 14 to 22 February 1999 and continued into the extraordinary meeting of the COP from 22 to 23 February 1999. At the start of the sixth session, Chair Koester noted that 30 of the 39 articles in the draft negotiating text were still unresolved. He identified the key concepts and core issues to be resolved: whether or not products derived from LMOs should be included in the scope of the protocol; whether or not contained use of LMOs should be included; and socio-economic considerations, the precautionary principle, liability and redress, and trade with non-parties. Negotiations were held in a number of informal groups and, when that failed, in a Friends of the Chair group. When the chair tried to introduce a new text on 18 February, the eve of the proposed negotiation deadline, he was met with extreme criticism. A number of delegates thought the chair was "trying to impose" an "unbalanced compromise." Others felt that the negotiations in the Friends of the Chair group were not transparent and that many countries were not represented in that group. They did not feel that the text should be thrust down delegates' throats without any discussion.

Therefore, when ExCOP opened on Monday, 22 February, there was still no protocol. Colombian Environment Minister Juan Mayr, the president of ExCOP, established a Working Group to consist of 10 spokespersons for the coalitions that had consolidated membership and positions: the Central and Eastern European states; the European Union; Central America and the Caribbean; the Miami Group (the world's major grain exporters minus the EU: Argentina, Australia, Canada, Chile, the United States, and Uruguay); the Like-minded Group (the majority of developing countries); and the Compromise Group (Japan, Mexico, Norway, South Korea, and Switzerland). The Working Group began its work on Monday night. It met all day Tuesday and into the early morning hours on Wednesday to continue negotiations in the hope of reaching consensus, but consensus remained elusive. At this point Mayr asked the various groups to give guidance on how to proceed. The European Union proposed a package that attempted to forge a middle ground on the core issues, but the Miami Group could not accept it. In the end, delegates agreed to suspend ExCOP and to hold interim meetings before its resumption to narrow differences between delegations.

Climate change

The final bargaining/details phase took place at the resumed session of AGBM-8 and in the Committee of the Whole at COP-3, in December 1997 in Kyoto, Japan. The remaining contentious issues included the number of gases to be included in the protocol, targets, timetables, policies and measures, the level of flexibility to be accorded to countries with economies in transition, and the question of voluntary commitments for developing countries. Three negotiating groups and numerous informal groups met throughout the first week and a half of the COP, including the weekend.

The final meeting of the Committee of the Whole began on Wednesday, 10 December at approximately 7:00 pm. The meeting was suspended to allow for distribution of the chair's final draft of the protocol and at 1:00 am delegates began an article-by-article review of the text, discussing the provisions related to quantified emissions limitation reduction objectives, emissions trading, and voluntary non-Annex I commitments at length. Throughout the night delegates worked to adopt all of the articles in the text. At times it appeared as though the negotiations would break down but finally, at 10:15 am, the Committee completed its work and agreed unanimously to submit the text of the protocol to the COP Plenary for formal adoption.

Turning point 5

More often than not, some type of time pressure, which forces delegates to make the necessary compromises to reach an agreement, affects this turning point. Sometimes this involves postponing consideration of a difficult issue and in other cases delegates are pressured into reaching an agreement on all issues.

Biosafety

ExCOP failed to reach turning point 5 and the negotiations reverted to the final bargaining/details phase. During the 11 months after suspension of ExCOP, its president, Juan Mayr, held three informal sessions to facilitate discussion on key outstanding issues and to enable the major coalitions to forge an agreement. The consultations focused on the issues of commodities, the protocol's relationship with other international agreements, the protocol's scope, and the application of the advance informed agreement procedure. These consultations achieved two important goals: they established a sense of ownership for the negotiating groups and they gradually clarified the core conflicts that bedeviled Cartagena. After a week of formal negotiations in Montreal in January 2000, ExCOP resumed and the major coalitions, with a lot of prodding from Mayr, were able to reach agreement and adopt the Cartagena Protocol on Biosafety at 4:50 am on Saturday, 29 January 2000. Thus, with a little help by postponing consideration of some issues, including liability, turning point 5, when it was finally reached, was based on final compromises that allowed the protocol to be adopted.

Climate change

The final turning point in the climate change negotiations was also triggered by internally motivated efforts towards compromise, particularly on the part of the chair. Throughout the final week of negotiations, the chair convened round-the-clock consultations aimed at reaching agreement on every article. Negotiations eventually concluded at 10:15 am on Thursday, 11 December, after an all-night session of the Committee of the Whole. The protocol was formally adopted on Thursday afternoon, 11 December 1997.

Ratification/implementation

In the more recent negotiations, the ratification/implementation phase has been characterized by the establishment of an interim mechanism so that governments can continue to discuss the issue and the agreement prior to its entry into force and the first Conference of the Parties. This was the case in both the biosafety negotiations and the climate change negotiations. The ExCOP in the biosafety negotiations adopted a decision establishing the Intergovernmental Committee for the Cartagena

Protocol on Biosafety. The first meeting of this committee was scheduled to meet in late 2000.

The climate change COP did not establish an interim body for the Kyoto Protocol, but asked the existing subsidiary bodies to the Convention – the Subsidiary Body for Implementation and the Subsidiary Body for Scientific and Technological Advice – to give guidance on a number of matters (including land use, land-use change, and forestry categories to be included as greenhouse gas sinks; definition of relevant principles, modalities, rules, and guidelines for emissions trading; elaboration of the concept of emissions reductions credits) and to discuss the programme of work for the meeting of the parties, once the Protocol entered into effect. The subsidiary bodies meet twice a year and have advanced the discussions on implementation of the Kyoto Protocol.

It is not certain yet when either of these protocols will enter into force. The Kyoto Protocol will enter into force on the ninetieth day after 55 parties to the Convention have ratified the Protocol, including Annex I countries, which accounted for 55 percent of total carbon dioxide emissions for 1990. The Cartagena Protocol will enter into force on the ninetieth day after 50 parties to the Convention have ratified it.

Process and outcome

Is there any discernible relationship between the process and the outcome in these two cases of post-UNCED negotiations? The correlation analysis in Chapter 6 did not provide many insights about the relationship between process and outcome. The only external characteristic that had any relationship with the outcome was the occurrence of a natural or human-induced disaster: when a disaster influenced the negotiating process, the ratification time tended to be longer. The only internal characteristic that had any relationship with the outcome was drafting: where the first draft of the agreement was prepared by the chair or the secretariat, the ratification time for the resulting agreement was shorter.

The biosafety and climate change negotiation processes were not precipitated by a disaster and the chair or the secretariat prepared the first draft, so the ratification time for the agreements may be shorter. However, because of the high economic stakes associated with these two protocols and the level of acrimony in the negotiating processes, it is unlikely that this correlation will hold.

It was also demonstrated in Chapter 6 that, when turning point 5 was brought about by postponing consideration of a difficult issue, 71 percent of the resulting agreements had a low Strength Index score (20 or below). The findings also suggested that, in 86 percent of the cases that postponed consideration of a difficult issue at the end of the negotiations, the ratification/implementation phase was characterized by inaction until the agreement entered into force. Neither the biosafety nor the climate change negotiations postponed consideration of a difficult issue. Rather, delegates worked late into the night to arrive at a final compromise. Thus, if these correlations continue to be accurate, the resulting Strength Index score should be above 20 and the ratification/implementation phase should not be characterized by inaction. This is indeed the case for the Kyoto Protocol, which has a Strength Index score of 24 (see Appendix I), and the resolution on interim arrangements ensured that the countries would meet to elaborate and operationalize the Protocol further, prior to its entry into force. The Cartagena Protocol, on the other hand, has a Strength Index score of only 16, although it does have a resolution establishing interim arrangements in the form of the Intergovernmental Committee for the Cartagena Protocol on Biosafety. However, it could be argued that the Cartagena Protocol did postpone consideration of difficult issues, including questions of liability, in order to reach an agreement.

Summary and conclusions

There have been a number of recent changes in the international environmental negotiating process that could affect the continued effectiveness and usefulness of the phased process model. In the process leading up to the UN Conference on Environment and Development and in the negotiations resulting from that watershed event, the international environmental negotiating process has been affected by the presence of more non-governmental actors, including NGOs, scientists, intergovernmental organizations, and UN agencies; more governmental actors; a number of emerging issues that are often more complicated and more interrelated than the subjects of negotiation in the 1970s and early 1980s; and the growing recognition of the relationship between environmental issues and the political, economic, and social context in which they should be addressed. The purpose of this chapter was to determine whether or not the model is effective in adapting to new developments and changing practices and continuing to explain and predict the evolution of ongoing and future negotiations. Two cases were used to test the model's adaptability: the negotiations to elaborate protocols to the Framework Convention on Climate Change and the Convention on Biological Diversity.

The model did provide a framework within which to analyze the process. This framework enables both practitioners and observers to look at the characteristics of a negotiating session and determine which phase the process is in, what its major focus is, and what events are necessary to move the negotiations closer to successful completion. By using the phased process model, it is possible to identify the characteristics of the phases and turning points in the biosafety and climate change negotiations as follows:

Precipitants: Concern about biological resources/economic concerns (biosafety); new scientific evidence (climate change).

Turning point 1: Decision of an intergovernmental body.

Issue definition: Within the framework of a UN agency/intergovernmental body/scientific body.

Turning point 2: Call for comments and/or proposals.

Statement of initial positions: Within a special negotiating group.

Turning point 3: Request for the chair or secretariat to prepare text.

Drafting/formula-building: Negotiations based on a text prepared by the chair and/or secretariat.

Turning point 4: Time pressure (both) and agreement on a single draft text (biosafety).

Final bargaining/details: Focus on outstanding core issues.

Turning point 5: Internally motivated efforts towards compromise (both) and, to some extent, postponement of consideration of difficult issues (biosafety).

Ratification/implementation: Meetings scheduled during the interim period until agreement enters into force.

The model has been useful in helping to analyze and test the progression of the phases in these two negotiating processes, but it can also be useful in assessing the path that future negotiations may take. The relationships that have been established between the early phases and the late phases in the process can be used to extrapolate trends that may guide the entire negotiation process. For example, the correlation analysis in Chapter 6 showed that there was a strong relationship between the characteristics of turning point 1, the issue definition phase, turning point 3, and turning point 4. In negotiations where the first turning point resulted from the decision of an intergovernmental body, the fourth turning point was characterized by the introduction of high-level officials, time pressure, or NGO/media pressure. In negotiations where the issue definition phase took place within the framework of a UN agency, the fourth turning point was also likely to be characterized by the introduction of high-level officials, time pressure, or NGO/media pressure. Likewise, in the four cases where turning point 3 was characterized by a request for the chair or the secretariat to prepare the negotiating text, turning point 4 resulted from either agreement on a single draft text, the introduction of high-level officials, time pressure, or NGO/media pressure. These trends definitely continued in these two post-UNCED cases.

Furthermore, some of the lessons learned by applying the phased process model may also help to ensure that the resulting agreements are stronger. For example, as negotiations enter the final bargaining/details phase with no agreement on a number of core issues, it is possible that one or more of these core issues will be postponed for "future" consideration. The model demonstrates that the resulting agreement may be more effective if governments work towards compromise language, even if it is weaker than either side may have preferred, yet incorporate provisions for renegotiation and amendment to adapt to changing circumstances in the future, perhaps even during the interim period before the agreement enters into force.

Notes

1. The Group of 77 now has 133 members but retains its name for historic reasons.
2. All of the information in this section about the negotiating process for these two protocols comes from the *Earth Negotiations Bulletin* coverage of the negotiations: for the biosafety negotiations, *Earth Negotiations Bulletin*, vol. 9, nos. 48, 67, 74, 85, 108, 117, and 137; for the climate change negotiations, *Earth Negotiations Bulletin*, vol. 12, nos. 22, 24, 27, 38, 39, 45, 55, 66, and 76. All issues can be found on the Internet at http://www.iisd.ca/.

8

Lessons learned for future multilateral environmental negotiations

Global environmental problems pose important diplomatic and legal challenges to the international community. The nature of these problems requires an unprecedented degree of international cooperation in terms of both scientific research and the harmonization of regulations that is achieved through negotiation. As Richard Benedick (1993, 222) notes:

[O]ne can regard contemporary environmental negotiations as the reflection of a modern society coping with new and dangerous uncertainties. Policymakers and diplomats confront the task of striking a balance between short-term costs and long-term but uncertain risks. Premature actions based on incomplete data and possibly erroneous scientific theories could impose unnecessary economic dislocations. But waiting for better evidence carries risks of larger and possible irreversible future damage and the need for even costlier countermeasures.

Environmental negotiations ... must reconcile complex and interconnected national interests and considerations – political, economic, commercial, technological, and scientific. In a sense the negotiators are designing international insurance policies: cooperative preventive actions among sovereign states. There are few formulas or guiding principles from other types of negotiations. Instead, there is a premium on innovation, flexibility, and pragmatic solutions.

Scientific uncertainty, the complexity of the issues, and the wide range of actors have shaped the negotiating process. Yet, given this rather complicated process, how can multilateral environmental negotiations be analyzed and explained? The purpose of this book was to develop a phased process model that can enable greater understanding of the process by which international environmental agreements are negotiated. By breaking down the negotiating process into a series of phases and turning points, it became easier to analyze the roles of different actors, the management of issues, the formation of groups and coalitions, and the art of consensus-building. Each phase features different actors, activities, forums, and purposes. By examining the relationships among different characteristics in the process, phases, turning points, and outcome, it is possible to reduce some of the complexities of multilateral negotiation to a more manageable level.

Trends and implications

During the development of the phased process model, six discernible phases and five associated turning points within the process of multilateral environmental negotiation were identified and explained: precipitants, issue definition, statement of initial positions, drafting/formula-building, final bargaining/details, and ratification/implementation. Each phase has its own characteristics, although the phase itself may not always be as well defined in practice as it is in theory. Even in cases of overlapping phases and backtracking, these phases can still be detected and can be useful in explaining and analyzing these complex multilateral negotiations.

After identifying and describing these phases and turning points, correlation analysis was used to determine if there are relationships among the phases and turning points and between the process and the outcome. In other words, is there anything that happens in the earlier phases of the negotiations that affects the later phases and is there anything in the process that may have an effect on the outcome? The overall goal of this analysis was to determine if and how one can adjust the process of multilateral negotiation to ensure stronger outcomes.

Relationship among phases

With regard to the relationship among the phases, two different negotiating paths or processes emerged. UN-centered negotiations are those where the United Nations or one of its specialized agencies initiates the negotiations and serves as the focal point throughout the negotiating process. State-centered negotiations are those where a state or group of states initiates the negotiating process and guides it through until there is agreement on a final treaty. There is no conclusive evidence that one of these paths is better or more effective than the other. The more recently negotiated environmental agreements, however, have taken the UN-centered path, rather than the state-centered one. In the 11 case studies, the more state-centered negotiations were the London Convention (1972), the MARPOL Protocol (1978), CITES (1973), and the Convention on Long-Range Transboundary Air Pollution (1979).

What are the implications of this apparent shift to UN-centered negotiations? Oran Young (1993, 250) points out that one of the major effects has been that international organizations can exercise considerable influence over the course of environmental negotiations, even when they are not key players during the negotiations themselves. Although international organizations have always been involved in environmental negotiations, they are now increasingly active in formulating negotiating texts, in some cases prior to the formal negotiations. However, international organizations, like states, may occasionally emerge as obstacles to the negotiation of environmental agreements. In some cases, they have exacerbated the collective action problems associated with such negotiations, rather than helped to solve them. In other cases, they have pushed for arrangements that seem attractive on paper but are unlikely to prove workable (Young 1993, 251; Susskind 1994, 33).

In most cases of multilateral environmental negotiations, the functions of the secretariat are carried out by one or more international organizations. As these organizations become more active in the negotiations, they run the risk of losing their status as an impartial mediator in the eyes of government delegates. Although the secretariat's major function is not always that of mediator, it can be in a position to perform functions that are similar to those of a third-party mediator. For example, it can supply objective information needed to clarify issues, summarize proceedings, and undertake systematic comparisons of key elements in national position papers. Such activities may help find common ground among the negotiators (Sjöstedt and Spector 1993, 299). The more active that a secretariat becomes, especially in the drafting of the agreement, the less effectively it is able to serve as an independent mediator. As a result, the role of mediator has to be played by a neutral government or by a highly respected individual acting in a personal capacity. This may be a positive or negative development, depending on the nature of the negotiations. Regardless of the outcome, this trend has a discernible influence on the dynamics of the negotiations.

In addition, in some cases the members of the secretariat/international organization may be looking out for their own best interests. The bureaucrats who staff international organizations have come to see themselves as having a direct stake in promoting the development and expansion of new international regimes under the convention that may fall under their auspices, often to protect or enhance their own careers. They have become actively involved in the negotiation process by forging strategic alliances with their counterparts in national governments, sponsoring and coordinating research, mobilizing technical expertise, raising public awareness, and playing a key leadership role (Hampson 1995, 349).

This shift towards UN-centered negotiations has also had a number of residual effects. For example, negotiations that take place within the framework of the UN system involve many of the same delegates. The implications of this are already apparent. As many of the same people are now negotiating multiple environmental agreements, they are able to capitalize on their past experiences, improve their negotiating techniques, and cite precedents in other negotiations to support their points. Non-traditional coalitions may also form as personal relationships begin to play a stronger role in the negotiations. The negative side, however, is that delegates support existing procedures and are often incapable of innovation or creative problem-solving. Furthermore, the easiest way to achieve consensus is often to revert to language agreed upon in previous negotiations. This may facilitate agreement, but it rarely advances the international response to a particular environmental problem.

Another effect is that developing countries are participating in environmental negotiations at a much higher level than ever before. The establishment of special funds within UN-sponsored negotiations enables greater participation by developing country delegates. The result is that the number of participants in the negotiations has grown (with well over 100 governments participating in any single negotiating session), the positions of developing countries are heard, and many negotiations are reduced to traditional North–South debates on financial assistance, technology transfer, economic development, and national sovereignty. This trend is positive in that developing countries have a greater degree of ownership in the resulting agreement and are more likely to ratify and implement it. The negative aspect is that many of these negotiations can get sidetracked away from the environmental problem on the table and towards a replay of North–South economic debates.

Finally, owing to the recent success of a number of UN-centered negotiations and the 1992 UN Conference on Environment and Development, there is a trend towards proliferation of negotiations. There have been far more multilateral environmental negotiations since 1992 than ever before. Calendars for environment- and development-related negotiations in the UN system have reached the point where nearly every single week of the year sees at least one sustainable development or environment-related conference, meeting, or specialized negotiating body. These have included negotiations on combating desertification and drought, climate change, biodiversity, the sustainable development of small island developing states, high seas fisheries, ozone depletion, hazardous wastes, population and development, tropical timber, land-based sources of marine pollution, human settlements, and the UN Commission on Sustainable Development, to name a few.

The implications are considerable. Many developing countries feel constrained by their lack of personnel adequately to cover the growing number of time-consuming negotiations abroad. The UN system itself is hard-pressed to service these negotiations adequately, given its current financial situation. In fact, because of budget constraints, several negotiations have been forced to meet without interpretation facilities or documents translated into all six working languages. And, with so many negotiations going on simultaneously, governments are now able to utilize a new delaying tactic, insisting that they cannot discuss a certain controversial subject in one forum until they see how it has been resolved in another. This only serves to prolong the process even further.

Process and outcome

From the discussion of the phases and turning points it appears that a great deal of attention is being given to procedure rather than negotiating tactics. Process and procedures are important elements in any negotiation; however, in multilateral environmental negotiations – especially UN-centered negotiations – procedures are actually the key elements. The complexity of these negotiations, as demonstrated by the large number of parties, the number of issues, the scientific uncertainty often surrounding these issues, and the variety of possible policy options to solve the environmental problem, demands that certain procedures be instituted to manage the negotiating process and ensure that the outcome is acceptable to all parties. This puts a lot of emphasis on procedures such as the use of deadlines, the use of drafting groups or asking the secretariat or chair to draft the agreement, and the entry of high-level officials into the process. As a result, the negotiations are guided from phase to phase through turning points that are often motivated by procedural events rather than agreements on formulas, stalemates, or details.

So, given this emphasis on procedure as well as the apparent relationship between some aspects of the process and the outcome, how do choices that negotiators make during the process influence the strength of the resulting agreement? In this analysis, the strength of the treaty was measured by the Strength Index, which was based on the actual language in the treaty, as well as on the nature of the ratification/implementation phase. Three of the phases and turning points had strong relationships with the outcome: statement of initial positions, final bargaining/details, and turning point 5. When the statement of initial positions phase took place within the context of the work of a UN agency working group or overlapped with the issue definition phase, the ratification/implementation phase was characterized by no action until the agreement entered into force. If the statement of initial positions phase took place within the context of meetings of an intergovernmental group established specifically for the negotiation of a convention, there was a greater chance that there would be an interim mechanism for meetings after the agreement was concluded and prior to its entry into force. In general, the outcome is considered to be stronger if there was some sort of interim mechanism for meetings since this serves to keep the issue and the convention in the forefront and, in some cases, tends to speed up the ratification process. In fact, in the three cases that included an interim mechanism for meetings (Montreal Protocol, Convention on Climate Change, and Convention on Biological Diversity), the average length of the ratification/implementation phase was 23 months, rather than the 32-month average of the 11 cases in the sample. Therefore, one could extrapolate that, if governments decide to set up an intergovernmental negotiating process early enough to include sufficient time for a quality statement of initial positions phase, the resulting convention may be stronger, at least in terms of its ratification time and the presence of an interim mechanism for meetings.

In the four of the five cases where the final bargaining/details phase focused on outstanding peripheral details in the final agreement (core issues and/or a formula had already been agreed upon in the previous phase), the final turning point was brought about by postponing consideration of a difficult issue. In all five of these cases, the ratification/implementation phase was characterized by inaction until the agreement entered into force. So, in cases where the process seemed to use a formula/detail approach (as described by Zartman and Berman 1982), the ratification/implementation phase tended to be weaker since no further action was taken until the agreement entered into force. This indicates that the inductive method of putting together an agreement in a piecemeal fashion may be more successful in cases of multilateral environmental negotiation. Yet, this is only one possible measurement of outcome and, since this sequence of events had no noticeable relationship to the Strength Index, it is possible that there might be different results if other measurements of outcome were used.

The only phase or turning point that had a significant relationship to the Strength Index was the final turning point. When turning point 5 was brought about by postponing consideration of a difficult issue, 71 percent of the cases had a Strength Index score of 22 or below out of a possible 45. In the three cases where turning point 5 was brought about by a vote or by internally motivated efforts towards compromise, the resulting agreements were among the strongest, with Strength Index scores above 26. These findings suggest that postponing consideration of a difficult issue towards the end of the process may result in a weaker agreement than when time pressure is the major factor. This relationship has two implications. First, postponing consideration of a difficult issue may decrease the substantive value of the agreement and, thus, make it weaker. Second, as time pressure at the end of the negotiating process is manifested in terms of a vote (consensus is impossible) or consensus brought about by delegates' desire to avoid failure, governments may be forced to make compromises that they would not have made given more time. So, in effect, time pressure may prevent the opportunity to weaken an agreement during the final phases of the negotiating process.

Although these findings have merit, this is not to say that if the outcome were measured in another way (such as speed of ratification, implementation record, or amendment record) the results would be the same. For example, if the strength of the outcome were measured by the length of time between adoption of the agreement and its entry into force, it is interesting to note that the four agreements with the shortest ratification time (less than two years)[1] were all characterized by the fact that turning point 1 was the result of a decision by an intergovernmental body and the statement of initial positions phase took place in a special negotiating group. Three of the four agreements with the longest ratification time (more than three years)[2] had certain characteristics of state-centered negotiations: turning point 1 was characterized by the initiative of a state or a group of states, the issue definition phase was characterized by discussion of a draft agreement (usually drafted by a state or group of states), turning point 5 was the result of postponing consideration of a difficult issue, and the ratification/implementation phase featured no action until the agreement entered into force. There is no correlation whatsoever between the time the convention took to enter into force and the Strength Index. These preliminary findings are fairly consistent with the earlier ones, measuring the outcome by the Strength Index and the ratification/implementation phase, and may also indicate that UN-centered negotiations may result in more rapid entry into force of the treaty. Needless to say, in theory, the sooner a treaty enters into force, the sooner it will be implemented and have a positive impact on the state of the planet.

Lessons learned for future negotiations

So, based on the development of the phased process model of multilateral environmental negotiation, what have we learned about the choices that negotiators make during the process that can influence the outcome? The model serves as a useful tool to help negotiators navigate the complex process of multilateral environmental negotiations, by providing a number of insights and observations that may help diplomats and other practitioners anticipate and avoid unnecessary pitfalls.

(1) If negotiations are influenced by the occurrence of a natural or human-induced disaster early in the process, ratification time tends to be longer. Governments should remember that, even once the causes and effects of a particular disaster fade from memory, another similar disaster or crisis could happen at any time. Thus, it is better to ratify the agreement and begin to implement it, rather than let complacency take over.

(2) Do not underestimate the importance of the issue definition phase. This phase not only provides government delegates with the opportunity to explore the scientific and technical dimensions of the issue, but also presents an opportunity for delegates to get to know each other and build trust. It is common for governments to send scientific and technical experts to the issue definition sessions and then send their diplomats to the first negotiating session. This defeats both potential benefits of this phase – educating diplomats and building trust. Thus, governments should encourage their diplomats who will be negotiating the treaty to participate in this phase.

(3) When the first draft of the agreement is prepared by the chair or the secretariat, the ratification time for the final agreement is shorter. This may be because, when the chair or the secretariat drafts the agreement, no one state or group of states has ownership. It may take longer to cultivate a sense of group ownership of the final treaty; once it is established, however, governments have a greater incentive to ratify the treaty as it is a testimonial to the success of the negotiations. Thus, although the negotiating time may take longer, it may be better in the long run to request the chair or the secretariat to prepare the first draft based on comments and proposals submitted by governments.

(4) When the negotiating time is shorter, the provisions in the resulting agreement are generally stronger. There are several possible explanations for this. Negotiations may take less time when there is greater agreement on the need to develop an international treaty to address a specific environmental problem. Second, there may be greater consensus in the scientific community about the causes and effects of the problem, thus eliminating the use of scientific uncertainty as a delaying tactic. Finally, a deadline may be established early in the process and, thus, governments, the secretariat, and the bureau are able to organize their strategies with this deadline in mind. When these factors are not present, governments should look for other mechanisms that will limit the negotiating time and improve the chances of a stronger agreement.

(5) If there are still outstanding core issues towards the end of the process, it is better to resolve them (even if the final compromise text is weak) rather than postpone further consideration of the issue. Agreements where a last-minute compromise is reached on outstanding core issues (turning point 5) are generally stronger than agreements where important issues are deferred. Therefore, if an issue proves difficult to resolve, include weak language in the text but also establish a mechanism for the negotiators to return to the table and re-address this issue after adoption of the agreement or ideally even before its entry into force.

(6) A recent trend in multilateral environmental negotiations is the establishment of mechanisms so that governments can meet during the interim period before the agreement enters into force. These meetings have important, positive implications for international environmental management as they keep the international dialogue alive, provide a forum for debating difficult issues, and may even facilitate the adoption of amendments or protocols that strengthen the agreement. This type of mechanism has proven its usefulness in the Montreal Protocol and FCCC regimes. Therefore, whenever possible, this trend should continue.

(7) Time pressure inevitably affects the negotiating process in turning points 4 and 5 and the final bargaining/details phase, but, if managed properly, deadlines can be beneficial to the process. Setting clear deadlines early in the process assists governments in preparing their negotiating strategies. The establishment of a deadline during the course of the process may strengthen the language in an agreement by putting greater pressure on blocking coalitions to compromise. On the other hand, deadlines may serve to weaken the final text of the treaty, since delegates may compromise integrity in exchange for last-minute consensus. Therefore, governments must be careful in how they use deadlines because it may not always work to their advantage.

(8) There are two approaches to negotiating an agreement: deductive and inductive. These approaches usually emerge during the drafting/ formula-building phase and continue until the agreement is adopted. The inductive process puts an agreement together paragraph-by-paragraph, often with no overriding framework. In the deductive process, delegates first negotiate a formula or the general principles that form the basis of the agreement and then tackle the implementing details. The inductive method of putting together an agreement in a piecemeal fashion tends to be more successful in cases of multilateral environmental negotiation. This may be because the complexities inherent in multilateral environmental nego-

tiation (multiple parties, roles, and issues) make agreement on an overarching formula nearly impossible to achieve.

(9) Although non-governmental actors appear to have had a minimal impact on the negotiations, governments should continue to encourage their participation in the negotiating process. NGOs and scientists often play a crucial role in bringing environmental issues to the attention of the world community. They usually have better technical expertise than many governments and, thus, can assist and clarify the issues in the issue definition phase. During the negotiations themselves, governments can benefit from updated scientific, technical, and human-focused reports prepared by the non-governmental community. As some governments have found, a non-governmental perspective may shine new light on a contentious issue. The participation of NGOs and the scientific community also serves to increase the transparency of the negotiating process. When there is greater transparency, governments are held accountable for their actions. Thus, the resulting agreements may be stronger than in cases where governments work in a vacuum.

(10) Finally, one of the most important ways for governments to improve the negotiation of environmental agreements is to keep abreast of the phases and the process. On many occasions governments enter the process late and try to reopen text where consensus may have already been achieved. This moves the negotiations backward instead of forward, prolongs the negotiating process, and thus is likely to weaken the resulting agreement. Another common problem is when delegates continue to state their government's general positions well into the drafting/formula-building phase, rather than commenting specifically on the immediate topic of discussion, usually drafting proposals. This also tends to slow the process down. Governments that have an interest in a particular environmental issue should try to participate in the negotiations from the very beginning and structure their comments so they are appropriate to the specific topic or text under discussion as well as the current phase. The model may serve as a useful guideline for this purpose.

Concluding thoughts on multilateral environmental negotiation

The process by which environmental agreements are negotiated in the international arena is not a perfect one. There is no shortage of scholars and practitioners who have commented on the faults and the lack of effectiveness of multilateral environmental negotiation. One of the most prevalent areas of criticism about the process is its duration. Lars Björkbom (1988) comments that many venues and paths have to be used to bring a problem to the attention of national decision makers and the international community. Once the problem is addressed in the international arena, it takes a long time to reach agreement, especially in cases where concrete, often expensive actions are presupposed to be taken by the parties to an agreement. Björkbom also points out that one of the risks of the slow pace of the work of multilateral diplomacy in the field of the environment is that it might delay action until such time as the problems involved are already beyond control.

Lawrence Susskind (1994) wholeheartedly agrees. In addition to the duration of the negotiation process, he argues that international environmental negotiations reinforce the tendency to seek lowest-common-denominator agreements, since most international environmental treaties impose the same requirements on all signatories. Other flaws in the negotiation of international environmental treaties, according to Susskind, include neglect of available scientific and technical information and the incorporation of requirements that turn out to be technically infeasible or illogical. Furthermore, the ad hoc nature of the "convention–protocol approach" to treaty-making fails to come to grips with important negotiation problems. It actually encourages countries to misrepresent or exaggerate their interests as part of their bargaining strategy and focuses insufficient attention on building informal agreements and coalitions prior to formal meetings. Susskind (1994, 34) also argues that "when negotiators are in the business of trading concessions (rather than engaging in a search for trades that maximizes joint gains), they must keep checking back with their leaders at home. Very little creativity is possible under these circumstances."

Beyond the actual negotiations, another concern about the process is that the ratification of treaties takes time. Peter Sand (1990) points out that the consequence of this is that the effectiveness of international agreements is deliberately delayed. Unlike national laws – which can fix their own dates of application – multilateral treaties can be brought into force, or amended, only after they are ratified by a specified number of signatories. The purpose of this practice is to ensure a measure of reciprocity and to avoid situations in which initial compliance by a few diligent parties creates disproportionate benefits to the "free-riders" remaining outside the treaty. Setting a threshold number, however, also delays implementation to the speed of the "slowest boat in the convoy."

Along these lines, Erwan Fouéré (1988) argues that, although some progress has been made, the response from governments in general is far from satisfactory. Whether because of a lack of political will or a lack of resources, or simply because they have been daunted by the very complexity of the situation, governments have yet to show the degree of determination and will to cooperate that is so necessary if environmental problems are to be dealt with adequately. This is still the case today. The increasing tendency of governments and elected leaders to delay the implementation of much-needed long-term solutions has led to short-term improvised decision-making, best described as crisis management. Governments often find it more convenient to hide behind scientific uncertainty in order to avoid taking decisions of a preventive or even curative nature.

These and other criticisms of the process have merit, but environmental negotiation does serve a purpose. Although the process may take a lot of time, it keeps the issue on the international agenda and ensures that there is a forum for discussion and, it is to be hoped, local, national, and regional action that will supplement any international treaty. Although it is not always clear if an agreement has any positive effect on the natural environment, the negotiating process has a number of residual effects. Contacts made among government delegates during negotiations may lead to bilateral agreements for technology cooperation or financial assistance for environmental protection. Many small-scale, local, or bilateral projects and programs may emerge from contacts made during the negotiations and these may ultimately have a greater impact on the environment than any multilateral treaty.

This analysis of the process has filled in one more piece of the complex puzzle of multilateral environmental negotiations. As in the mating of elephants, closer study has made the once mysterious process of gestation more comprehensible. Until there are advances in genetic engineering (or the development of new methods for international environmental management), the birth of an elephant (or a treaty) will still take approximately 23 months and the health of the offspring cannot be guaranteed.

Notes

1. These four agreements are the Convention on the Conservation of Antarctic Marine Living Resources, the International Tropical Timber Agreement, the Convention on Climate Change, and the Convention on Biological Diversity.
2. These four agreements are the London Convention, MARPOL, the Convention on Long-Range Transboundary Air Pollution, and the Basel Convention.

Appendix I

The Strength Index

The Strength Index was developed to measure the theoretical strength of a legally binding international environmental agreement. The list of 12 variables was developed in consultation with academics and diplomats who have been involved in negotiating environmental treaties, in addition to a review of relevant literature. Each of the agreements was rated on the basis of its contents, not on its implementation record or evaluations of its effectiveness. The twelfth variable, information about amendments or protocols adopted since the treaty was ratified, was included to measure if the treaty continues to be adjusted, modified, or strengthened over time to respond to increased scientific certainty and changing attitudes. Certain variables have been given more weight than others (see table I.1). These measure the criteria directly relating to environmental protection or natural resources management, rather than the administration of the convention or protocol. Although the administrative provisions may make the treaty stronger by facilitating the implementation of the agreement, they are one step removed from the provisions that directly address the actual objectives of the agreement.

1. Provisions for a secretariat/commission

Provision for an administrative body is necessary to promote the effective implementation of the convention. An independent secretariat or commission was considered to be superior to an existing organization because

Table I.1 The Strength Index

Variable	Weighting
1. Provisions for a secretariat/ commission	(0) None (2) Existing organization (3) Independent secretariat/commission
2. Provisions for reporting by parties	(0) None (2) No reporting dates specified (4) Regularly scheduled reporting
3. Provisions for reservations to parts of conventions or annexes	(0) Yes (2) No
4. Provisions for the secretariat to monitor states' compliance	(0) No (1) Somewhat (3) Yes
5. Mechanisms for dealing with non-compliance	(0) None or to be determined (1) Each party can determine its own mechanisms (3) Report to the commission – no specified action (5) Recommendation or imposition of trade restrictions and/or sanctions
6. Provisions for observations or inspections	(0) None or to be determined (2) Observations/inspections by individual parties (4) Observations/inspections by secretariat or independent authority
7. Dispute settlement mechanisms (highest option recommended)	(0) None or to be determined (1) Negotiation by parties (2) Settlement by commission/secretariat (3) Settlement by the International Court of Justice or arbitrator
8. Provisions for amendments, protocols, or annexes (not including amendments to annexes)	(0) None (2) Commission or secretariat decisions (3) Vote by parties followed by ratification or acceptance by governments (4) Vote by parties, ratification not necessary, in some cases
9. Explicit performance standards	(0) None (2) Procedural only (4) Procedural and measurable
10. Liability provisions	(0) None (1) Recommended for future elaboration (3) Present in text
11. Financial resources, arrangements, or mechanisms	(0) None (3) Recommended for future elaboration (5) Present in text
12. If the agreement has been in force for 5 years or more, have the parties adopted protocols or amendments?	(0) No protocols or amendments (1) Protocols and/or amendments under negotiation (2) Amendments but no protocols (3) Protocols (and amendments) (5) Protocols (and/or amendments) with measurable performance standards

it would not run the risk of being buried under existing bureaucratic problems. An independent organization – or at least one that is supported administratively by another organization but guaranteed a certain degree of independence – has the ability to focus totally on the convention.

2. Provisions for reporting by parties

Provisions in a convention that promote reporting and exchange of data can formalize the scientific input and establish the basis for future consensus on protocols or amendments that will strengthen the agreement and improve the environment. Regularly scheduled reporting is considered to be superior to ad hoc reporting since it serves to encourage governments to report back to the Conference of the Parties and it holds parties responsible for fulfilling their obligations under the convention.

3. Provisions for reservations to parts of conventions or annexes

Provisions for reservations enable more countries to sign and ratify a treaty; however, they also have a negative impact. As a result of reservations, not all parties are held responsible for implementing all measures contained in the treaty. This has the potential seriously to limit the effectiveness or strength of the treaty. Therefore, an agreement is considered to be stronger if there are no provisions for reservations.

4. Provisions for the secretariat to monitor states' compliance

In many environmental negotiations, states are wary of being monitored by other states or an independent body such as the secretariat. However, without the existence of some monitoring body, states cannot really be held responsible for fulfilling their obligations under the treaty. If the secretariat or another independent body is given this power, there is a greater chance that parties will better implement the convention.

5. Mechanisms for dealing with non-compliance

Although the effect of non-compliance with different provisions in different conventions varies, a convention with no mechanisms for dealing with non-compliance does not have the ability to "punish" the transgressors. A treaty can deal with non-compliance in a number of different ways, including decisions by parties on a case-by-case basis, a report to the commission or Conference of the Parties, or the recommendation or imposition of trade restrictions and/or sanctions. The last method is being challenged by free trade advocates, but it remains a strong mechanism for improving compliance.

6. Provisions for observations or inspections

Provisions for observations or inspections may not be relevant in all cases; however, they do increase a party's accountability under the convention. In some cases, such observations or inspections can be done by parties, but a stronger option is for observations or inspections to be undertaken by an independent authority.

7. Dispute settlement mechanisms (highest option recommended)

Many international environmental agreements list a number of options for dispute settlement, including negotiation by the parties of the dispute, settlement by the commission or secretariat, or settlement by an arbitrator or the International Court of Justice. Although these provisions may never come into use, their presence has the potential to improve both the administration of the convention as well as its implementation.

8. Provisions for amendments, protocols, or annexes

Provisions for amending a convention can be the key to a strong international environmental agreement. At the time of negotiation, there may still be scientific uncertainty or skepticism about the nature of a particular environmental problem, leading to the adoption of a less than optimal agreement. As scientific knowledge increases or the implications of the environmental problem become more apparent, there may be a need to change some of the provisions of the agreement. The easier it is to strengthen the agreement through amendments or protocols, the more likely it is that governments will take the initiative to do so.

9. Explicit performance standards

Another characteristic of a strong treaty is the presence of performance standards, in the form of emissions reduction targets, timetables for emissions reduction, etc. Many conventions – especially framework conventions – do not contain such performance standards and, thus, may not be as effective in improving the environment or conserving natural resources.

10. Liability provisions

Questions of liability are not relevant to all environmental issues, but there are cases where the action of one party may have a negative effect on the natural environment of another, particularly where pollution and wastes are concerned. If a convention explicitly sets forth procedures for the assessment of liability and the settlement of disputes, it can serve to prevent environmental damage, thus increasing the treaty's effectiveness and strength.

11. Financial resources, arrangements, or mechanisms

In many cases, developing countries do not have the capacity to implement a convention effectively. Although this could prevent them from signing and ratifying a convention, it more likely will impede the successful implementation of the agreement by developing countries. The provision of financial resources for the purposes of implementing environmental agreements has led to a marked North–South fissure in recent years. Nevertheless, the presence of guidelines for arrangements for the provision of financial resources or the establishment of a financial mechanism should increase compliance by developing countries. In some cases, agreement cannot be reached on financial issues and instead the convention contains recommendations for the future establishment of a financial mechanism. Although this decreases the potential strength of the convention at the time of entry into force, the treaty is still stronger than if there is no reference to financial provisions at all.

12. Adoption of protocols or amendments

This variable relates to the "life" of the agreement: have the parties adopted protocols or amendments? The scientific uncertainties and the increasingly preventive objectives of environmental negotiations dictate a pragmatic and flexible approach. If the agreement continues to adapt to changing circumstances and is improved over time, it is stronger than an agreement that remains static. Therefore, the adoption of protocols or amendments that strengthen the convention contributes to the overall effectiveness of the agreement.

The next section details the information gathered to score each case study on the variables of the Strength Index.[1] The scores are shown in table I.2. The ratification, amendment, and protocol information was provided by the United Nations Treaty Section and/or the convention secretariats. The citation of articles and paragraphs is directly from the

Table I.2 Strength Index coding

Strength Index	LDC	MAR	CIT	MED	TAP	CCA	ITTA	OZO	BAS	FCCC	CBD	KYO	CAR
							Cases[a]						
1. Secretariat	2	2	2.5[b]	2	2	3	3	2	2	3	2	2	2
2. Reporting	2	4	4	2	2	4	4	4	4	4	2	2	2
3. Reservations	2	0	0	2	0	2	2	2	2	2	2	2	2
4. Monitoring	0	3	3	0	0	3	0	0	0	1	0	3	0
5. Compliance	1	5	5	0	0	5	0	5	3	0	0	0	0
6. Inspections	2	2	0	0	0	4	0	0	0	0	0	0	0
7. Disputes	0	3	3	3	1	3	2	3[c]	3	3	3[c]	3[c]	3[c]
8. Amendment	3	3	4	3	3	3	3	4	4	3	3	3	2
9. Standards	4	4	4	0	0	0	0	4	0	0	0	4	0
10. Liability	1	0	0	1	0	0	0	0	1	0	0	0	0
11. Finance	0	0	0	3	0	5	5	3	3	5	5	5	5
12. Protocols	3	3	2	5	5	0	0	5	3	5	3	0	0
Total score	20	29	27.5	21	13	32	19	32	25	26	20	24	16

a. Key to abbreviations of treaties:
LDC Convention on the Prevention of Marine Pollution by Dumping of Wastes and Other Matters
MAR 1978 Protocol to the International Convention for the Prevention of Pollution from Ships
CIT Convention on International Trade in Endangered Species
MED Convention for the Protection of the Mediterranean Sea against Pollution
TAP Convention on Long-Range Transboundary Air Pollution
CCA Convention on the Conservation of Antarctic Marine Living Resources
ITTA International Tropical Timber Agreement
OZO Montreal Protocol on Substances That Deplete the Ozone Layer
BAS Basel Convention on the Control of Transboundary Movements of Hazardous Wastes and Their Disposal
FCCC Framework Convention on Climate Change
CBD Convention on Biological Diversity
KYO Kyoto Protocol to the Framework Convention on Climate Change
CAR Cartagena Protocol on Biosafety
   The Convention establishes an independent secretariat that can be assisted by existing intergovernmental or non-governmental organizations.
b. Part of the Framework Convention.
c.

239

text of each convention, which can be found in *International Legal Materials* or at the United Nations Treaty Section.

The basis for Strength Index scores

1972 Convention on the Prevention of Marine Pollution by Dumping of Wastes and Other Matters (London Convention)

1. Provisions for a secretariat/commission: Article 14.2

   "The Contracting Parties shall designate a competent Organisation existing at the time of that meeting to be responsible for secretariat duties in relation to this Convention."

2. Provision for reporting by parties: Article 6.4

   "Each Contracting Party, directly or through a Secretariat established under a regional agreement, shall report to the Organisation, and where appropriate to other Parties, the information specified in sub-paragraphs c and d of paragraph 1 above, and the criteria, measures and requirements it adopts in accordance with paragraph 3 above. The procedure to be followed and the nature of such reports shall be agreed by the Parties in consultation."

3. Provisions for reservations to parts of convention or annexes: none.
4. Provisions for the secretariat to monitor states' compliance: none.
5. Mechanisms for dealing with non-compliance: Article 7.2

   "Each party shall take in its territory appropriate measures to prevent and punish conduct in contravention of the provisions of this Convention."

6. Provisions for observations or inspections: Article 7.3

   "The Parties agree to cooperate in the development of procedures for the effective application of this Convention particularly on the high seas, including procedures for the reporting of vessels and aircraft observed dumping in contravention of the Convention."

7. Dispute settlement mechanisms: Article 11

   "The Contracting Parties shall at their first consultative meeting consider procedures for the settlement of disputes concerning the interpretation and application of this Convention."

8. Provisions for amendments, protocols or annexes: Article 15

"At meetings of the Contracting Parties called in accordance with Article XIV amendments to this Convention may be adopted by a two-thirds majority of those present. An amendment shall enter into force for the Parties which have accepted it on the sixtieth day after two-thirds of the Parties shall have deposited an instrument of acceptance of the amendment with the Organisation."

9. Explicit measurable performance standards:
   Annex I: list of wastes or other matter whose dumping is prohibited
   Annex II: list of wastes and other matter whose dumping requires a prior special permit
   Annex III: provisions to be considered in establishing criteria governing the issue of permits for the dumping of matter at sea
10. Liability provisions: Article 10

"In accordance with the principles of international law regarding state responsibility for damage to the environment of other States or to any other area of the environment, caused by dumping of wastes and other matter of all kinds, the Contracting Parties undertake to develop procedures for the assessment of liability and the settlement of disputes regarding dumping."

11. Financial resources, arrangements, or mechanisms: none.
12. Protocols and/or amendments:
   1978 amendments concerning settlement of disputes and incineration
   1980 amendments to Annexes
   1989 amendments to Annex III
   1993 amendments to ban the disposal of low-level radioactive wastes, ocean incineration, and the ocean dumping of industrial wastes
   1996 protocol prohibiting the dumping of wastes or other matter with the exception of those listed in Annex 1

1973 International Convention for the Prevention of Pollution from Ships as modified by the Protocol of 1978

1. Provisions for a secretariat/commission: not specified in a single article, but it is implied that the Intergovernmental Maritime Consultative Organization will perform secretariat functions.
2. Provision for reporting by parties: Article 11.1

"The Parties to the Convention undertake to communicate to the Organization:
(a) the text of laws, orders, decrees and regulations ...
(f) an annual statistical report, in a form standardized by the Organization, of penalties actually imposed for infringement of the present Convention."

3. Provisions for reservations to parts of convention or annexes: Article 14.1

"A State may at the time of signing, ratifying, accepting, approving or acceding to the present Convention declare that it does not accept any one or all of Annexes III, IV and V (hereinafter referred to as 'Optional Annexes') of the present Convention."

4. Provisions for the secretariat to monitor states' compliance: Article 6.4

"Upon receiving such evidence, the Administration so informed shall investigate the matter, and may request the other Party to furnish further or better evidence of the alleged contravention. If the Administration is satisfied that sufficient evidence is available to enable proceedings to be brought in respect of the alleged violation, it shall cause such proceedings to be taken in accordance with its law as soon as possible."

5. Mechanisms for dealing with non-compliance: Article 4.1

"Any violation of the requirements of the present Convention shall be prohibited and sanctions shall be established therefore under the law of the Administration of the ship concerned wherever the violation occurs."

6. Provisions for observations or inspections: Article 5.2

"A ship required to hold a certificate in accordance with the provisions of the Regulations is subject, while in the ports or off-shore terminals under the jurisdiction of a Party, to inspection by officers duly authorized by that Party."

7. Dispute settlement mechanisms: Article 10

"Any dispute between two or more Parties to the Convention concerning the interpretation or application of the present Convention shall, if settlement by negotiation between the Parties involved has not been possible, and if these Parties do not otherwise agree, be submitted upon request of any of them to arbitration as set out in Protocol II to the present Convention."

8. Provisions for amendments, protocols, or annexes: Article 16.1(d) and (f)

"[A]mendments shall be adopted by a two-thirds majority of only the Parties to the Convention present and voting."

"[A]n amendment to an Article of the Convention shall be deemed to have been accepted on the date on which it is accepted by two-thirds of the Parties, the combined merchant fleets of which constitute not less than fifty percent of the gross tonnage of the world's merchant fleet."

9. Explicit measurable performance standards:
   Annex I: Regulations for the Prevention of Pollution by Oil
   Annex II: Regulations for the Control of Pollution by Noxious Liquid Substances in Bulk
   Annex III: Regulations for the Prevention of Pollution by Harmful Substances Carried by Sea in Packaged Forms, or in Freight Containers, Portable Tanks or Road and Rail Tank Wagons
   Annex IV: Regulations for the Prevention of Pollution by Sewage from Ships
   Annex V: Regulations for the Prevention of Pollution by Garbage from Ships
10. Liability provisions: none.
11. Financial resources, arrangements, or mechanisms: none.
12. Protocols and/or amendments: numerous amendments to both the treaty and the annexes since 1984. Three protocols have been adopted, one making it an explicit requirement to report incidents involving discharge into the sea of harmful substances in packaged form, a second addressing arbitration procedures and a third on the prevention of air pollution from ships.

1973 Convention on International Trade in Endangered Species

1. Provisions for a secretariat/commission: Article 12

"Upon entry into force of the present Convention, a Secretariat shall be provided by the Executive Director of the United Nations Environment Programme. To the extent and in the manner he considers appropriate, he may be assisted by suitable inter-governmental or non-governmental inter-national or national agencies and bodies technically qualified in protection, conservation and management of wild fauna and flora."

2. Provision for reporting by parties: Article 8.7

"Each Party shall prepare periodic reports on its implementation of the present Convention and shall transmit to the Secretariat:
(a) an annual report containing a summary of the information specified in sub-paragraph (b) of paragraph 6 of this Article; and
(b) a biennial report on legislative, regulatory and administrative measures taken to enforce the provisions of the present Convention."

3. Provisions for reservations to parts of convention or annexes: Article 23

"1. The provisions of the present Convention shall not be subject to general reservations. Specific reservations may be entered in accordance with the provisions of this Article and Articles XV and XVI.
2. Any State may, on depositing its instrument of ratification, acceptance, approval or accession, enter a specific reservation with regard to:
(a) any species included in Appendix I, II or III; or
(b) any parts or derivatives specified in relation to a species included in Appendix III."

4. Provisions for secretariat to monitor states' compliance: Article 12.1

"(d) to study the reports of the Parties and to request from Parties such further information with respect thereto as it deems necessary to ensure implementation of the present Convention."

5. Mechanisms for dealing with non-compliance: Article 8.1

"The Parties shall take appropriate measures to enforce the provisions of the present Convention and to prohibit trade in specimens in violation thereof. These shall include measures:
(a) to penalize trade in, or possession of, such specimens, or both; and
(b) to provide for the confiscation or return to the State of export of such specimens."

6. Provisions for observations or inspections: none.
7. Dispute settlement mechanisms: Article 18

"1. Any dispute which may arise between two or more Parties with respect to the interpretation or application of the provisions of the present Convention shall be subject to the negotiation between the Parties involved in the dispute.

2. If the dispute cannot be resolved in accordance with paragraph 1 of this Article, the Parties may, by mutual consent, submit the dispute to arbitration."

8. Provisions for amendments, protocols, or annexes: Articles 15, 16, and 17

   Article 15 deals with amendments to Appendices I and II: amendments shall be adopted by a two-thirds majority of the parties present and voting. "Amendments adopted at a meeting shall enter into force 90 days after that meeting for all Parties except those which make a reservation in accordance with paragraph 3 of this Article." It also sets up methods for amendment between meetings of the parties.

   Article 16 deals with amendments to Appendix III: any party can submit a list of species and it shall take effect 90 days after the date of such communication.

   Article 17 deals with amendments to the Convention: "An extraordinary meeting of the Parties shall be convened by the Secretariat on the written request of at least one-third of the Parties to consider and adopt amendments to the present Convention. Such amendments shall be adopted by a two-thirds majority of Parties present and voting ... An amendment shall enter into force for the Parties which have accepted it 60 days after two-thirds of the Parties have deposited an instrument of acceptance."

9. Explicit measurable performance standards: Articles 2, 3, 4, and 5

   Article 2 explains the fundamental principles of the Convention and what species should be contained in each appendix. Appendix I includes all species threatened by extinction which are or may be affected by trade. Appendix II includes species that are not necessarily threatened with extinction but may become so. Appendix III includes all species which any party identifies as being subject to regulation within its jurisdiction.

   Article 3 explains the regulation of trade in specimens of species included in Appendix I.

   Article 4 explains the regulation of trade in specimens of species included in Appendix II.

   Article 5 explains the regulation of trade in specimens of species included in Appendix III.

10. Liability provisions: none.

11. Financial resources, arrangements, or mechanisms: none.

12. Protocols and/or amendments:

    1979 Bonn amendments

    1983 Gaborone amendments

    Amendments to the annexes containing lists of protected species

1976 Barcelona Convention for the Protection of the Mediterranean Sea against Pollution

1. Provisions for a secretariat/commission: Article 13

   "The Contracting Parties designate the United Nations Environment Programme as responsible for carrying out the following secretariat functions ..."

2. Provision for reporting by parties: Article 20

   "The Contracting Parties shall transmit to the Organization reports on the measures adopted in implementation of this Convention and of Protocols to which they are Parties, in such form and at such intervals as the meetings of the Contracting Parties may determine."

3. Provisions for reservations to parts of convention or annexes: none.
4. Provisions for the secretariat to monitor states' compliance: none.
5. Mechanisms for dealing with non-compliance: Article 21

   "The Contracting Parties undertake to co-operate in the development of procedures enabling them to control the application of the Convention and the Protocols."

6. Provisions for observations or inspections: Article 10

   "The Contracting Parties shall endeavour to establish, in close cooperation with the international bodies which they consider competent, complementary or joint programmes including, as appropriate, programmes at the bilateral and multi-lateral levels, for pollution monitoring in the Mediterranean Sea Area and shall endeavour to establish a pollution-monitoring system for that Area."

7. Dispute settlement mechanisms: Article 22

   "1. In case of a dispute between Contracting Parties as to the interpretation or application of this Convention or the Protocols, they shall seek a settlement of the dispute through negotiation or any other peaceful means of their own choice.
   2. If the parties concerned cannot settle their dispute through the means mentioned in the preceding paragraph, the dispute shall upon common agreement be submitted to arbitration under the conditions laid down in Annex A to this Convention."

8. Provisions for amendments, protocols, or annexes: Articles 15–17
   Article 15 addresses adoption of additional protocols: a diplomatic conference for the purpose of adopting additional protocols shall

be convened by the Organization at the request of two-thirds of the contracting parties.

Article 16 addresses amendment of the Convention or Protocols: amendments shall be adopted by a diplomatic conference which shall be convened by the Organization at the request of two-thirds of the contracting parties; amendments shall be adopted by a three-fourths majority vote; amendments shall enter into force 30 days after the acceptance by at least three-fourths of the contracting parties.

Article 17 addresses annexes and amendments to annexes: amendments to annexes may be proposed at any meeting of the parties and shall be adopted by a three-fourths majority vote of the contracting parties; any party that cannot approve an amendment must notify the Depositary within a period determined by the contracting parties; on expiry of the period referred, the amendment to the annex shall become effective for all contracting parties which have not submitted notification.

9. Explicit measurable performance standards: none.
10. Liability provisions: Article 12

"The Contracting Parties undertake to co-operate as soon as possible in the formulation and adoption of appropriate procedure for the determination of liability and compensation for damage resulting from the pollution of the marine environment deriving from violations of the provisions of this Convention and applicable protocols."

11. Financial resources, arrangements, or mechanisms: Article 18.2

"The Contracting Parties shall adopt financial rules, prepared in consultation with the Organization, to determine, in particular, their financial participation."

12. Protocols and/or amendments:
    1976 Protocol for the Prevention of Pollution of the Mediterranean Sea by Dumping from Ships and Aircraft
    1976 Protocol Concerning Cooperation in Combating Pollution of the Mediterranean Sea by Oil and Other Harmful Substances in Cases of Emergency
    1980 Protocol for the Protection of the Mediterranean Sea against Pollution from Land-Based Sources (amended in 1996 and now called Protocol for the Protection of the Mediterranean Sea against Pollution from Land-Based Sources and Activities)
    1982 Protocol Concerning Mediterranean Specially Protected Areas (amended in 1995 and now called Protocol Concerning Specially Protected Areas and Biological Diversity in the Mediterranean)

1994 Protocol for the Protection of the Mediterranean Sea against Pollution Resulting from Exploration and Exploitation of the Continental Shelf and the Seabed and its Subsoil

1995 Action Plan for the Protection of the Marine Environment and the Sustainable Development of the Coastal Areas of the Mediterranean (MAP Phase II)

1996 Protocol on the Prevention of Pollution of the Mediterranean Sea by Transboundary Movements of Hazardous Wastes and their Disposal

1979 Convention on Long-Range Transboundary Air Pollution

1. Provisions for a secretariat/commission: Article 11

"The Executive Secretary of the Economic Commission for Europe shall carry out, for the Executive Body, the following secretariat functions ..."

2. Provision for reporting by parties: Article 8

"The Contracting Parties, within the framework of the Executive Body referred to in article 10 and bilaterally, shall, in their common interests, exchange available information on ..."

3. Provisions for reservations to parts of convention or annexes: not specified; however, some reservations have been made.
4. Provisions for the secretariat to monitor states' compliance: none.
5. Mechanisms for dealing with non-compliance: none.
6. Provisions for observations and inspections: none.
7. Dispute settlement mechanisms: Article 13

"If a dispute arises between two or more Contracting Parties to the present Convention as to the interpretation or application of the Convention, they shall seek a solution by negotiation or by any other method of dispute settlement acceptable to the parties to the dispute."

8. Provisions for amendments, protocols, or annexes: Article 12

"An amendment to the present Convention shall be adopted by consensus of the representatives of the Contracting Parties, and shall enter into force for the Contracting Parties which have accepted it on the ninetieth day after the date on which two-thirds of the Contracting Parties have deposited their instruments of acceptance."

9. Explicit measurable performance standards: none.
10. Liability provisions: none.
11. Financial resources, arrangements, or mechanisms: none.
12. Protocols and/or amendments:

> 1984 Protocol on Long-Term Financing of the Cooperative Programme for Monitoring and Evaluation of the Long-Range Transmission of Air Pollutants in Europe (EMEP)
>
> 1985 Protocol on the Reduction of Sulphur Emissions or Their Transboundary Fluxes by at Least 30 Percent
>
> 1988 Protocol Concerning the Control of Emissions of Nitrogen Oxides or Their Transboundary Fluxes
>
> 1991 Geneva Protocol Concerning the Control of Emissions of Volatile Organic Compounds or Their Transboundary Fluxes
>
> 1994 Oslo Protocol on Further Reduction of Sulphur Emissions
>
> 1998 Aarhus Protocol on Persistent Organic Pollutants
>
> 1998 Aarhus Protocol on Heavy Metals
>
> 1999 Gothenburg Protocol to Abate Acidification, Eutrophication and Ground-level Ozone

1980 Convention on the Conservation of Antarctic Marine Living Resources

1. Provisions for a secretariat/commission: Article 7

   "The Contracting Parties hereby establish and agree to maintain the Commission for the Conservation of Antarctic Marine Living Resources."

2. Provision for reporting by parties: Article 20

   "1. The Members of the Commission shall, to the greatest extent possible, provide annually to the Commission and to the Scientific Committee such statistical, biological and other data and information as the Commission and the Scientific Committee may require in the exercise of their functions."

3. Provisions for reservations to parts of convention or annexes: none.
4. Provisions for the secretariat to monitor states' compliance: Article 10.2

   "The Commission shall draw the attention of all Contracting Parties to any activity which, in the opinion of the Commission, affects the implementation by a Contracting Party of the objective of this Convention or the compliance by that Contracting Party with its obligations under this Convention."

5. Mechanisms for dealing with non-compliance: Article 21

> "1. Each Contracting Party shall take appropriate measures within its competence to ensure compliance with the provisions of this Convention and with conservation measures adopted by the Commission to which the Party is bound in accordance with Article IX of this Convention.
> 2. Each Contracting Party shall transmit to the Commission information on measures taken pursuant to paragraph 1 above, including the imposition of sanctions for any violation."

6. Provisions for observations or inspections: Articles 22 and 24

> "Each Contracting Party undertakes to exert appropriate efforts, consistent with the Charter of the United Nations, to the end that no one engages in any activity contrary to the objective of this Convention."

> "In order to promote the objective and ensure observance of the provisions of this Convention, the Contracting Parties agree that a system of observation and inspection shall be established."

7. Dispute settlement mechanisms: Article 25

> "If any dispute arises between two or more of the Contracting Parties concerning the interpretation or application of this Convention, those Contracting Parties shall consult among themselves with a view to having the dispute resolved by negotiation, inquiry, mediation, conciliation, arbitration, judicial settlement or other peaceful means of their own choice."

8. Provisions for amendments, protocols, or annexes: Article 30

> "1. This Convention may be amended at any time.
> 2. If one-third of the Members of the Commission request a meeting to discuss a proposed amendment the Depositary shall call such a meeting.
> 3. An amendment shall enter into force when the Depositary has received instruments of ratification, acceptance or approval thereof from all the Members of the Commission."

9. Explicit measurable performance standards: none.
10. Liability provisions: none.
11. Financial resources, arrangements, or mechanisms: Article 19

> "1. At each annual meeting, the Commission shall adopt by consensus its budget and the budget for the Scientific Committee ...
> 3. Each Member of the Commission shall contribute to the budget. Until the expiration of five years after the entry into force of this Convention, the contribution of each Member of the Commission shall be equal ..."

12. Protocols and/or amendments: none.

1983 International Tropical Timber Agreement

1. Provisions for a secretariat/commission: Articles 6 and 16

   "The highest authority of the Organization shall be the International Tropical Timber Council, which shall consist of all the members of the Organization."

   "The Council shall, by special vote, appoint the Executive Director."

2. Provision for reporting by parties: Article 28

   "1. The Council shall, within six months after the close of each calendar year, publish an annual report ...
   3. The review shall be carried out in the light of:
   (a) Information supplied by members in relation to national production, trade, supply, stocks, consumption and prices of tropical timber."

3. Provisions for reservations to parts of convention or annexes: Article 43

   "Reservations may not be made with respect to any of the provisions of this Agreement."

4. Provisions for the secretariat to monitor states' compliance: none.
5. Mechanisms for dealing with non-compliance: none.
6. Provisions for observations or inspections: none.
7. Dispute settlement mechanisms: Article 29

   "Any complaint that a member has failed to fulfil its obligations under this Agreement and any dispute concerning the interpretation or application of this Agreement shall be referred to the Council for decision. Decisions of the Council on these matters shall be final and binding."

8. Provisions for amendments, protocols, or annexes: Article 38

   "1. The Council may, by special vote, recommend an amendment of this Agreement to its members.
   2. The Council shall fix a date by which members shall notify the depositary of their acceptance of the amendment.
   3. An amendment shall enter into force 90 days after the depositary has received notifications of acceptance from members constituting at least two-thirds of the producing members and accounting for at least 85 percent of the votes of the producing members, and from members constituting at least two-thirds of the consuming members and accounting for at least 85 percent of the votes of the consuming members."

9. Explicit measurable performance standards: none.
10. Liability provisions: none.
11. Financial resources, arrangements or mechanisms: Chapter VI
    Article 18: Financial Accounts
    Article 19: Administrative Account
    Article 20: Special Account
    Article 21: Forms of Payment
    Article 22: Audit and publication of accounts
12. Protocols and/or amendments: none (although the agreement was renegotiated and adopted in 1994).

1987 Montreal Protocol on Substances that Deplete the Ozone Layer

1. Provisions for a secretariat/commission: Article 12 (uses the Convention secretariat).
2. Provision for reporting by parties: Article 7

   "1. Each Party shall provide to the secretariat, within three months of becoming a Party, statistical data on its production, imports and exports of each of the controlled substances for the year 1986, or the best possible estimates of such data where actual data are not available.
   2. Each party shall provide statistical data to the secretariat on its annual production (with separate data on amounts destroyed by technologies to be approved by the Parties), imports, and exports to Parties and non-Parties, respectively, of such substances for the year during which it becomes a Party and for each year thereafter. It shall forward the data no later than nine months after the end of the year to which the data relate."

3. Provisions for reservations to parts of convention or annexes: Article 18

   "No reservations may be made to this Protocol."

4. Provisions for the secretariat to monitor states' compliance: none.
5. Mechanisms for dealing with non-compliance: Article 8 and Article 4 re trade sanctions

   "The Parties, at their first meeting, shall consider and approve procedures and institutional mechanisms for determining non-compliance with the provisions of this Protocol and for treatment of Parties found to be in non-compliance."

6. Provisions for observations or inspections: none.

7. Dispute settlement mechanisms: within Convention.
8. Provisions for amendments, protocols, or annexes: Article 2.9

> "(b) Proposals for such adjustments shall be communicated to the Parties by the secretariat at least six months before the meeting of the Parties at which they are proposed for adoption;
> (c) In taking such decisions, the Parties shall make every effort to reach agreement by consensus. If all efforts at consensus have been exhausted, and no agreement reached, such decisions shall, as a last resort, be adopted by a two-thirds majority vote of the Parties present and voting representing at least fifty per cent of the total consumption of the controlled substances of the Parties;
> (d) The decisions, which shall be binding on all Parties, shall ... enter into force on the expiry of six months from the date of the circulation of the communication by the Depositary."

9. Explicit measurable performance standards: Articles 2, 4, and 5
   Article 2: Control Measures
   Article 4: Control of Trade with Non-Parties
   Article 5: Special Situation of Developing Countries
10. Liability provisions: none.
11. Financial resources, arrangements, or mechanisms: Article 13

> "1. The funds required for the operation of this Protocol, including those for the functioning of the secretariat related to this Protocol, shall be charged exclusively against contributions from the Parties.
> 2. The Parties, at their first meeting, shall adopt by consensus financial rules for the operation of this Protocol."

12. Protocols and/or amendments:
    1990 London amendments
    1992 Copenhagen adjustments
    1993 Bangkok adjustments
    1997 Montreal amendment
    1999 Beijing amendments

1989 Basel Convention on the Control of Transboundary Movements of Hazardous Wastes and Their Disposal

1. Provisions for a secretariat/commission: Article 16.3

> "At its first meeting, the Conference of the Parties shall designate the Secretariat from among those existing competent intergovernmental organizations which have signified their willingness to carry out the secretariat functions under this Convention."

2. Provision for reporting by parties: Article 13.3

"The Parties, consistent with national laws and regulations, shall transmit, through the Secretariat, to the Conference of the Parties established under Article 15, before the end of each calendar year, a report on the previous calendar year, containing the following information ..."

3. Provisions for reservations to parts of convention or annexes: Article 26

"No reservation or exception may be made to this Convention."

4. Provisions for secretariat to monitor states' compliance: none.
5. Mechanisms for dealing with non-compliance: Article 19

"Any Party which has reason to believe that another Party is acting or has acted in breach of its obligations under this Convention may inform the Secretariat thereof, and in such an event, shall simultaneously and immediately inform, directly or through the Secretariat, the Party against whom the allegations are made. All relevant information should be submitted by the Secretariat to the Parties."

6. Provisions for observations and inspections: none.
7. Dispute settlement mechanisms: Article 20

"1. In case of a dispute between Parties as to the interpretation or application of, or compliance with, this Convention or any protocol thereto, they shall seek a settlement for the dispute through negotiation or any other peaceful means of their own choice.
 2. If the Parties concerned cannot settle their dispute through the means mentioned in the preceding paragraph, the dispute, if the parties to the dispute agree, shall be submitted to the International Court of Justice or to the arbitration under the conditions set out in Annex VI on Arbitration."

8. Provisions for amendments, protocols, or annexes: Articles 17 and 18
 Article 17 addresses amendment of the Convention: amendments should be reached by consensus or, as a last resort, a three-fourths majority vote; amendments to protocols need a two-thirds majority vote; amendments must be ratified by three-fourths of the parties to enter into force; amendments to protocols must be ratified by two-thirds of the parties to enter into force.
 Article 18 addresses amendment and adoption of annexes: any party that is unable to accept an additional annex shall notify the Depositary in writing, within six months from the date of commu-

nication of the adoption by the Depositary; after six months the annex shall become effective for all parties that have not submitted a notification.

9. Explicit measurable performance standards: none.
10. Liability provisions: Article 12

"The Parties shall cooperate with a view to adopting, as soon as practicable, a protocol setting out appropriate rules and procedures in the field of liability and compensation for damage resulting from the transboundary movement and disposal of hazardous wastes and other wastes."

11. Financial resources, arrangements, or mechanisms: Article 14

"1. The Parties agree that, according to the specific needs of different regions and subregions, regional or sub-regional centres for training and technology transfers regarding the management of hazardous wastes and other wastes and the minimization of their generation should be established. The Parties shall decide on the establishment of appropriate funding mechanisms of a voluntary nature.
2. The Parties shall consider the establishment of a revolving fund to assist on an interim basis in case of emergency situations to minimize damage from accidents arising from transboundary movements of hazardous wastes or during the disposal of those wastes."

12. Protocols and/or amendments:
    1995 Basel Ban amendment
    1999 Protocol on Liability and Compensation for Damage Resulting from the Transboundary Movement of Hazardous Wastes and their Disposal

1992 Framework Convention on Climate Change

1. Provisions for a secretariat/commission: Article 8.3

"The Conference of the Parties, at its first session, shall designate a permanent secretariat and make arrangements for its functioning."

2. Provision for reporting by parties: Article 4

"All Parties, taking into account their common but differentiated responsibilities and their specific national and regional development priorities, objectives and circumstances, shall:
(a) Develop, periodically update, publish and make available to the Conference of the Parties, in accordance with Article 12, national inventories of

anthropogenic emissions by sources and removals by sinks of all green-house gases not controlled by the Montreal Protocol, using comparable methodologies to be agreed upon by the Conference of the Parties."

3. Provisions for reservations to parts of convention or annexes: Article 24

   "No reservations may be made to the Convention."

4. Provisions for the secretariat to monitor states' compliance: Article 10 establishes a Subsidiary Body for Implementation.
5. Mechanisms for dealing with non-compliance: none.
6. Provisions for observations or inspections: none.
7. Dispute settlement mechanisms: Article 14

   "1. In case of a dispute between any two or more Parties concerning the interpretation or application of the Convention, the Parties concerned shall seek a settlement for the dispute through negotiation or any other peaceful means of their own choice....

   5. ... if the Parties concerned have not been able to settle their dispute through the means mentioned in paragraph 1 above, the dispute shall be submitted, at the request of any of the parties to the dispute, to conciliation."

8. Provisions for amendments, protocols, or annexes: Articles 15, 16, and 17

   Article 15 addresses amendments to the Convention: adopted at an ordinary session of the Conference of the Parties; agreement by consensus or as a last resort a three-fourths majority; enter into force on the ninetieth day after the acceptance by at least three-fourths of the Parties.

   Article 16 addresses adoption and amendment of annexes to the Convention. Annexes will enter into force six months after the date of the communication by the depositary to such parties of the adoption of the annex (same as in Article 15), except those parties that have notified the depositary, in writing, within that period of their non-acceptance of the annex.

   Article 17 addresses protocols. The Conference of the Parties can adopt protocols at any ordinary session.

9. Explicit measurable performance standards: none.
10. Liability provisions: none.
11. Financial resources, arrangements, or mechanisms: Article 11

    "A mechanism for the provision of financial resources on a grant or concessional basis, including for the transfer of technology, is hereby defined ..."

12. Protocols and/or amendments:
    1997 Kyoto Protocol

1992 Convention on Biological Diversity

 1. Provisions for a secretariat/commission: Article 24.2 (interim arrangements in Article 40)

    "At its first ordinary meeting, the Conference of the Parties shall designate the secretariat from amongst those existing competent international organizations which have signified their willingness to carry out the secretariat functions under this Convention."

 2. Provision for reporting by parties: Article 26

    "Each Contracting Party shall, at intervals to be determined by the Conference of the Parties, present to the Conference of the Parties, reports on measures which it has taken for the implementation of the provisions of this Convention and their effectiveness in meeting the objectives of this Convention."

 3. Provisions for reservations to parts of convention or annexes: Article 37

    "No reservations may be made to this Convention."

 4. Provisions for the secretariat to monitor states' compliance: none.
 5. Mechanisms for dealing with non-compliance: none.
 6. Provisions for observations or inspections: none.
 7. Dispute settlement mechanisms: Article 27

    "1. In the event of a dispute between Contracting Parties concerning the interpretation or application of this Convention, the parties concerned shall seek solution by negotiation.
     2. If the parties concerned cannot reach agreement by negotiation, they may jointly seek the good offices of, or request mediation by, a third party."

 8. Provisions for amendments, protocols, or annexes: Articles 28, 29, and 30
    Article 28 addresses the adoption of protocols, which can be adopted at a meeting of the Conference of the Parties.
    Article 29 addresses amendment of the Convention or Protocols: must be adopted by consensus or as a last resort a two-thirds ma-

jority vote of the parties; will enter into force on the ninetieth day following the receipt of acceptance by two-thirds of the parties.

Article 30 addresses adoption and amendment of annexes. On the expiry of one year from the date of the communication of adoption of an annex (same procedure as in Article 29), the annex shall enter into force for all parties to this Convention or to any Protocol concerned that have not submitted a notification of objection.

9. Explicit measurable performance standards: none.
10. Liability provisions: none.
11. Financial resources, arrangements, or mechanisms: Articles 20 and 21

Article 20 sets out the responsibilities of developed country parties to the Convention with regard to the provision of new and additional financial resources to enable developing country parties to meet the agreed full incremental costs to them of implementing the Convention.

Article 21 states that the Conference of Parties will be responsible for determining the policy, strategy, and program priorities for a mechanism for the provision of financial resources to developing country parties for the purposes of this Convention.

12. Protocols and/or amendments:
2000 Cartagena Protocol on Biosafety

1997 Kyoto Protocol to the United Nations Framework Convention on Climate Change

1. Provisions for a secretariat/commission: Article 14

"The secretariat established by Article 8 of the Convention shall serve as the secretariat of this Protocol."

2. Provision for reporting by parties: Articles 6 and 17

The Conference of the Parties serving as the meeting of the parties to this Protocol may, at its first session or as soon as practicable thereafter, further elaborate guidelines for the implementation of various aspects of the Protocol, including for verification and reporting.

3. Provisions for reservations to parts of convention or annexes: Article 26

"No reservations may be made to this Convention."

4. Provisions for the secretariat to monitor states' compliance: Article 8

The secretariat coordinates expert review teams that shall provide a thorough and comprehensive technical assessment of all aspects of the implementation by a party of this Protocol.

5. Mechanisms for dealing with non-compliance: Article 18

"The Conference of the Parties serving as the meeting of the Parties to this Protocol shall, at its first session, approve appropriate and effective procedures and mechanisms to determine and to address cases of non-compliance with the provisions of this Protocol, including through the development of an indicative list of consequences, taking into account the cause, type, degree and frequency of non-compliance. Any procedures and mechanisms under this Article entailing binding consequences shall be adopted by means of an amendment to this Protocol."

6. Provisions for observations or inspections: none.
7. Dispute settlement mechanisms: Article 19

"The provisions of Article 14 of the Convention on settlement of disputes shall apply *mutatis mutandis* to this Protocol."

8. Provisions for amendments, protocols, or annexes: Articles 20 and 21

Any Party may propose amendments or annexes to this Protocol. Amendments or annexes to this Protocol shall be adopted at an ordinary session of the Conference of the Parties serving as the meeting of the parties to this Protocol.

"The Parties shall make every effort to reach agreement on any proposed amendment to this Protocol by consensus. If all efforts at consensus have been exhausted, and no agreement reached, the amendment shall as a last resort be adopted by a three-fourths majority vote of the Parties present and voting at the meeting. The adopted amendment shall be communicated by the secretariat to the Depositary, who shall circulate it to all Parties for their acceptance."

"Instruments of acceptance in respect of an amendment shall be deposited with the Depositary. An amendment adopted in accordance with paragraph 3 above shall enter into force for those Parties having accepted it on the ninetieth day after the date of receipt by the Depositary of an instrument of acceptance by at least three fourths of the Parties to this Protocol."

9. Explicit measurable performance standards: Article 3

This article contains 14 paragraphs and refers to Annexes A and B. Annex A lists six greenhouse gases (GHG) – carbon dioxide, methane, nitrous oxide, hydrofluorocarbons, perfluorocarbons and sulphur hexafluoride – to which reduction or limitation targets should apply and includes GHG source categories and sectors such as fuel combustion, industrial processes, agriculture, and waste. Annex B lists quantified emission limitation or reduction commitments for Annex I parties, which range from an 8 percent decrease to a 10 percent increase of GHG emissions from 1990 levels to be reached in a period between 2008 and 2012. The EU countries are to reduce GHG emissions from 1990 levels by 8 percent, the United States by 7 percent, and Japan by 6 percent, whereas Australia and Iceland are allowed increases by 8 percent and 10 percent, respectively. The Russian Federation is to maintain its emissions at 1990 levels.

10. Liability provisions: none.
11. Financial resources, arrangements, or mechanisms: Article 11

Developed country parties to the Convention will continue to provide financial resources and technology to developing country parties to help them implement existing commitments under the Convention.

12. Protocols and/or amendments: none.

2000 Cartagena Protocol on Biosafety

1. Provisions for a secretariat/commission: Article 31

"The Secretariat established by Article 24 of the Convention shall serve as the secretariat to this Protocol."

2. Provision for reporting by parties: Article 33

"Each Party shall monitor the implementation of its obligations under this Protocol, and shall, at intervals to be determined by the Conference of the Parties serving as the meeting of the Parties to this Protocol, report to the Conference of the Parties serving as the meeting of the Parties to this Protocol on measures that it has taken to implement the Protocol."

3. Provisions for reservations to parts of convention or annexes: Article 38

"No reservations may be made to this Protocol."

4. Provisions for the secretariat to monitor states' compliance: Articles 33 and 34

"Each Party shall monitor the implementation of its obligations under this Protocol, and shall, at intervals to be determined by the Conference of the Parties serving as the meeting of the Parties to this Protocol, report to the Conference of the Parties serving as the meeting of the Parties to this Protocol on measures that it has taken to implement the Protocol."

"The Conference of the Parties serving as the meeting of the Parties to this Protocol shall, at its first meeting, consider and approve cooperative procedures and institutional mechanisms to promote compliance with the provisions of this Protocol and to address cases of non-compliance."

5. Mechanisms for dealing with non-compliance: Article 34

"The Conference of the Parties serving as the meeting of the Parties to this Protocol shall, at its first meeting, consider and approve cooperative procedures and institutional mechanisms to promote compliance with the provisions of this Protocol and to address cases of non-compliance."

6. Provisions for observations or inspections: none.
7. Dispute settlement mechanisms: none, although the dispute settlement mechanisms in Article 27 of the Convention apply.
8. Provisions for amendments, protocols, or annexes: Article 29

The Conference of the Parties serving as the meeting of the Parties to this Protocol shall "consider and adopt, as required, amendments to this Protocol and its annexes, as well as any additional annexes to this Protocol, that are deemed necessary for the implementation of this Protocol."

9. Explicit measurable performance standards: none.
10. Liability provisions: none.
11. Financial resources, arrangements, or mechanisms: Article 28

"The financial mechanism established in Article 21 of the Convention shall, through the institutional structure entrusted with its operation, be the financial mechanism for this Protocol."

"... the Parties shall also take into account the needs of the developing country Parties, in particular the least developed and the small island developing States among them, and of the Parties with economies in transition, in their efforts to identify and implement their capacity-building requirements for the purposes of the implementation of this Protocol."

"The developed country Parties may also provide, and the developing country Parties and the Parties with economies in transition avail themselves of, financial and technological resources for the implementation of the provisions of this Protocol through bilateral, regional and multilateral channels."

12. Protocols and/or amendments: none.

Note

1. I have included the Kyoto Protocol and the Cartagena Protocol in this section – although not part of the case-study analysis in Chapters 4, 5, and 6, they are discussed in Chapter 7.

Appendix II

Correlation analysis

In Chapter 6, correlation analysis is used to examine relationships among different characteristics within the multilateral environmental negotiation process. The purpose of this appendix is to explain in greater detail the nature of the statistical techniques and how they were used in Chapter 6.

Correlation analysis is used to identify, analyze, and verify the relationships between two or more characteristics or variables. A coefficient of correlation is a statistical formula that expresses the degree of relationship between two variables or characteristics. It is a pure number that has no connection with the units in which the variables or characteristics are measured. Different coefficients have different limits. The one used in the analyses in Chapter 6 varies from a value of +1.00, which means a perfect positive relationship, down through the value zero, which indicates no relationship at all, until it reaches its lower limit of −1.00, indicating perfect negative correlation.

For ordinal- or interval-level variables, degree of similarity of a pair of variables X, Y is dependent on the extent to which high scores on variable X tend to be associated with high scores on variable Y, and, at the same time, low scores on X tend to be associated with low scores on Y. If two variables give similar or equivalent information about subjects, then, if you know the subjects' scores on X, you have a better idea of their status on Y than if you did not know their X scores or the relationship between X and Y. It is important to understand, however, that the degree of relationship is not proportional to the size of the coefficient. A coefficient of 0.60 does not mean that the relationship is exactly twice as strong as one indicated by a coefficient of 0.30. The correlation coefficient is an index number, not a measurement like inches, dollars, or tons. The correct interpretation depends on the particular problem being investigated and the purpose for which the coefficient is being calculated. What would be considered a high correlation in one investigation may be considered a low one in another. The following is a rough guide to the degree of relationship indicated by the size of the coefficients:

0.90–1.00	Very high correlation – very strong relationship
0.70–0.90	High correlation – marked relationship
0.40–0.70	Moderate correlation – substantial relationship
0.20–0.40	Low correlation – a definite relationship but a small one
less than 0.20	Slight correlation – relationship so small as to be negligible

In the analysis in Chapter 6, the type of correlation computed is the gamma coefficient. This is a measure of non-parametric correlation that makes few assumptions about the scaling of variables or frequency distributions.[1] The gamma coefficient was also used in Druckman's (1993) study, which developed a comparative methodology for analyzing negotiations using these statistical techniques. The gamma coefficient can be used with variables that cannot be stated precisely enough to be capable of quantification. Yet, such variables as human preferences, judgments, or attitudes, or the characteristics of a negotiating process, may manifestly correlate with one another to a greater or lesser extent. Although not strictly measurable, the characteristics or cases to be judged may simply be arranged in order according to some quality that they all possess (Connolly and Sluckin 1971, 178).

The gamma coefficient can be used in situations when scores are tied on one or more variables because it has the advantage of being easily calculated and interpreted. The formula for gamma is

$$\gamma = \frac{S}{A + D}$$

where

A = the sum of the number of agreements
D = the sum of the number of disagreements
$S = A - D$ (the sum of agreements minus the sum of disagreements)

For example, in an attempt to understand a couple's marital difficulties, a marriage counselor asks both husband and wife to rate 20 stimulus words on a scale from passive (1) to active (7).[2] The results are shown in table II.1, where each tally represents a stimulus word. ΣA_i and ΣD_i are

Table II.1 Use of the gamma coefficient

Wife (Y)	Husband (X)							ΣA_i	ΣD_i
	1	2	3	4	5	6	7		
1	|							18	0
2		||					|	28	0
3			|		|			14	2
4		|		||			|	22	8
5	|		|		|||			16	20
6				|	|	|		3	9
7				|			|	0	8
Σ								101	47

summed across all stimuli in a row of the table. For row 1, there is only one stimulus word, at $(X = 1, Y = 1)$, so $\Sigma A_i = A_i$ for that stimulus, which is equal to 18 (the number of tallies to the right and below the tally for this stimulus). For the second row, there are three stimuli, so $A_i = 2(14) + 0$; that is, 14 for each of the stimuli at $(X = 2, Y = 2)$, plus 0 for the stimulus at $(X = 7, Y = 2)$, because there are no tallies to the right and below the tally for this stimulus. D_i values are calculated by the number of tallies above and to the right of each stimulus, that is, stimuli rated higher by the husband and lower by the wife.

In this example, gamma is calculated as follows:

$$S = A - D = 101 - 47 = 54$$

$$A + D = 101 + 47 = 148$$

$$\gamma = \frac{S}{A + D} = \frac{54}{148} = .365$$

The significance test for the gamma coefficient in cases where there are tied scores (as in Chapter 6) is as follows. Where the number of cases (or stimulus words, to use the above example) is greater than 10, S is approximately normally distributed under H_0 (the null hypothesis), and hypotheses can be tested using the statistic

$$z = \frac{S}{\sigma_s},$$

where

$$\sigma_s^2 = \frac{1}{18} \left\{ N(N-1)(2N+5) - \sum_j N_j(N_j-1)(2N_j+5) \right.$$

$$- \sum_k N_k(N_k-1)(2N_k+5)$$

$$+ \frac{\sum_j N_j(N_j-1)(N_j-2) \sum_k N_k(N_k-1)(N_k-2)}{9N(N-1)(N-2)}$$

$$\left. + \frac{\sum_j N_j(N_j-1) \sum_k N_k(N_k-1)}{2N(N-1)} \right\}$$

N_j is the number of objects at level j of variable X, N_k is the number of objects at level k of variable Y, N is the total number of objects rated, and σ_s is the positive square root of $\sigma^2{}_s$.

For example,[3] suppose for the data above that this was testing the two-tail hypothesis H_0: $\Gamma = 0$ and H_m: $\Gamma \neq 0$, at $\alpha = .05$. We would need the calculations in table II.2 in addition to the ones already completed.

$$\sigma_s^2 = \frac{1}{18} \left\{ 20(19)(45) - 594 - 624 + \frac{90(96)}{9(20)(19)(18)} + \frac{46(48)}{2(20)(19)} \right\}$$

$$= \frac{1}{18} (17,100 - 1,218 + 0.14 + 2.90)$$

$$= \frac{15,885.04}{18} = 882.5.$$

$$\sigma_s = \sqrt{882.5} \doteq 29.7.$$

Then $z = 54/29.7 = 1.82$. The critical values of the standard normal distribution (taken from any statistical table of standard normal distribution) are $z_{.05}$ (two-tail) $= \pm 1.96$. The computed values of z lie between these limits, so the null hypothesis is not rejected.

In the analysis in Chapter 6, the gamma coefficient was used to identify relationships among the various characteristics of the international negotiation process. The correlations were calculated using the statistical software package SYSTAT. For more information on the gamma coefficient,

Table II.2 Significance test of the gamma coefficient

X_j	$N_j(N_j - 1)$	$N_j(N_j - 1)(2N_j + 5)$	$N_j(N_j - 1)(N_j - 2)$
1	2	18	0
2	6	66	6
3	2	18	0
4	12	156	24
5	20	300	60
6	2	18	0
7	2	18	0
Σ	46	594	90

Y_k	$N_k(N_k - 1)$	$N_k(N_k - 1)(2N_k + 5)$	$N_k(N_k - 1)(N_k - 2)$
1	0	0	0
2	6	66	6
3	2	18	0
4	12	156	24
5	20	300	60
6	6	66	6
7	2	18	0
Σ	48	624	96

see Goodman and Kruskal (1954) and Harshbarger (1977). For additional information on the use of correlation analysis for the comparison of international negotiations, see Druckman (1993).

I assigned numerical values to the characteristics of each phase and turning point (as elaborated in Chapter 5) for quantitative analysis. These values were assigned solely for the purpose of comparing the cases. Wherever possible the numerical values were assigned to the different characteristics of each phase on a gradated scale so that similar characteristics are at one end of the scale. For example, in the Precipitants phase, the characteristics ranged from those that are external to the international community (incidents of human-induced pollution and growing scientific evidence) to those indicating more government concern (concern about overexploiting biological resources and economic concerns). Similarly, in Turning Point 1, the characteristics were scaled from institutionalized (decision of an intergovernmental body) to ad hoc (initiative of a non-governmental organization).

In addition to the phases and turning points, the Strength Index, as derived in Chapter 6, was included in this analysis as a measurement of the outcome of the negotiations. To determine the primary characteristic of each phase and turning point, I examined each of the 11 cases in detail

Table II.3 The data matrix

Variables	LDC	MAR	CIT	MED	TAP	CCA	ITTA	OZO	BAS	FCCC	CBD
						Cases					
Precipitant	2	1	3.5	1	2	3	4	2	1	2	3
TP1	2	2	3	1	2	1	1	1	1	1	1
Issue definition	1	1	1	2	1	3	2	2	2	3	2
TP2	0	3	0	1	2	1	1	1	4	4	1
Statement	0	3	0	1	2	2	2	2	2	2	2
TP3	2	4	4	2	4	1	3	2	1	1	1
Drafting	2	3	4	3	2	1	3	3	1	1	4
TP4	2	1	2	2	1	2	1	3	3	4	4
Final bargaining	3	2	3	3	3	3	1	2	2	2	2
TP5	1	3	3	1	1	1	1	3	1	1	4
Ratification	1	3	1	1	1	1	1	2	1	2	2
Strength	2	4	4	2	1	4	2	4	3	3	2

Table II.4 Matrix of gamma coefficients

	PRECIP	TP1	ISSUE	TP2	STATE	TP3	DRAFT-ING	TP4	FINAL-BAR	TP5	RATIF	STRENGTH
PRECIP	1.00											
TP1	0.04	1.00										
ISSUE	0.13	-1.00	1.00									
TP2	-0.59	-0.33	0.33	1.00								
STATE	-0.26	-0.33	0.33	0.86	1.00							
TP3	0.03	0.93	-0.94	-0.23	-0.11	1.00						
DRAFTING	-0.03	0.57	-0.61	-0.49	-0.33	0.84	1.00					
TP4	-0.06	-0.67	0.67	0.12	-0.08	-0.89	-0.58	1.00				
FINALBAR	0.07	0.46	-0.18	-0.53	-1.00	0.03	0.00	-0.11	1.00			
TP5	0.26	0.30	-0.33	-0.36	0.14	0.20	0.44	0.38	-0.30	1.00		
RATIF	-0.33	-0.18	0.14	0.50	1.00	-0.13	-0.09	0.43	-0.78	0.68	1.00	
STRENGTH	0.09	0.20	0.00	-0.24	0.08	0.06	0.38	0.03	-0.11	0.62	0.27	1.00

and coded them appropriately. Information about each case was gathered from primary source material, such as UN documents, secondary source material (including articles and books written about the subject), and interviews conducted by me.[4] Although it is desirable to have different people with knowledge of each case perform the coding, in this analysis the evaluation and coding were done solely by me. This analysis was conducted primarily to see if cases could be compared on the basis of the nature of different phases and turning points.

In some of the cases, more than one of the options characterized a particular phase or turning point. For example, the CITES negotiations were precipitated by some countries' concerns about overexploiting biological resources and other countries' economic concerns. In such cases, the average of the two responses was used. For CITES, the numerical value used in the data matrix was 3.5. The values assigned to the data collected are shown in the data matrix in table II.3. The resulting matrix of gamma coefficients is in table II.4.

Although not all of the results were conclusive, this is not a reason to abandon this approach. Weaknesses in this analysis relate to the use of only 11 cases and to the ratio of variables to cases, which is nearly 1:1. Perhaps if more cases were analyzed and coded across the variables the results would be more conclusive and/or reliable. Nevertheless, the use of correlation analysis does provide some insights into the process of environmental negotiation that the descriptive case-study method does not.

Notes

1. A non-parametric statistical procedure is one that satisfies at least one of the following criteria: (1) the method deals with enumerative data (data that are frequency counts); (2) the method does not deal with specific population parameters; and (3) the method does not require assumptions about population distributions (in particular, the assumption of normality)(Aczel 1989).
2. This example is from Harshbarger (1977).
3. This example is from Harshbarger (1977).
4. For more information on the cases, see the summaries in Chapter 4.

References

Aczel, Amir D. 1989. *Complete Business Statistics*. Boston, Mass.: Irwin.

Antarctic Treaty. 1980. Convention on the Conservation of Antarctic Marine Living Resources, drawn up at Canberra on 20 May 1980 (AT20051980B).

Arbose, Jules. 1972. "91 Nations Agree on Convention to Control Dumping in Oceans." *New York Times*, 14 November.

Barnes, James N. 1982. "The Emerging Convention on the Conservation of Antarctic Marine Living Resources: An Attempt to Meet the New Realities of Resource Exploitation in the Southern Ocean." In *The New Nationalism and the Use of Common Spaces*, edited by Jonathan I. Charney. New Jersey: Allanheld Osmun Publishers.

Barrett, Scott. 1990. "The Problem of Global Environmental Protection." *Oxford Review of Economic Policy*, 6(1): 68–79.

Bartos, Otomar J. 1974. *Process and Outcome of Negotiation*. New York: Columbia University Press.

Benedick, Richard E. 1991. *Ozone Diplomacy*. Cambridge, MA: Harvard University Press.

———. 1993. "Perspectives of a Negotiation Practitioner." In *International Environmental Negotiation*, edited by Gunnar Sjöstedt. Newbury Park, CA: Sage Publications.

Bernstein, Johannah, et al. 1992. "Climate Change Talks Adjourn in New York." *Earth Negotiations Bulletin*, 1(1): 1.

Bilderbeek, Simone. 1992. "Report of the Sixth Negotiating Session on the Convention on Biological Diversity." Unpublished report.

Birnie, Patricia W. 1992. "International Environmental Law: Its Adequacy for Present and Future Needs." In *The International Politics of the Environment*, edited by Andrew Hurrell and Benedict Kingsbury. New York: Oxford University Press.

———. 1993. "The UN and the Environment." In *United Nations, Divided World*, edited by Adam Roberts and Benedict Kingsbury. New York: Oxford University Press.

Birnie, Patricia W., and Alan E. Boyle. 1992. *International Law and the Environment*. New York: Oxford University Press.

Björkbom, Lars. 1988. "Resolution of Environmental Problems: The Use of Diplomacy." In *International Environmental Diplomacy*, edited by John E. Carroll. New York: Cambridge University Press.

Bliss-Guest, Patricia A. 1981. "The Protocol against Pollution from Land-Based Sources: A Turning Point in the Rising Tide of Pollution." *Stanford Journal of International Law*, 17(2): 261–279.

Boardman, Robert. 1981. *International Organization and the Conservation of Nature*. Bloomington: University of Indiana Press.

Bodansky, Daniel. 1994. "Prologue to the Climate Change Convention." In *Negotiating Climate Change: The Inside Story of the Rio Convention*, edited by Irving M. Mintzer and J. A. Leonard. Cambridge: Cambridge University Press.

Brams, Steven. J., Ann E. Doherty, and Matthew L. Weidner. 1994. "Game Theory: Focusing on the Players, Decisions and Agreements." In *International Multilateral Negotiation*, edited by I. William Zartman. San Francisco: Jossey-Bass.

Brenton, Tony. 1994. *The Greening of Machiavelli*. London: Royal Institute of International Affairs.

Bureau of National Affairs. 1988a. "UNEP Working Group Reaches Agreement on Question of Prior Informed Consent." *International Environment Reporter*, 9 March: 165.

———. 1988b. "Developed, Developing Countries Disagree over Elements of Waste Shipment Agreement." *International Environment Reporter*, 13 July: 376–377.

———. 1988c. "UNEP Transboundary Transport Draft Bogged down over Prior-Consent Issue." *International Environment Reporter*, December: 660–661.

———. 1989a. "Delegates of 50 Countries Fail to Agree on Draft Covering Movement of Toxic Wastes." *International Environment Reporter*, February: 49–50.

———. 1989b. "Thirty-four Countries Sign Convention on Transport, Disposal of Hazardous Wastes." *International Environment Reporter*, April: 159–161.

Caldwell, Lynton Keith. 1984. *International Environmental Policy*. Durham, NC: Duke University Press.

Chasek, Pamela, Langston J. Goree, and Wagaki Mwangi. 1993. *Earth Negotiations Bulletin*, 4(2–11).

Chayes, Abram, and Antonia H. Chayes. 1991. "Adjustment and Compliance Processes in International Regulatory Regimes." In *Preserving the Global Environment*, edited by Jessica Tuchman Mathews. New York: W.W. Norton.

Chertkoff, J. M., and M. Conley. 1967. "Opening Offer and Frequency of Concession as Bargaining Strategies." *Journal of Personality and Social Psychology*, 7: 181–185.

Chossudovsky, Evgeny M. 1989. *East–West Diplomacy for Environment in the United Nations*. New York: UNITAR.

Connolly, T. G. and W. Sluckin. 1971. *An Introduction to Statistics for the Social Sciences*, 3rd edition. London: Macmillan.

Demsetz, H. 1967. "Toward a Theory of Property Rights." *American Economic Association Papers and Proceedings*, 57(2): 347–359.

Dorfman, Robert, and Nancy S. Dorfman, eds. 1993. *Economics of the Environment*. New York: W.W. Norton.

Druckman, Daniel. 1986. "Stages, Turning Points and Crises: Negotiating Base Rights, Spain and the United States." *Journal of Conflict Resolution*, 30: 327–360.

———. 1990. "The Social Psychology of Arms Control and Reciprocation." *Political Psychology*, 11: 553–581.

———. 1993. "A Comparative Methodology for Analyzing Negotiations." Working Paper WP-93-34. Laxenburg, Austria: IIASA.

Dupont, Christopher. 1994. "Coalition Theory: Using Power to Build Cooperation." In *International Multilateral Negotiation*, edited by I. William Zartman. San Francisco: Jossey-Bass.

Dupont, Christopher, and Guy-Olivier Faure. 1991. "The Negotiation Process." In *International Negotiation: Analysis, Approaches, Issues*, edited by Victor A. Kremenyuk. San Francisco: Jossey-Bass.

ECO. 1991a. "Negotiations Face Failure?" *ECO Newsletter*. Climate Change Negotiations – Chantilly, INC 1(4), 14 February.

———. 1991b. "Rio Looks Little Closer." *ECO Newsletter*. Climate Change Negotiations – Nairobi, INC 3(10), 20 September.

Elliot, David. 1993. Interview by author, Geneva, Switzerland, 21 September.

Elliott, Lorraine M. 1994. *International Environmental Politics: Protecting the Antarctic*. New York: St. Martin's Press.

Falk, Richard. 1971. *This Endangered Planet: Prospects and Proposals for Human Survival*. New York: Vintage Books.

Fouéré, Erwan. 1988. "Emerging Trends in International Environmental Agreements." In *International Environmental Diplomacy*, edited by John E. Carroll. Cambridge: Cambridge University Press.

Frank, Ronald F. 1983. "The Convention on the Conservation of Antarctic Marine Living Resources." *Ocean Development and International Law Journal*, 13(3): 291–345.

Friedheim, Robert L. 1987. "The Third United Nations Conference on the Law of the Sea: North–South Bargaining on Ocean Issues." In *Positive Sum: Improving North–South Negotiations*, edited by I. William Zartman. New Brunswick, NJ: Transaction Books.

Galtung, Johan. 1968. "Small Group Theory and the Theory of International Relations: A Study of Isomorphism." In *New Approaches to International Relations*, edited by Morton A. Kaplan. New York: St. Martin's Press.

GAO. 1992. *International Agreements Are Not Well Monitored*. Report GAO/ RCED-92-43, Washington, DC: US General Accounting Office.

Gardner, Richard N. 1972. "The Role of the UN in Environmental Problems." In *World Eco-Crisis*, edited by David A. Kay and Eugene B. Skolnikoff. Madison, WI: University of Wisconsin Press.

Goodman, Leo A., and William H. Kruskal. 1954. "Measures of Association for Cross Classifications." *Journal of the American Statistical Association*, 49: 732–764.

Gulliver, P. H. 1979. *Disputes and Negotiations: A Cross-Cultural Perspective*. New York: Academic Press.

Haas, Peter M. 1989. "Do Regimes Matter? Epistemic Communities and Mediterranean Pollution Control." *International Organization*, 43(3): 377–403.

———. 1990. *Saving the Mediterranean: The Politics of International Environmental Cooperation*. New York: Columbia University Press.

Haas, Peter M., with Jan Sundgren. 1993. "Evolving International Environmental Law." In *Global Accord*, edited by Nazli Choucri. Cambridge, MA: MIT Press.

Hamner, W. Clay. 1974. "Effects of Bargaining Strategy and Pressure to Reach Agreement in a Stalemated Negotiation." *Journal of Personality and Social Psychology*, 30(4): 458–467.

Hampson, Fen Osler. 1995. *Multilateral Negotiations: Lessons from Arms Control, Trade and the Environment*. Baltimore, MD: Johns Hopkins University Press.

Hardin, Garrett. 1968. "The Tragedy of the Commons." *Science*, 162: 1243–1248.

Harshbarger, Thad R. 1977. *Introductory Statistics: A Decision Map*. New York: Macmillan.

Hinton, Bernard L., W. Clay Hamner, and Michael F. Pohlen. 1974. "The Influence of Reward Magnitude, Opening Bid and Concession Rate on Profit Earned in a Managerial Negotiation Game." *Behavioral Science*, 19(3): 197–203.

Homans, George C. 1961. *Social Behavior*. San Diego: Harcourt Brace Jovanovich.

Hopmann, P. Terrence. 1996. *The Negotiation Process and the Resolution of International Conflicts*. Columbia, SC: University of South Carolina Press.

Hurley, Brad. 1991. "Climate Convention Negotiations Start to Take Shape." *Global Environmental Change Report*, 18 January.

Hurrell, Andrew, and Benedict Kingsbury, eds. 1992. *The International Politics of the Environment*. New York: Oxford University Press.

IMO. 2000. "Marine Pollution." International Maritime Organization at ⟨http:// www.imo.org/imo/convent/pollute.htm⟩ [31 July 2000].

Jervis, Robert. 1978. "Cooperation under the Security Dilemma." *World Politics*, 30(2): 167–214.

Kaufmann, Johan. 1996. *Conference Diplomacy: An Introductory Analysis*, 3rd revised edition. London: Macmillan.

Kjellén, Bo. 1992. Interview by author, Washington, DC, 14 December.

Kolb, Deborah M., and Guy-Olivier Faure. 1994. "Organization Theory: The Interface of Structure, Culture, Procedures, and Negotiation Processes." In *International Multilateral Negotiation*, edited by I. William Zartman. San Francisco: Jossey-Bass.

Kunugi, Tatsuro. 1982. "Consensus on Elements of International Timber Agreement – Negotiating Conference Expected Early Next Year." *UNCTAD Monthly Bulletin*, 185.

Lang, Winfried. 1991. "Negotiations on the Environment." In *International Negotiation: Analysis, Approaches, Issues*, edited by Victor A. Kremenyuk. San Francisco: Jossey-Bass.

Leitzell, Terry L. 1973. "The Ocean Dumping Convention – A Hopeful Beginning." *San Diego Law Review*, 10(3): 502–513.

McConnell, Fiona. 1996. *The Biodiversity Convention: A Negotiating History*. London: Kluwer Law International.

McManus, Robert J. 1983. "Ocean Dumping: Standards in Action." In *Environmental Protection: The International Dimension*, edited by David A. Kay and Harold K. Jacobson. Totowa, NJ: Allanheld, Osmun & Co.

Mäler, Karl-Göran. 1990. "International Environmental Problems." *Oxford Review of Economic Policy*, 6(1): 80-108.

M'Gonigle, R. Michael, and Mark W. Zacher. 1979. *Pollution, Politics and International Law*. Berkeley: University of California Press.

Midgaard, Knut, and Arild Underdal. 1977. "Multiparty Conferences." In *Negotiations: Social-Psychological Perspectives*, edited by Daniel Druckman. Beverly Hills, CA: Sage Publications.

Mitchell, Ronald B. 1993. "Intentional Oil Pollution of the Oceans." In *Institutions for the Earth*, edited by Peter M. Haas, Robert O. Keohane, and Marc A. Levy. Cambridge, MA: MIT Press.

———. 1994. *Intentional Oil Pollution at Sea*. Cambridge, MA: MIT Press.

Molina, Mario, and Sherwood Rowland. 1974. "Stratospheric Sink for Chlorofluoromethanes: Chlorine Atom Catalyses Destruction of Ozone." *Nature*, 249: 810–812.

Morgenthau, Hans J. and Kenneth W. Thompson. 1985. *Politics among Nations: The Struggle for Power and Peace*. New York: Knopf.

New York Times. 1972. "Dispute on Coastal Limits Perils Sea-Pollution Pact," 11 November.

Nicolson, Harold. 1961. *The Congress of Vienna*. New York: Viking Press.

Nye, Joseph S., Jr. 1986. "The Diplomacy of Nuclear Proliferation." In *Negotiating World Order*, edited by Alan K. Henrikson. Wilmington, Del.: Scholarly Resources, Inc.

OECD. 1990. *Monitoring and Control of Transfrontier Movement of Hazardous Wastes.* OECD Environmental Monographs No. 34.

Olson, Mancur. 1971. *The Logic of Collective Action.* Cambridge, MA: Harvard University Press.

Pearson, Charles S. 1975. *International Marine Environment Policy: The Economic Dimension.* Baltimore, MD: Johns Hopkins University Press.

Porter, Gareth, Janet Welsh Brown, and Pamela Chasek. 2000. *Global Environmental Politics*, 3rd edition. Boulder, CO: Westview Press.

Princen, Thomas. 1994. "NGOs: Creating a Niche in Environmental Diplomacy." In *Environmental NGOs in World Politics*, edited by Thomas Princen and Matthias Finger. New York: Routledge.

Pruitt, Dean C., and Jeffrey Z. Rubin. 1986. *Social Conflict: Escalation, Stalemate and Settlement.* New York: McGraw-Hill.

Raghavan, Chakravarthi. 1991. "Climate Change Negotiating Committee Meets June 19." *South–North Development Monitor* (Third World Network), 19 June.

Raiffa, Harold. 1985. "Post-Settlement Settlements." *Negotiation Journal*, 1: 9–12.

Rapoport, Anatol. 1970. *N-Person Game Theory.* Ann Arbor: University of Michigan Press.

Rittberger, Volker. 1983. "Global Conference Diplomacy and International Policy-Making: The Case of UN-Sponsored World Conferences." *European Journal of Political Research*, 11: 167–182.

Rothstein, Robert L. 1987. "Commodity Bargaining: The Political Economy of Regime Creation." In *Positive Sum: Improving North–South Negotiations*, edited by I. William Zartman. New Brunswick, NJ: Transaction Books.

Rubin, Jeffrey Z. 1991. "Psychological Approach." In *International Negotiation: Analysis, Approaches, Issues*, edited by Victor A. Kremenyuk. San Francisco: Jossey-Bass.

Sánchez, Vicente. 1994. "The Convention on Biological Diversity: Negotiations and Contents." In *Biodiplomacy: Genetic Resources and International Relations*, edited by Vicente Sánchez and Calestous Juma. Nairobi, Kenya: ACTS Press.

Sand, Peter H. 1990. *Lessons Learned in Global Environmental Governance.* Washington, DC: World Resources Institute.

Sattaur, Omar. 1990. "Convention Breaks down over Protecting Gene Pool." *New Scientist*, 15 December.

Saunders, Harold. 1985. "We Need a Larger Theory of Negotiation: The Importance of Pre-negotiating Phases." *Negotiation Journal*, 1: 249–262.

Schonfeld. Alan H. 1985. "International Trade in Wildlife: How Effective Is the Endangered Species Treaty?" *California Western International Law Journal*, 15: 111–160.

Scott, Norman. 1985. "The Evolution of Conference Diplomacy." In *International Geneva, 1985*, edited by L. Dembinski. Lausanne: Payot Lausanne.

Sielen, Alan B., and Robert J. McManus. 1983. "IMCO and the Politics of Ship Pollution." In *Environmental Protection: The International Dimension*, edited by David A. Kay and Harold K. Jacobson. Totowa, NJ: Allanheld, Osmun & Co.

Sjöstedt, Gunnar, and Bertram I. Spector. 1993. "Conclusion." In *International Environmental Negotiations*, edited by Gunnar Sjöstedt. Beverly Hills, CA: Sage.

Sjöstedt, Gunnar, et al. 1994. "The Dynamics of Regime-building Negotiations." In *Negotiating International Regimes: Lessons Learned from the United Nations Conference on Environment and Development*, edited by Gunnar Sjöstedt, Bertram I. Spector, and I. William Zartman. London: Graham & Trotman.

Spector, Bertram I. 1992. *International Environmental Negotiation: Insights for Practice*. Executive Report 21, Laxenburg, Austria: International Institute for Applied Systems Analysis.

———. 1993. "Post-Agreement Negotiation: Conflict Resolution Processes in the Aftermath of Successful Negotiations." Unpublished paper.

———. 1994. "Decision Theory: Diagnosing Strategic Alternatives and Outcome Trade-Offs." In *International Multilateral Negotiation*, edited by I. William Zartman. San Francisco: Jossey-Bass.

Stairs, Kevin, and Peter Taylor. 1992. "Non-Governmental Organizations and the Legal Protection of the Oceans: A Case Study." In *The International Politics of the Environment*, edited by Andrew Hurrell and Benedict Kingsbury. New York: Oxford University Press.

Stein, Janice Gross. 1989. "Getting to the Table: The Triggers, Stages, Functions and Consequences of Prenegotiation." In *Getting to the Table*, edited by Janice Gross Stein. Baltimore, MD: Johns Hopkins University Press.

Susskind, Lawrence. 1994. *Environmental Diplomacy*. New York: Oxford.

Susskind, Lawrence, and Connie Ozawa. 1992. "Negotiating More Effective International Environmental Agreements." In *The International Politics of the Environment*, edited by Andrew Hurrell and B. Kingsbury. New York: Oxford University Press.

Thacher, Peter S. 1992. "Institutional and Legal Issues for Roundtable in Preparation of UNCED '92." Presentation given at the Vienna Institute for Development and Cooperation, 31 January.

———. 1993. "The Mediterranean: A New Approach to Marine Pollution." In *International Environmental Negotiations*, edited by Gunnar Sjöstedt. Beverly Hills, CA: Sage.

Thomas, Caroline. 1992. *The Environment in International Relations*. London: Royal Institute of International Affairs.

Tolba, Mostafa K., with Iwona Rummel-Bulska. 1998. *Global Environmental Diplomacy: Negotiating Environmental Agreements for the World, 1973–1992*. Cambridge, MA: MIT Press.

Tomlin, Brian. W. 1989. "The Stages of Prenegotiation: The Decision to Negotiate North American Free Trade." In *Getting to the Table*, edited by Janice Gross Stein. Baltimore, MD: Johns Hopkins University Press.

Touval, Saadia. 1991. "Multilateral Negotiation: An Analytic Approach." In *Negotiation Theory and Practice*, edited by J. William Breslin and Jeffrey Z. Rubin. Cambridge, MA: Program on Negotiation at Harvard Law School.

Train, Russell. 1973. "Report of the U.S. Delegation." As reprinted in *Department of State Bulletin*, 68: 613–618.

Trexler, Mark C. 1990. "The Convention on International Trade in Endangered Species of Wild Fauna and Flora: Political or Conservation Success?" Ph.D. dissertation, University of California, Berkeley.

UNCTAD. 1977. "Report of the Second Preparatory Meeting on Tropical Timber Held at the Palais des Nations, Geneva, from 24 to 28 October 1977." TD/B/IPC/TIMBER/5.
———. 1978. "Report of the Third Preparatory Meeting on Tropical Timber Held at the Palais des Nations, Geneva, from 23 to 27 January 1978." TD/B/IPC/TIMBER/11.
———. 1979. "Report of the Fifth Preparatory Meeting on Tropical Timber Held at the Palais des Nations, Geneva, from 22 to 26 October 1979." TD/B/IPC/TIMBER/26.
———. 1980. "Report of the Fifth Preparatory Meeting on Tropical Timber on its Second Part Held at the Palais des Nations, Geneva, from 7 to 18 July 1980." TD/B/IPC/TIMBER/32.
———. 1983a. "Report of the Meeting on Tropical Timber Held at the Palais des Nations, Geneva, from 29 November to 3 December 1982." TD/B/IPC/TIMBER/42.
———. 1983b. "Conference on Tropical Timber Makes Substantial Progress." *UNCTAD Monthly Bulletin*, 192.
———. 1983c. "International Tropical Timber Agreement." TD/TIMBER/11/Rev.1.
———. 1993. "Background, Status and Operation of the International Tropical Timber Agreement, 1983, and Recent Developments of Relevance to the Negotiation of a Successor Agreement." TD/TIMBER.2/3.
Underdal, Arild. 1991. "The Outcomes of Negotiation." In *International Negotiation: Analysis, Approaches, Issues*, edited by Victor A. Kremenyuk. San Francisco: Jossey-Bass.
———. 1994. "Leadership Theory: Rediscovering the Arts of Management." In *International Multilateral Negotiation*, edited by I. William Zartman. San Francisco: Jossey-Bass.
UNEP. 1991a. *Environmental Law in UNEP*. Nairobi: UNEP.
———. 1991b. "Report of the Intergovernmental Negotiating Committee for a Convention on Biological Diversity on the Work of Its Third Session." UNEP/Bio.Div./INC.3/11, 4 July.
United Nations. 1991. "Conservation of Biological Diversity: Progress Report of the Secretary-General of the Conference." A/CONF.151/PC/28.
———. 1992. *Agenda 21: The United Nations Programme of Action from Rio*. New York: United Nations.
US Congress. 1978. Senate. Committee on Commerce, Science, and Transportation. *Antarctic Living Marine Resources Negotiations: Hearing before the National Ocean Policy Study of the Committee on Commerce, Science and Transportation*. 95th Cong., 2nd Sess., 14 June.

Wasserman, Ursula. 1984. "UNCTAD: International Tropical Timber Agreement." *Journal of World Trade Law*, 18(1): 89–91.

Wetstone, Gregory S., and Armin Rosencranz. 1983. *Acid Rain in Europe and North America: National Responses to an International Problem*. Washington, DC: Environmental Law Institute.

Williams, Abiodun. 1992. *Many Voices: Multilateral Negotiations in the World Arena*. Boulder, CO: Westview Press.

Winham, Gilbert R. 1977. "Complexity in International Negotiation." In *Negotiations: Social-Psychological Perspectives*, edited by Daniel Druckman. Beverly Hills, CA: Sage.

Winham, Gilbert R., and Karin L. Kizer. 1993. *The Uruguay Round: Midterm Review*. Washington, DC: Johns Hopkins Foreign Policy Institute.

Young, Oran R. 1989. "The Politics of International Regime Formation." *International Organization*, 43(3): 349–376.

———. 1991. "Political Leadership and Regime Formation: On the Development of Institutions in International Society." *International Organization*, 45(3): 281–308.

———. 1993. "Perspectives on International Organizations." In *International Environmental Negotiations*, edited by Gunnar Sjöstedt. Beverly Hills, CA: Sage.

———. 1994. *International Governance*. Ithaca, NY: Cornell University Press.

Zartman, I. William. 1978. *The Negotiation Process: Theories and Applications*. Beverly Hills, CA: Sage.

———. 1983. *The 50% Solution*. New Haven, CT: Yale University Press.

———. 1987. *Positive Sum: Improving North–South Negotiations*. New Brunswick, NJ: Transaction Books.

———. 1989. "Prenegotiation: Phases and Functions." In *Getting to the Table*, edited by Janice Gross Stein. Baltimore, MD: Johns Hopkins University Press.

———. 1994. "Two's Company and More's a Crowd: The Complexities of Multilateral Negotiation." In *International Multilateral Negotiation*, edited by I. William Zartman. San Francisco: Jossey-Bass.

Zartman, I. William, and Berman, Maureen R. 1982. *The Practical Negotiator*. New Haven, CT: Yale University Press.

Biographical Note

Pamela S. Chasek has a PhD in international studies from the Paul H. Nitze School of Advanced International Studies, The Johns Hopkins University. She is the founder and editor of the *Earth Negotiations Bulletin*, a reporting service on United Nations environment and development negotiations. She is currently a visiting assistant professor and director of international studies at Manhattan College.

Index